The Cultural Memory of Georgian Glasgow

The Cultural Memory of Georgian Glasgow

Craig Lamont

EDINBURGH
University Press

For Sarah and Rhona

Edinburgh University Press is one of the leading university presses in the UK. We publish academic books and journals in our selected subject areas across the humanities and social sciences, combining cutting-edge scholarship with high editorial and production values to produce academic works of lasting importance. For more information visit our website: edinburghuniversitypress.com

© Craig Lamont, 2021, 2022

Edinburgh University Press Ltd
The Tun – HolyroodRoad
12 (2f) Jackson's Entry
Edinburgh EH8 8PJ

First published in hardback by Edinburgh University Press 2021

Typeset in 10.5/13pt Sabon by
Servis Filmsetting Ltd, Stockport, Cheshire

A CIP record for this book is available from the British Library

ISBN 978 1 4744 4327 2 (hardback)
ISBN 978 1 4744 4328 9 (paperback)
ISBN 978 1 4744 4329 6 (webready PDF)
ISBN 978 1 4744 4330 2 (epub)

The right of Craig Lamont to be identified as author of this work has been asserted in accordance with the Copyright, Designs and Patents Act 1988 and the Copyright and Related Rights Regulations 2003 (SI No. 2498).

Index compiled by Carol Baraniuk

Contents

List of Figures vi
Acknowledgements viii
Timeline of Georgian Glasgow x
Plan of the City of Glasgow (1778) xiii

Introduction 1

PART I GEORGIAN GLASGOW
1 Georgian Glasgow: A History 15

PART II REMEMBERING THE GLASGOW ENLIGHTENMENT
2 Glasgow as a Centre for the Arts, Science and Medicine 37
3 'Unimpaired remembrance reigns' 62

PART III EMPIRE AND THE DISPLACEMENT OF MEMORY
4 'That barbarous traffic' 87
5 'Then went forth our Scots' 114

PART IV COMMEMORATING GLASGOW AS THE 'SECOND CITY'
6 Literary Tourists and Soldier Heroes 143
7 The Great Exhibitions: 1888–1938 169

Conclusion 191

Bibliography 209
Index 232

Figures

	Plan of the City of Glasgow (1778)	xiii
1	Arbuckle Coffee Company card no. 86, *Scotland* (1889)	35
2	David Allan, *Fine Art Exhibition in the Court of the Old College* (1761)	44
3	David Allan, *The Foulis Academy of Fine Arts* (1760)	47
4	Thomas Annan, photographic reproduction of *The Foulis Academy of Fine Arts* by David Allan	47
5	James Fittler, *Glasgow Infirmary* (1804)	71
6	Joseph Swan, *View of the Hunterian Museum, &c. from the West* (1829)	72
7	John Mossman, sculpture of James Watt and Youth, Nelson Mandela Place, Glasgow (1886)	76
8	John Blake MacDonald, *James Watt* (1858)	78
9	Adam Smith statue, Royal Mile, Edinburgh	96
10	David Livingstone statue, Cathedral Square, Glasgow	98
11	Cropped section from *Description of a Slave Ship* (1789)	101
12	Medallion by Josiah Wedgwood, *Am I Not a Man and a Brother?*	102
13	Archibald McLauchlan, *John Glassford and his Family* (c.1767)	107
14	John Knox, *Old Glasgow Cross or The Trongate* (1826)	127
15	J. & C. Walker, *Plan of the Town of Guelf, Upper Canada* (1831)	130
16	Sir John Moore statue, George Square, Glasgow	156
17	John Knox, *The Nelson Monument Struck by Lightning* (c.1810)	157

Figures

18 Miniature enamelled book locket from the 1901 Glasgow Exhibition   185
19 Marketing poster design for *How Glasgow Flourished: 1714–1837* (2014)   200

Acknowledgements

I began writing my PhD thesis in late October 2012, in the Kildonan Hotel, Arran, following initial meetings with Murray Pittock. I had secured the PhD studentship on Murray's AHRC-funded project 'Georgian Glasgow', a Collaborative Doctoral Award (CDA) shared between the University of Glasgow and Glasgow Life. It was designed to combine supervised academic study and the best practices of the city's cultural sector, with insight into the development of a major exhibition. I had just completed an MRes in Creative Writing, so this journey to the Georgian period was a leap of faith. The only common threads between the Master's and PhD were 'Glasgow' and 'memory'. Good threads to have, but without the support of Murray I doubt I would have made the leap convincingly. Once the writing began my second supervisor Gerard Carruthers helped guide me through the wonderful maze of Scottish literature in the eighteenth century. In my sessions with both I was able to draft ideas and encounter new realms at an exciting pace. It is firstly to the credit of these excellent mentors that I have been able to reconfigure a successful PhD thesis (winner of the 2016 Roy Medal) into the book you hold now. I am very grateful to the Andrew Tannahill Fund for the Furtherance of Scottish Literature, whose support went towards image digitisation and licensing fees for this work.

I am extremely grateful to my colleagues and friends in the University and beyond who have been instrumental in all my postdoctoral activity to date, especially Alexander Broadie, Rhona Brown, Ian Brown, Carol Baraniuk, Duncan Jones, Alison Lumsden, Anthony Lewis, Kirsteen McCue, Pauline Mackay, Stephen Mullen, Christopher Whatley and Ronnie Young. By reading early drafts of this work or by simply being a helpful part of the journey, I thank you. I am also extremely grateful for the sharp and inquisitive eye of Anita Joseph whose excellent copyediting skills go beyond the surface details and into the heart of the book itself.

For all the work that went into this and the countless other things that comprise any working day, I owe most thanks of all to my wife Sarah. Her support and compassion is boundless. Our daughter, Rhona, was born on 10 June 2019.

Timeline of Georgian Glasgow

1700   The population of Glasgow is estimated at around 12,000.

1706   A series of anti-Union riots break out on 7 November, lasting several days.

1714   George I ascends the throne on 1 August: the Georgian era begins.

1715   Glasgow's first newspaper, the *Glasgow Courant*, is printed on 14 November, one day after the Battle of Sheriffmuir. During this first Jacobite rising Glasgow prepared to defend itself but the city was never attacked.

1724   The printing of Daniel Defoe's *Tour Through the Whole Island of Great Britain* begins. In it, he describes Glasgow as 'a very fine city . . . the cleanest and beautifullest, and best built city in Britain, London excepted.'

1725   On 24 June, rioters sack Shawfield Mansion, home of Daniel Campbell MP, whom they blamed for raising the Malt Tax. The rioting continued on 25 June, and several people were killed by soldiers trying to disperse the rabble.

1733   The first hospital in the city, the Toun's/Town's, is opened on Clyde Street.

1734   A statue of William of Orange is unveiled in the Trongate.

1736   The first history of the city, John M'Ure's *A View of the City of Glasgow*, is published. Construction on the Town Hall building in the Trongate begins.

1737   Work begins on the Tontine Hotel, Trongate.

1745   During the second Jacobite rising, Prince Charles Edward Stuart leads his troops through Glasgow, which was predominantly Hanoverian.

1750   The population of Glasgow is estimated at around 21,000.

Timeline

1753   Robert and Andrew Foulis, printers to the University of Glasgow, open an Academy of Fine Arts to students in December.

1756   The building of St Andrew's Church in the Square, near Glasgow Cross, is completed. It was designed by Allan Dreghorn, based on St Martin-in-the-Fields, in London.

1757   The Macfarlane Observatory is built near the University of Glasgow.

1759   Adam Smith's *The Theory of Moral Sentiments* is published, based largely on his lectures in Glasgow University.

1761   Joseph Black introduces his doctrine on 'latent heat,' developed during his time at the University. During this high point in the Glasgow Enlightenment, Black worked with James Watt and Alexander Wilson, Glasgow's first Professor of Astronomy.

1777   The next extensive *History of Glasgow*, by John Gibson, is published.

1778   John McArthur's excellent map *Plan of the City of Glasgow: Gorbells and Caltoun* is published.

1779   On 2 February, a riot breaks out in protest of the government's plans to pass a Catholic Relief Act.

1782   Glasgow's chief civic space, George Square, is laid out by the town council.

1783   *The Glasgow Advertiser* is printed for the first time on 23 January by John Mennons. It would become the *Glasgow Herald*, recognised as the longest-running national newspaper in the world.

1787   Class tensions grew in the Calton district, east of the city centre. Cotton weavers went on strike for several weeks, and on 3 September troops shot at the belligerent crowd, killing a number of protestors.

1791   A Glasgow anti-slavery society publish a pamphlet, *An Address to the Inhabitants of Glasgow, Paisley, and the Neighbourhood, Concerning the African Slave Trade*. The building of Glasgow's Trades Hall, still standing in Glassford Street, commences.

1794   The building of Trades Hall, designed by Robert Adam, is completed. The Royal Infirmary, near Glasgow Cathedral, is opened.

1796   Professor John Anderson leaves plans in his will for a new university. Anderson's Institution opens in November, evolving over time into the University of Strathclyde.

1801   The population of Glasgow grows to over 77,000.

1807   The Hunterian, Scotland's first public museum, is opened on the grounds of the University of Glasgow. The Slave Trade Act is passed in Parliament.

1812 Henry Bell's paddle steamer, PS *Comet*, begins a passenger service on 15 August.

1814 Through a Royal Charter, the Glasgow Asylum for Lunatics opens.

1816 The first ship to India from Glasgow is dispatched. St Andrew's Roman Catholic Chapel, now Cathedral, is built on Clyde Street.

1819 The first statue to be erected in George Square is completed: Sir John Moore of Corunna.

1820 Several strikes and marches are staged in Glasgow by members of the working class, especially those working in factories, during the first few days in April. The ensuing Radical War leads to skirmishes and risings across Scotland.

1827 The Argyle Arcade is built in Argyle Street, making it one of the oldest covered shopping centres, or arcades, in the world. It is still in use.

1830 The James Watt statue in George Square is unveiled.

1831 The population of Glasgow more than doubles since the turn of the century, estimated at over 202,000.

1832 In July, the Reform Act for Scotland passed, changing the political landscape of the nation. There would be several more reforms, but for the first time in its democratic history, more Glaswegians could cast a vote.

1833 The Slavery Abolition Act is passed in Parliament, bringing further sanctions against slavers.

1837 Victoria becomes Queen on 20 June. The Georgian era ends.

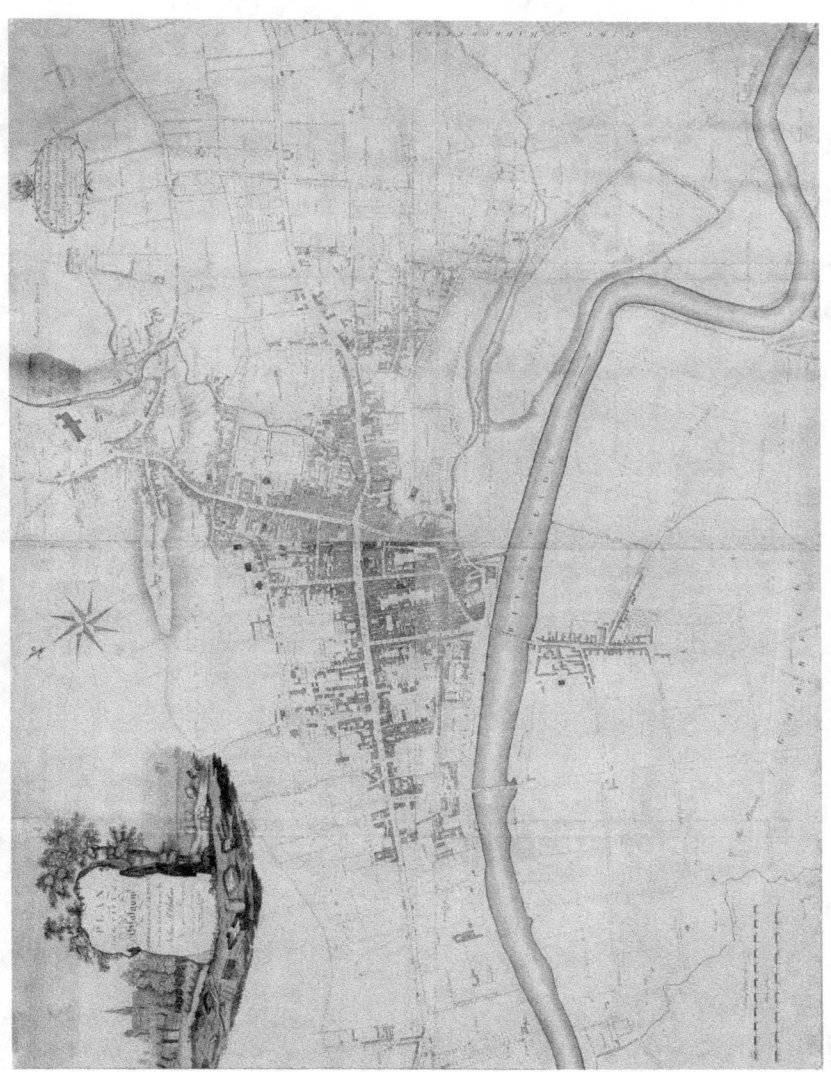

John McArthur, *Plan of the City of Glasgow* (1778). Image courtesy of the University of Glasgow Library: Case Maps C18:45 GLA1.

Introduction

WHERE IS GEORGIAN GLASGOW?

This book focuses on Glasgow during one of the most important periods in Scottish history. The Georgian era commenced when George I ascended the throne in 1714 and ended in 1837 when Victoria became Queen. Throughout this time Lowland Scotland was transformed into a network of burgeoning hubs, open to the increased traffic of commerce and industry. It was a century of unprecedented sociability, invention and Enlightenment. But before George took up the throne, British people were still coming to terms with their new identity. Following the Regal Union of 1603 the Stuart Kings ruled from England. Scotland had lost the royal court in Edinburgh where poetry and song had previously flourished. When William of Orange led the so-called 'Glorious Revolution' at the end of the seventeenth century the Catholic monarch was ousted and the Protestant ideology that unravelled during the Reformation flew high in Scottish skies. But before long the Union Acts were passed and in 1707 Scotland ceased to function as a politically independent nation. Culturally, the journey to 'Britishness' was longer and more complicated than the passing of any Act. Between two Jacobite risings in the first half of the eighteenth century and an aggressively growing Empire in the second half, the social and cultural dynamic of Scotland was reconfigured. This book considers this history with a special focus on the surprisingly neglected terrain of Glasgow.

There have been scores of landmark books that have traversed the national landscape of the long eighteenth century. For example, Christopher Whatley's *Scottish Society: 1707–1830* (2000) and Michael Fry's *Scottish Empire* (2001) help us come to terms with the unprecedented winds of change sweeping Scotland during the period and untangle Scotland's unique history from the catch-all British narrative that had persisted for decades.[1] In some cases, scholars have in fact narrowed their focus to the metropolis itself. Unsurprisingly, London was central in several studies all entitled *Georgian London*, by John Summerson (1945), G. E. Mingay (1975), and Lucy Inglis (2013).[2] *Georgian Dublin* by Desmond Guinness (1975) and a collection of essays under the same title, edited by Gillian O'Brien and Finola O'Kane (2008) show us that there is already a strong tradition of scholarship on the Georgian period through the prism of one place.[3] It is therefore surprising that no Scottish city has been given this same treatment. Of course, there have been several key books on the Scottish Enlightenment, and how it transformed not only the cultural aspects but the physical environment of towns and cities. But more often than not these texts focus on Edinburgh as the hotbed of ideas and invention in which we can celebrate Scottish genius. This will be one of the primary issues analysed in Chapter 2, where we will delve into the Glasgow Enlightenment and take stock of just how influential the scientific, artistic and philosophical work coming out of Glasgow truly was. It is not that this picture of Glasgow has *never* been painted, but it has certainly been overshadowed. The first volume of Tom Devine and Gordon Jackson's series on Glasgow, *Beginnings to 1830* (1995) and, more recently, Robert Crawford's *On Glasgow and Edinburgh* (2013) have helped recover some of the forgotten aspects of Glasgow's rich history. No text, however, has focused solely on the Georgian period. Many modern books about Glasgow – ranging from Jack House's ever-popular *The Heart of Glasgow* (1965) to Alan Taylor's *Glasgow: An Autobiography* (2016) – have focused on anecdote, popular history and 'character'.[4] Only Michael Fry's *Glasgow: A History of the City* (2017) gives the eighteenth century due diligence, covering a good deal of ground including slavery and the Scottish Enlightenment.[5] Even so, when the Georgian era does feature it tends to fall away to the more recognisable image of Glasgow which we remember today: the smoky, industrial, canny city of the late Victorian and early twentieth century. Despite the associations in street names and extant architecture, Georgian Glasgow remains surprisingly absent from the story of Glasgow.

This dearth of history is manifested visually on the large wall murals in the Banqueting Hall of Glasgow City Chambers, arguably the city's most impressive Victorian building. These murals were painted between 1899 and 1901 by the Glasgow Boys, and their scope of history reveals the historical glossing over of the Georgian period in favour of a sudden and as-yet-unchallenged pride in Victorian achievement. Beginning with the sixth century miracles of St Mungo, *Legendary Glasgow* was painted by Alexander Ignatius Roche. This was followed by the centre mural depicting the twelfth century *Glasgow Fair*, painted by Edward Arthur Walton. The final panel sees a massive leap to *Modern Glasgow* by John Lavery, a depiction of teeming workers labouring around a large ship. This triptych completely omits large portions of Glasgow's history, none more glaring than the Scottish Enlightenment. As crucial as St Mungo remains to Glasgow's civic image (the city motto and iconography are designed into many different council notices and properties), the progression from medieval to Victorian Glasgow in this pictorial timeline gives the impression that nothing important happened in-between.

And yet, we get so much of this story in literature and the visual arts. The work of Moira Burgess has been crucial in gathering together the various impressions of Glasgow in the literature of and about the city. Her well-edited *Imagine a City* (1998) and her seminal bibliography *The Glasgow Novel* (1972) show us that Georgian Glasgow has often been a focus for many writers.[6] In the pages of Edward Gaitens's *Dance of the Apprentices* (1948), buried in his tale of communism in the working classes, the author imagines the growth of Glasgow through its streets, as a postman might encounter the different epochs of history on his route: 'Where the working women of Glasgow had worked for men and families, continuing the generations there since the great industrial city was a small, charming town . . . Those streets that still have memories of olden days when the Tobacco Lords swaggered the pavements.'[7] Topography of this kind in fiction (the narrative extends to almost 500 words) is symbolic of the place of memory in literature. It is especially useful in cases where traditional scholarship has failed to recognise the importance of a particular time and place. As with Gaitens, the same foreshortening of time is used in other novels, such as the classic work by Archie Hind, *The Dear Green Place* (1966). One scene in particular places main character Mat Craig on a bridge, 'looking over the parapet into the dirty water, at the very spot where Boswell had stood and looked at the widest streets in the whole of Europe'. This harkening back to Defoe's version of eighteenth-century Glasgow is something of a consolation for Mat, who sees instead 'a vehicular sclerosis, a congestion of activity . . . [feeling] again a wave of nostalgia for another kind of existence – waxed fruit, sword sticks, snuff, tobacco . . .'[8] In *Lanark* (1981) Alasdair Gray considers the city's faltering legacy in modern terms, contrasting it with London, Paris, Florence and New York. Once hailed as home to 'the world's foremost makers of several useful things',

Glasgow's magnificence is sardonically reduced to 'a music hall song and a few bad novels'.[9]

Remarks like this are shrewd reminders, perhaps, of our over-reliance on that single – chiefly industrial – generation to give an image of Glasgow to the world. But even this image is worth protecting. In an alternate universe, Gray's imagined cityscape might have been completely different. Known today simply as the Bruce Report or Plan, Robert Bruce's *First Planning Report to the Highways and Planning Committee of the Corporation of Glasgow* was published in 1945. His plan was to change the face of Glasgow completely, proposing a metropolis without Central Station, the old historic core, without even George Square and the grand City Chambers. In Bruce's vision for Glasgow, Queen Street Station and George Square form a unified L-shaped green at the heart of a new business district. A new city chambers would take the place of St Enoch Square and its minor roads, looking onto the Clyde.[10] One can only imagine how differently the city would have manifested in art, books, and popular culture if these plans had come to fruition. The cultural memory of Glasgow would have been set on a completely new course.

As it stands, the cultural memory of Georgian Glasgow is there to be found in the city's literature, its architecture, and its museums. The term itself is gaining momentum: following the successful 2014 exhibition *How Glasgow Flourished* in Kelvingrove Art Gallery and Museum, a new permanent display of objects from Georgian Glasgow faces those from the Victorian period in the popular Glasgow Stories section.[11] The interdisciplinary nature of this book will not only fix Glasgow's eighteenth century in place, it will help us understand more about why it has been obscured from view for so long. Tracing a line from the beginning of the eighteenth century to the first few decades of the nineteenth century, the chronological approach will draw out some of the neglected people and events of Scottish history. A timeline of Georgian Glasgow has been supplied in the preliminary pages, and Chapter 1 offers a curtailed history of the period as a guide to the core of the book. Chapters 2 and 3 are studies of the diverse culture of the Scottish Enlightenment as it developed in Glasgow. A new strand of classical humanism, instilled in the students of the University, came up against a traditionally Presbyterian culture, which, for all its merit, was often intolerant of emerging ideas. The key players and institutions are central here, but there is a new focus on *why* certain Enlightenment-era figures such as James Watt (1736–1819) have been so revered while others are practically forgotten. In Chapter 4 there is a progression in the Georgian timeline, with a shift of focus from the scientific and cultural achievements in Glasgow to the influence of the city on the wider world. The city's deep involvement in transatlantic slavery is examined first, with a consideration of how we have only recently begun to fully recognise the ills of imperialism closer to home. Chapter 5, on the other hand, tracks the journeys of Scots going out to the New World. Looking back on the tumultuous eighteenth century, authors like John Galt (1779–1839) cast several impressions of Glasgow in their works, often inspired by their own colonial exploits. In Chapter 6 we will see how a new age of monuments was carved out and how commemoration became a mainstay of civic identity and national pride. It was in these final years of the Georgian period that Glasgow recreated itself and stood alone to become the 'Second City of the Empire'. In Chapter 7 we move beyond the Georgian period to consider how the Great Exhibitions of 1888, 1901, 1911 and 1938 helped solidify the image of Glasgow as an industrial stronghold for generations to come.

READING CULTURAL MEMORY

As the title of this book suggests, cultural memory is crucial in telling the story of Georgian Glasgow. To offer a definition: cultural memory is the shared understanding or interpretation of any one thing built up over several generations. The extant Georgian architecture of Glasgow, such as the Trades Hall, and the street names that commemorate people from that time (i.e. Glassford Street, Ingram Street) all feed into the cultural memory of Georgian Glasgow. It might be helpful to think in terms of 'images' or 'scenes' woven into the great tapestry of that cultural memory. The predominant Glasgow scenes of shipbuilding (think of the city's River Clyde) and heavy industry (the vast cranes that comprise the city skyline) belong to a more recent, modern age. Understanding cultural memory depends on recognising these images and how often they are repeated or reworked in various media. Rome, for example, tends to conjure a very classical image and time. Each city has a multifaceted identity, comprised of mnemonic landmarks of places, people and ideas that create a cultural memory. There have been studies of other cities that follow similar lines of thought to this book, such as Fenlon with Venice (2007), O'Connor with Florence (2008), and Thomas with Prague (2010).[12] Each with their own special focus (the Renaissance, the nineteenth century), these works use memory to harness the perceived histories of these places over time. By challenging the traditional view of Glasgow and embracing its neglected Georgian period, this book aims to engage with cultural memory theory.

As an academic field, memory studies has been growing in volume since it became entrenched in historiography in the second half of the twentieth century.[13] One of the central motivations in the field was to interrogate documented histories in order to establish how perceptions of the past have shaped society. These new interpretations often seek living witnesses, and so histories of World War II and the Holocaust have been highly represented. This gave rise to the subfield of 'trauma memory', which, as we will see in Chapter 4, can also be used to handle discussions of genocide and slavery.[14] Given the focus here on the long eighteenth century, memory itself must be dealt with using a different set of rules. No one alive today can remember an event that took place in Georgian Glasgow. What we have are letters, objects, paintings, novels, historical accounts: an accumulated *cultural* memory.

As a term in its own right, cultural memory evolved from 'collective memory', the principal term in the lineage of memory studies coined by the French philosopher and sociologist Maurice Halbwachs. Influenced by Durkheim and Bergson, Halbwachs is regarded as the pioneer in the field, defining collective memory as the 'result, or sum, or combination of *individual recollections* of many members of the same society'.[15] Bear in mind that 'individual recollections' suggests a short-term, generational memory. In the early days of memory theory there was a greater emphasis on using memory for sociological rather than historical purposes. A major development in the field was Pierre Nora's *Les Lieux de mémoire*: a project undertaken in the late 1970s with contributions from around sixty leading French historians.[16] Its main concern is the lasting identity of France and the problematic perceptions of France's national history. Communicative memory (i.e. generational, lived) and cultural memory (i.e. transgenerational, archival) are branches of this principal term.[17] The key to discussing cultural memory in this book is its layered, *out-of-time* presence. By definition, it has passed from the stage of 'communicative' or 'live' in order to become 'cultural'. This means that cultural memory can change: new statues can be built; old ones destroyed. In other words, the tapestry of scenes may become damaged over time, just as hitherto neglected histories might be newly woven into the story.

The growth of memory studies in academia has accelerated since the new millennium. In 2003 one of the first major collections of essays concerning cultural memory was published. *Cultural Memory*, edited by Edric Caldicott and Anne Fuchs, engages with the emerging strands of memory studies through literature and art. In the same year, Barbara A. Misztal's *Theories of Social Remembering* was published. As an overview of the development of memory studies, Misztal successfully highlights the different media and transmission of memory using the differences to broaden the field into other disciplines of social science. And yet, for all the work done on defining, expanding and explaining memory, Jeffrey K. Olick and Joyce Robbins declared in 2004 that 'social memory studies is a nonparadigmatic, transdisciplinary, centerless enterprise'.[18] The slippery nature of memory studies therefore leaves room for potential problems. One of these is the unreliability of histories or personal accounts that inform historical events. To this end, the theory of 'composure' was introduced in Graham Dawson's *Soldier Heroes* (1994). Based on the idea that storytelling is of cultural importance – because we tell stories to locate ourselves within a cultural framework – while reflecting on the past, 'composure' is caused by the pressures of group dynamics on the individual's (re)construction of collective memory. For, surely, no memory can pass from the event to the mind and out again without some alteration, however unintentional. A new academic train of thought concerned with oral history has since gained momentum.[19] Composure and oral history help us ground and personalise the often abstract theories of memory which can often become disorienting.

In the past decade there have been several key books taking this new mode of memory into account, such as Blaikie's *The Scots Imagination and Modern Memory* (2010) and Coleman's *Remembering the Past in Nineteenth-Century Scotland* (2014). Books like these forge a new culture of interdisciplinary scholarship in which Scotland can be understood in an uncertain cultural landscape. In many ways, these new works on memory are a response to the referendums, the hoisting of flags and the destruction of statues across the world. On the tercentenary of the Georgian era, Scotland voted to remain in the United Kingdom: an event which revealed more than just the friction of political identities in the heat of debate. Old prejudices, centuries old, were on show in Glasgow's George Square as opposing groups clashed. The Brexit vote stoked these flames once again, as Scotland's place in Europe was thrown into question: that same relationship with the Continent which was so fruitful during the heyday of the Scottish Enlightenment. These are some of the connections between the Georgian era and our lives today. By placing a lens over Glasgow we see how important these connections are, and just how vital it is to remember them.

NOTES

1. Christopher A. Whatley, *Scottish Society, 1707–1830: Beyond Jacobitism, Towards Industrialisation* (Manchester: Manchester University Press, 2000); Michael Fry, *The Scottish Empire* (Phantassie, East Lothian: Tuckwell Press, 2001).
2. George Summerson, *Georgian London* (London: Pleiades Books, 1945); G. E. Mingay, *Georgian London* (London: Batsford, 1975); Lucy Inglis, *Georgian London: Into the Streets* (London: Penguin/Viking, 2013).
3. Desmond Guinness, *Georgian Dublin* (London: Batsford, 1979); Gillian O'Brien and Finola O'Kane, eds, *Georgian Dublin* (Dublin and Portland, OR: Four Courts, 2008).
4. Jack House, *The Heart of Glasgow* (London: Hutchinson, 1965); Alan Taylor, ed., *Glasgow: An Autobiography* (Edinburgh: Birlinn, 2016).
5. As Fry points out himself, he mirrors his history of Edinburgh (2009), working thematically rather than chronologically. The effect is rather impressive, and the Georgian period – peppered throughout the work – does come to life. It should be noted that despite Fry's writing on Glasgow and slavery, more or less missing from previous histories, he has come under scrutiny from Sir Geoff Palmer for seeming to minimise the role of Henry Dundas in delaying the abolition of slavery. See <https://www.commonspace.scot/articles/13143/completely-unacceptable-historian-michael-fry-slammed-fellow-plaque-panellist-slavery> (last accessed 30 August 2020).
6. Moira Burgess, *Imagine a City: Glasgow in Fiction* (Glendaruel: Argyll Publishing, 1998); Moira Burgess, *The Glasgow Novel, 1870–1970: A Bibliography* (Glasgow: Scottish Library Association, 1972).
7. Edward Gaitens, *Dance of the Apprentices* (Edinburgh: Canongate Classics, 2001 [1948]), 247–8.
8. Archie Hind, *The Dear Green Place & Fur Sadie* (Edinburgh: Polygon, 2008 [1966]), 62.
9. Alasdair Gray, *Lanark: A Life in Four Books* (Edinburgh: Canongate, 2007 [1981]), 243–4.
10. Robert Bruce, *Folio of maps, plans and drawings accompanying the First Planning Report to the Highways and Planning Committee* (Glasgow: Corporation of the City of Glasgow, 1945), folios 7–8.
11. The research that led to the writing of this book featured as one of the many academic partnerships with Glasgow Life during the planning of the exhibition.
12. Iain Fenlon, *The Ceremonial City: History, Memory and Myth in Renaissance Venice* (New Haven, CT and London: Yale University Press, 2007); Anne O'Connor, *Florence: City and Memory in the Nineteenth Century* (Florence: Città di Vita, 2008); Alfred Thomas, *Prague Palimpsest: Writing, Memory, and the City* (Chicago: University of Chicago Press, 2010).

13. Patrick Hutton, 'Recent Scholarship on Memory and History', *The Memory Teacher*, 33:4 (2000), 533–48 (533).
14. In Chapter 4, the unique case of cultural memory and slavery will be elucidated fully.
15. Maurice Halbwachs, *On Collective Memory*, ed. Lewis A. Coser (Chicago: University of Chicago Press, 1992 [1941]), 39
16. Hutton, 'Recent Scholarship', 538; The English-language edition is a translation of seven volumes published between 1984 and 1992 into the three-volume *Realms of Memory*.
17. For an excellent flow chart of terms, cf. Christina West, 'Memory—Recollection—Culture—Identity—Space: Social Context, Identity Formation, and Self-construction of the Calé (Gitanos) in Spain', in Peter Meusburger, Michael Heffernan and Edgar Wunder, eds, *Cultural Memories: The Geographical Point of View* (London: Springer, 2011), 101–19 (104). The key terms first distinguished in Jan Assmann, 'Communicative and Cultural Memory', in Astrid Erll and Ansgar Nünning, eds, *Media and Cultural Memory: An International and Interdisciplinary Handbook* (Berlin: Walter de Gruyter GmbH & Co., 2008), 109–18 (110).
18. Jeffrey K. Olick, 'Social Memory Studies: From "Collective Memory" to the Historical Sociology of Mnemonic Practices', *Annual Review of Sociology*, 24 (1998), 105–40 (105).
19. Penny Summerfield's article 'Culture and Composure: Creating Narratives of the Gendered Self in Oral History Interviews' in *Cultural and Social History* 1:1 (2004) deals with this theory expertly, looking forward to Lynn Abrams' seminal text *Oral History Theory* (2010).

PART I
Georgian Glasgow

Glasgow was founded by Saint Kentigern (or, more popularly, 'Mungo'), probably in the middle of the sixth century. Saint Mungo and his miracles are immortalised in a rhyme known to most Glaswegians: 'Here is the bird that never flew / here is the tree that never grew / here is the bell that never rang / here is the fish that never swam.' These symbols have comprised Glasgow's coat of arms through the centuries and can still be seen today on city council documents and in the crest of the University of Glasgow. Before Saint Mungo, the area we know as Glasgow was part of the Kingdom of Strathclyde, with Dumbarton Rock its stronghold.[1] Glasgow flourished as a small religious town. In the twelfth century a cathedral was built on the site of Saint Mungo's church and an annual fair was initiated. There were Dominican and Franciscan friaries set up in the thirteenth and fifteenth centuries respectively, and the Castle in which the Glasgow bishops lived (also known as the Bishop's Palace) was built at some point before 1258, when it first appeared in charters. The ruins of this castle, on which the Royal Infirmary now stands, were there to be seen until the last year of the Georgian era which this history will cover in detail. In 1451 the University was founded, though a campus of new College buildings was not complete until the 1650s. All this activity spread outward from the cathedral on the hill, and it was this burgeoning centre of religion and learning that would withstand the test of time and remain as Glasgow's centre.

In the second half of the sixteenth century the Protestant Reformation swept through Scotland. Its leader John Knox is commemorated with the highest-standing statue in the Glasgow Necropolis. Led by Andrew Melville, the Principal of the University, religious reformers made an attempt to demolish the ancient cathedral in the spring of 1579 and use the stones to build new Protestant churches across town. Members of the Trades House took up arms and defended the building from destruction. In 1600 church records accounted for a population of 7,000, and over the next hundred years Glasgow came under several threats in the form of fire, famine, plague and civil war. Glasgow's first book was printed in 1638, being an account of the General Assembly of the Church of Scotland which took place in the cathedral. The shallow River Clyde hampered an increase in trade and so Glasgow merchants utilised the deeper waters eighteen miles north-west at Port Glasgow, first recorded as named in 1668. Towards the end of the century two major events impacted the nation. The first was the overthrow of the Catholic King James II and VII by William of Orange.

The predominantly Protestant town of Glasgow enjoyed new freedoms – choosing magistrates, provosts and bailies as the people saw fit. As the Darien scheme was put into place, Glasgow faced the Atlantic with confidence and readied itself to become the new trading headquarters of Scotland. Around 120 Glasgow merchants subscribed to the Company of Scotland and, despite its failure, pamphlets were churned out warning readers that France's persecution of European Protestants would increase if Scotland did not hold steady ground in the New World. With the Darien scheme eventually abandoned, Scotland entered the eighteenth century under a shadow. Scholarly work on the Union has often had to combat the simplistic notion that the Darien disaster led directly to the Acts of Union being passed: that Scotland went bankrupt, and that the England had to bail Scotland out.[2] Regarding Glasgow, historians have also had to handle the event of the Union with care, often dissenting from the notion that Glasgow was an insignificant market town with no real commercial activity before 1707.[3] We can only speculate as to how Glasgow's 12,000 inhabitants would have fared if Scotland had remained independent during the eighteenth century. What we do know about the Georgian period can be pieced together by looking at the people, events and architecture that reflect Glasgow during this time. In the end we are left with a fascinating portrait of the city rarely observed by historians or popular culture. This brief history seeks to outline some of the main events and offer a map of Georgian Glasgow with which we can navigate the main case studies of this book.

NOTES

1. Norman Davies offers a vivid account of this in the second chapter of his *Vanished Kingdoms: The History of Half-Forgotten Europe* (London: Allen Lane/Penguin, 2011), 35–83.
2. For some of the best, most up-to-date scholarship on a variety of issues from a Scottish perspective, see Gerard Carruthers and Colin Kidd, eds, *Literature and Union: Scottish Texts, British Contexts* (Oxford: Oxford University Press, 2018).
3. T. C. Smout, 'The Glasgow Merchant Community in the Seventeenth Century', *The Scottish Historical Review*, 47:143, Part 1 (1968), 53–71 (55).

1

Georgian Glasgow: A History

On 6 November 1706, one of the town's more popular preachers, Rev. James Clark, held his 11 o'clock service in the Tron Kirk. The impending Union with England hung in the air, and Clark struck a match with his words. 'Up and be valiant,' he declared, 'for the city of our God!'[1] The congregation responded and a mob formed quickly in the streets. They marched to the Tolbooth to a beating drum, but Provost Aird, who had refused to sign the anti-Union address drawn up by Glaswegians, had fled to Edinburgh. The Articles of the Union were burned at the Cross and the provost's house was sacked for arms. The rabble lasted weeks; the threat of the mob rose up just when quiet had been restored. The same magistrates the people had elected were now at the mercy of an armed and angry populace. Soldiers were sent from Edinburgh and prisoners were taken, though most were released without charge. It is quite remarkable to consider this anti-Unionist mentality so widespread in Glasgow, the same proud Hanoverian town which gave Charles Edward Stuart one of the most hostile receptions in Scotland a mere forty years later. It was with this fear and suspicion that Glaswegians began life in the newly forged nation of Great Britain, but it did not take long before the town began to reap the benefits of a new cultural dynamic. Whatever part the Union played in opening this up, there is no doubting that the character of Glasgow evolved dramatically as the century progressed. What was once a small religious town became a compact metropolis, home to the chief figures of the Scottish Enlightenment and a cast of merchants who set Glasgow up as an entrepôt between Britain and the Atlantic world.

George I ascended the throne of Great Britain on 1 August 1714. In September his son, George Augustus, became the Prince of Wales, effectively replacing the title worn by James Francis Edward Stuart, illegally or not, since 1688. To the Hanoverian monarchy Glasgow soon pledged its allegiance. Word had spread that the new royals rather liked Glasgow, and Glasgow responded in kind. In August 1715 Provost Aird, now secure and unthreatened, had sent the Princess of Wales 'a swatch of plaids' made in the town as a token of goodwill.[2] It was also a token of loyalty. Talk of a rebellion during this time was at large in Scotland, not even a decade after the Union, and on 6 September the standard of James III and VIII was famously raised at Braemar. The former Prince of Wales led the Jacobite rising of 1715 primarily in the north and the east. Glasgow offered to raise an army of 500 men to fend off the Jacobite threat, but no opposing army came to town. Instead, a regiment was sent to Stirling. Some prisoners were brought back to Glasgow for a short time, and although the city itself stayed clear of attack, what began as a gesture of allegiance to the Hanoverian government in the form of some plaid was now a steady show of strength. Glasgow had chosen a side. On 14 November of the same year, the *Glasgow Courant* was first published in the College printing house. Like most Glasgow newspapers of the eighteenth century, the *Courant* was comprised mostly of news from London, some from abroad, and very little from Glasgow. Local news was introduced gradually, as was the news of the Glasgow regiment's actions in Stirling during the Battle of Sheriffmuir. As such, the name of the paper was changed at one point to the *West Country Intelligence*. Perhaps the French word was offensive to those still wary of the Jacobite threat.

During the next decade there were sure signs of growth in the town. In 1718 the first Glasgow street lamps were put in place and the University inaugurated the first professorship of Anatomy. The College buildings were being extended with new lodgings for the growing faculty in 1720. More trading voyages left Port Glasgow than ever before, including some early slaving activity. Three vessels – *George* (1717), *Loyalty* (1719) and *Hanover* (1720) – left Port Glasgow and crossed the Atlantic, embarking a combined total of around 300 slaves.[3] Not all of these slaves survived the crossing, and as slavery increased towards the end of the century the people of Glasgow became all too aware of the horrors of the trade, many of them calling for abolition. While the town undoubtedly flourished, the early days of Union were sometimes tense. Glasgow's canny merchants were staking a larger claim in the transatlantic trade than the English expected. After London, Liverpool and Bristol were – and continued to be – Glasgow's chief rivals in trade. Unhappy with their Scottish counterparts competing for business, their complaints to Parliament led to the presence of officers at Port Glasgow and Greenock in 1723.⁴ But the restrictions these officers levied on the ports were only the first sign of trouble.

On 23 June, the new Malt Tax took effect in Scotland and scenes not unlike the Union riots broke out in the town once again. The Scottish ministers in the House of Commons had negotiated the original tax down from sixpence to threepence on every barrel of beer brewed. Glasgow's representative, Daniel Campbell, had travelled with his family to their country house the day before. The mob saw his home in the town as an easy target. The Shawfield Mansion, built 1711, was sacked by a Glasgow mob the next day; cries of 'Down with Shawfield's house!' and 'No Malt Tax!' were heard. Troops were sent for from Edinburgh and the entryways to the Mansion were closed off, but the people were still up in arms. Stones were thrown and the soldiers were ordered to fire. Two men were killed by the shots but the mob fought back, arming themselves and rising up against the soldiers. All told, nine of the mob were killed in the skirmishes. Unlike the Union riots, these were treated as an insurrection. General Wade came to Glasgow with an army. Some of the rioters were found and tried, punished with banishment or public whipping.⁵

During the 1730s Glasgow returned to its path of progress, beginning, fittingly, with the appointment of Francis Hutcheson (1694–1746) as the new Professor of Moral Philosophy. As the next chapter will show, Hutcheson's influence on the University of Glasgow was immense. But Hutcheson's coming to Glasgow is quite special even without the context of his students. Before then, the town was still very much in the early days of its cultural development. Hutcheson's teachings were controversial: not only did he revolutionise his lectures by introducing English over Latin, he also leaned towards a humanist set of morals that were unheard of in Glasgow before. His was the idea that humans 'have a notion of moral goodness prior in the order of knowledge to any notion of the will or law of God.'⁶ Given the town's staunch Presbyterian stance, it is perhaps unsurprising that in 1738 he was accused of heresy. In the same year that Hutcheson came to Glasgow, the first glass-bottle works was established in the town near the bank of the River Clyde and a school to teach girls to spin flax was established.⁷ In 1731 an additional number of spinning wheels for the school were bought by the town council and a teacher was appointed. This increased manufacturing and commercial activity led to the Bank of Scotland opening a branch in Glasgow, the first since 1697. Though it only ran for two years, it gives us a sense of a perceived high moment of trade in the town.⁸ The Toun's/Town's Hospital, Glasgow's first, was opened on 15 November 1733 facing the Clyde. It was paid for by the town council and several professional incorporations to meet the demands of an increasing population, and is said to have held over 150 old men, widows and orphans. It was also an educational hospital, a training place for new physicians and surgeons to learn from the experienced medical practitioners and the University teachers.[9] William Cullen (1710–90), Joseph Black (1728–99) and John Moore (1729–1802) would all have worked in the Town's during their time in Glasgow.

The next year an equestrian statue of William of Orange was presented to the town and placed in the Trongate. The beloved 'King Billy' was sculpted in traditional Roman attire, brandishing a baton. It was the only new portrait sculpture to come to Glasgow in the eighteenth century.[10] As we will see throughout this book, the process of commemoration in Glasgow escalated in the late Georgian period. But this symbol said more about Glasgow's sense of identity than the influx of business and wealth. Donated by James Macrae, a native of the town, William's 'Glorious Revolution' was celebrated by many Glaswegians who held their religion as the highest mark of civic pride. The statue is described in John M'Ure's *A View of the City of Glasgow* (1736), together with a booster poem exalting William. M'Ure's book was the first ever history of Glasgow, covering ground from the foundation story of St Mungo through to the most recent sugar refineries in the city – which, rather than 'town' – we may now begin to call it. After all, Daniel Defoe, had described it as such, at length, in his *Tour Through the Whole Island of Great Britain* (1724):

> Glasgow is, indeed, a very fine city; the four principal streets are the fairest for breadth, and the finest built that I have ever seen in one city together. The houses are all of stone, and generally equal and uniform in height, as well as in front; the lower story [sic] generally stands on vast square dorick columns, not round pillars, and arches between give passage into the shops, adding to the strength as well as beauty of the building; in a word, 'tis the cleanest and beautifullest, and best built city in Britain, London excepted.[11]

By 1740 there were around 17,000 inhabitants in Glasgow. New churches and factories were put up, and in 1742 a group of merchants, including John Glassford and Archibald Ingram, established Pollokshaws Printfield Company.[12] But for the first half of the eighteenth century Glasgow was only ever at peace for a short while. A shift in the fate of Britain would weigh down on the city once again, and this time the Jacobite threat was not in the distance.

Charles Edward Stuart wrote to the civic leaders of Glasgow on

13 September 1745, demanding £15,000 and whatever arms, clothes or supplies could be provided. He said that 'all those who love their Country and the *true* interest of Britain ought to wish for [his] success, and do what they can to promote it'.[13] The council ignored the letter, but it was sent again. The whole amount was not realised but Glasgow did manage to raise about a third of the cash and a large amount in clothes and supplies. The Highland army came to the city on Christmas Day and the Prince arrived the day after. Many of the magistrates and clergy moved their families out of Glasgow in the build up to the Jacobites' arrival. Once landed, Charles took up residence in the same Shawfield Mansion where the Malt Tax riots had ended in bloodshed. While he entertained his supporters and Clementine Walkinshaw at the Mansion, his troops postured in the city streets and proclaimed him Regent of Scotland at the Cross, in sight of William's statue. The soldiers were mostly unwelcome, and in some histories it is said that a shot was fired at the Prince on one of his public outings (it missed) and that a joiner, refusing to give up his shoes to a bedraggled Highlander, struck and killed the soldier with his hammer when he tried to pull them from the joiner's feet.[14] The Jacobites left Glasgow on 3 January 1746 to continue their march north. One writer, Dougal Graham, seems to have followed the army. If ever we wanted an indication as to how little we have remembered about the Georgian period, it is that Graham was the most popular Scottish chapbook writer and a little-known Glasgow poet simultaneously.[15] His eyewitness accounts were printed in vulgar rhyme in 1746 as *A Full, Particular and True Account of the Rebellion in the Years 1745–1746*. His account of the ragged and shoeless soldiers in his city is a lengthy one, but one aspect in particular is worth quoting:

> Eight days they did in Glasgow rest
> Until they were all clothed and drest:
> And though they on the best o't fed,
> The town they under tribute laid,
> Ten thousand sterling made it pay,
> For being of the Georgian way.[16]

The last line in particular confirms what we know about Glasgow's opposition to the Jacobite cause. It is a curious remark nonetheless, worth pausing at, for seeing the civic identity of Glasgow ascribed as being not just 'loyal' or 'Hanoverian' but, specifically, 'Georgian'. Historians have long considered the value, if not the readability, of Graham's history of the '45, which, though printed cheaply and often, was read almost 'out of existence'.[17]

Glasgow began to make strides of progress in manufacturing towards the middle of the century, producing copper and white iron for the first time in 1747. Business grew steadily, and in 1749 the Ship Bank opened, followed by the Glasgow Arms Bank (1753) and the Thistle Bank (1761). In 1750 the population broke through the 20,000 mark and the first theatre since the Reformation opened up near the College. A second, this time purpose-built, playhouse opened up 'against the wall of the Bishop's Castle' in 1752, and a third was erected in 1763 in the village of Grahamston, on which Glasgow Central Station was later built.[18] Drama had long been denounced by the church, but Edinburgh (and Allan Ramsay senior in particular) led the way towards a more tolerant culture in Scotland. Following the Academy of St Luke in Edinburgh (1729) the brothers Robert (1707–76) and Andrew Foulis (1712–75), who were the official and revered printers to the University, opened their Academy of Fine Art in late 1753 or early 1754. This venture exemplified a truly classical take on the Scottish Enlightenment, explored in detail in the next chapter. Its importance to Glasgow cannot be understated: it was supported by the merchants Glassford, Ingram and Cunninghame and it sought to teach young artists the practical, as well as aesthetical, skills that could be deployed effectively in Glasgow's commercial society.

After almost twenty years of construction, Allan Dreghorn's St Andrew's Church, south of the Cross in the Saltmarket, was finally completed in 1756. This is one of the finest Georgian Glasgow buildings to have survived. Its six distinct pillars and tall steeple were captured by the artists of the day. A year later the Macfarlane Observatory was built on the College grounds, east of the main buildings on the High Street. It was soon to be used by Alexander Wilson (1714–86), the Professor of Astronomy, who doubled up as the Foulis brothers' type founder. Many of these new buildings on the Glasgow skyline were described by Tobias Smollett (1721–71) in his *Expedition of Humphry Clinker* (1771). Some of the taller structures can be identified within the new views or prospects of the city, many of which were done in the Foulis Academy. Generally speaking, this was a rich period for Glasgow in terms of its intellectual and architectural development. New philosophical and literary clubs and societies were formed, attended by scholars, merchants and clergymen alike.[19] In this sense, Glasgow was nothing like Edinburgh, whose own cast of literati were without that unique injection of commercial and industry-led debate. Indeed, many historians have cited Glasgow's melting pot as a key influence on Smith's *Wealth of Nations*.[20] But, as we will explore in Chapter 4, this rise in good fortune for Glasgow's inhabitants was linked to the misery of transatlantic slavery. Over time this connection became more and more visible. As new streets were laid out to accommodate the growing city in 1763, the exploits of Glasgow's merchants, whom we remember in Glasgow's popular Merchant City district, were made clear with names like Jamaica Street and Havannah Street (Virginia Street had already been so-named). A new class of merchants were born in Glasgow as the tobacco trade brought them unprecedented wealth. Known as Tobacco Lords, there merchants styled themselves cultured and refined gentlemen as their empire swelled overseas. John Glassford, who was arguably the most prominent (he is certainly the best remembered) of these men, took up residence in the infamous Shawfield Mansion. It was Glassford, we should note, who helped establish the Foulis Academy of Fine Art. In Glassford a connection is also made between Glasgow's Enlightenment and its more nefarious history, for not only did these men put slaves to work on their plantations, some kept indentured servants in their Glasgow mansions.[21]

Despite the outbreak of the American War of Independence, which cut off the supply of these merchants' tobacco trade, the city witnessed further growth in the latter decades of the eighteenth century. Some merchants were, of course, ruined by the American war, but others saw the loss coming and invested in new businesses. William Cunninghame of Lainshaw went as far as to buy up the remaining tobacco stock from his compeers and sell it for a massive profit when the price inevitably rose. This enabled him to build his own mansion in 1778, which was later extended to become the Royal Exchange (1830), later the Stirling Library, and, as now, the Gallery of Modern Art.

Before the end of the 1770s there were more riots in Glasgow. In January 1779, the long-standing anti-Catholic sentiment spilled over into disorder following the passing in London of the Papists Act 1778. Eighty-five separate societies opposed the bill, the Saltmarket presses churned out sectarian pamphlets, and church elders inflamed the minds of the people with their sermons.[22] The mob in turn destroyed holy images in the High Street chapel and tried to burn down the house of Robert Bagnall, a potter and prominent Catholic.[23] Bagnall's warehouse also came under attack as the mob attempted to put him out of business, but the city magistrates paid him compensation.[24] Glasgow was a Protestant city for sure, but this view towards Catholics was not just a Glasgow problem. In Edinburgh there were riots to the same effect. James Boswell, who was living in the capital during this time, recorded similar actions in his journal. His wife gave refuge to an Italian dancing-mistress as the mob ran loose in the street and tried to burn down a small Catholic chapel. Boswell quipped: 'I loved a mob, but was ashamed of them now, for what could the papists do worse than this?'[25]

From 1780 onwards Glasgow entered a new phase in its development. The days of big tobacco were over and the brightest days of the Scottish Enlightenment had come and gone.[26] In 1782 the new Tontine Buildings were completed, comprising part of the Town Hall joining up with the old Tolbooth steeple, on which the heads of martyrs could be seen during the Restoration. Only the allegorical Tontine heads, or plaster masks, were on show in this new Glasgow. These symbols of status became famous, linking the new class of merchants with those who first brought real wealth into the city. The same year, George Square was laid out, signalling yet another shift in Glasgow's eloquent self-awareness. The green haven would soon be peopled with statues of civic heroes, presided over by the colossal City Chambers of Victorian Glasgow.

It was in the 1780s that David Dale began to make his mark in the city. Born in Ayrshire, Dale moved to Paisley and then to Glasgow, where he worked as a clerk to a silk mercer. In 1783 he was a founder member of the Glasgow Chamber of Commerce, commissioned Robert Adam to build his house in Charlotte Street, and set up the first branch of the Royal Bank of Scotland from a shop at the Cross. Despite all this success in Glasgow he is best remembered for his New Lanark project. By 1793 it was Britain's largest water-powered spinning mill and it is now one of only six UNESCO World Heritage sites in Scotland. Many historians have commented on the socially experimental thinking on Dale's part: with houses and schools fit for workers and their families, the almost utopian scheme became a community in itself with a population of over 1,300, out of sight of the burgeoning, and, often insanitary, centre of Glasgow.[27] Of course, such best-laid schemes gang aft agley, to quote Burns's immortal poem 'To a Mouse', which appeared in his first book of *Poems, Chiefly in the Scottish Dialect* in 1786. Not all workers considered their wages fair. During 1787 there were growing tensions between the weavers in the Calton district, east of the city centre, and their employers. Unsettled workers were said to have cut webs from the looms in the workshops and set bonfires in the streets as protest. On 3 September there were clashes between the workers who formed a mob and soldiers who were sent to quell the threat. Three of the weavers were killed by musket fire, three more died from their wounds. This was the first industrial dispute in Scotland to end in bloodshed: a sure sign of the rising power of the industrial elite when, previously, the only riots had been religious or political in nature. Many more class wars would follow; even today the word 'Calton' is synonymous with the plight of the working class.

In 1790 the Forth and Clyde Canal opened, signalling another shift in the industrial dynamic of Scotland. Among its many uses it joined up with the Monkland Canal, which greatly increased the amount of coal that could reach the city from Lanarkshire. The Forth and Clyde project had a long history rooted in the 1760s when plans began to take shape. Central to these plans was James Hutton, the Edinburgh-based geologist. The Company of the Proprietors of the Forth and Clyde Navigation had long held their meetings in the capital but by 1787 they conducted their business almost exclusively in Glasgow.[28] As with many of these large, cross-city partnerships the scheme was not without its setbacks, but it did boost Glasgow's trading profile significantly in the early nineteenth century.[29] In 1791 the last of the Bishop's Castle, lying in ruin for decades, was cleared for Glasgow's new hospital. The Royal Infirmary and the Trades Hall opened in 1794, two of the few surviving buildings from this time. But the Castle was not the only Glasgow landmark to lose its place in the cityscape. The Shawfield Mansion was also removed in 1793. John Glassford, the merchant and last owner of the Mansion, had died in serious debt and his son was forced to sell it. He is remembered by the new street that was built through the site: Glassford Street. As the century came to a close the city was far from the unified metropolis that these improvements might suggest. Britain and France were engaged in naval combat during the Revolutionary Wars and on 2 May 1794 Thomas Muir of Huntershill, the famous radical reformer, was banished to Botany Bay.[30] Small communities of artisan weavers met secretly during these tense times to discuss the uprising in France, but most Glaswegians remained loyal to Britain and their Hanoverian monarchs. One of the city's obscure poets, William Campbell, recorded the following lines in his manuscript:

> With Jacobin Monsters in Britain & France
> Your adoption may do very well
> But depend on't you'll never lead me such a dance
> As to kick up a Riot in H[ell] . . .[31]

The Royal Glasgow Volunteers were raised in case France invaded. Yet another riot broke out in December 1794 when a deserter escaped from the guard-house and found a mob of sympathisers willing to dissent. The cost of war and faltering trade were compounded with an incessant spell of crop failure so disastrous that in 1799 and 1800 the Glasgow magistrates footed the bill to give cheaper grain to the poorer inhabitants of the city. And so, as at the beginning of the eighteenth century, Glasgow entered the nineteenth century with many social problems in tow.

In 1801 there were 77,000 people living in the city. Weaving was fast becoming Glasgow's most valuable asset: a 200-loom factory was established in Pollokshaws in 1801 and, three years later, Archibald Buchanan made improvements to the power loom, effectively boosting John Monteith's enterprise and quickening the rate of output in the new mills. From the ashes of the Scottish Enlightenment the nation's first public museum came home to Glasgow. The Hunterian Museum was opened in 1807 in the University campus on the High Street. Renowned anatomist and physicist William Hunter (b. 1718) had died in London in 1783 and his collections were to stay in London for a set period for the continuation of their use particular to the teaching provisions he helped establish. But his connections to Glasgow, which we will explore in Chapter 2, were eventually honoured when his collections were moved north to form the core of the new museum. This new museum was nothing short of a monument to the city's rich contribution to scientific, literary and philosophical innovation during the previous century. In 1809, Sir John Moore died after sustaining wounds in combat. He requested to be buried where he died, in Corunna. In Glasgow's West End there is a Corunna Street, and the first statue to be erected in George Square (1810–19) was dedicated to one of the nation's beloved sons. Sir John Moore's father, Dr John Moore, was a well-respected surgeon, author, and famous correspondent of Robert Burns.[32] Along with the 8th Duke of Hamilton, father and son went on a Grand Tour of the Continent in 1772, but by the time he became a soldier the younger Moore stood for an imperial Britain with a greater need for brave soldiers than learned travellers. In his diaries Moore is often quite open about his actions, many of which reveal the horrors of slavery in the Caribbean islands. Glasgow's long arm of empire became increasingly useful in the city's quest to be the 'Second City', but the moral implications of this legacy are perhaps too grave to discuss in this brief chapter. We will encounter these more fully in Chapter 4.

Throughout the next decade there were several new ventures worth noting. 1812 is best known for being the year in which Henry Bell's PS *Comet* began running services from Glasgow to Greenock and Helensburgh. The vessel was named after 'The Great Comet' had appeared in Scottish skies at the end of the previous year and, though it was by no means the most impressive steam engine to be launched during the late Georgian period, it was certainly an exciting spectacle. Two years later the Glasgow Asylum for Lunatics was opened in

Parliamentary Road. It goes without saying that mental health care during this period was far from advanced, but we must remember that before the asylum was opened people were simply thrown into the Town's Hospital without much chance of recovery. The asylum was built in the panopticon – or, radial – style, allowing for complete observation. As the population of the city increased and resources stretched, a new building was needed and in 1842 the asylum was moved to Gartnavel, where it could cater for around 500 patients.

As we know, Roman Catholics had been far from accepted into the social fold of Glasgow since the Reformation. At every opportunity the city pledged itself beside William of Orange and, later, the Hanoverians. But the centuries-old Protestant city was growing in number by the year and the Catholic population along with it. This is evident from the construction of St Andrew's Roman Catholic Church, or Cathedral, built on Clyde Street beside the Town's Hospital in 1816.[33] The building is still in use today, and while it represents a positive step in the direction of Glasgow's tolerant society, religious tensions would surface time and again. Sadly, Glasgow's sectarianism is one of the prominent cultural markers which survives its long history.

Towards the close of the decade a new class war was brewing. As before, many Glaswegians were agonised by a lack of work and, when work was offered, painfully low wages. Many of these were the same handloom weavers whose efforts were lining the pockets of the new business elite in the city who had replaced the famous Tobacco Lords. In 1820 these tensions boiled over: a bill was posted on the streets by the radicals with a view of organising a Provisional Government. It was read by all who passed, including the preacher Thomas Chalmers, who in turn delivered a sermon on 'the slumbering ferocities of man'.[34] Three names are usually cited in this short-lived uprising: James Wilson, John Baird and Andrew Hardie. For their role in the war these men were executed and became known as the Radical Martyrs. The People's Palace in Glasgow is home to Hardie's brush from his cell in Edinburgh where, while waiting out his last days, he carved his name, date and location into the wood, adding a thistle and the coat of arms of Glasgow. At the other end of the social spectrum, Queen Caroline was at the receiving end of the Pains and Penalties Bill 1820. Like many other British cities, a strong support grew in Glasgow in favour of Caroline, and when the bill was withdrawn the people celebrated with bonfires and displayed candles in their windows. The next year William McGavin, who is remembered by his pseudonym 'The Protestant', was summoned to court in Edinburgh by his accuser Andrew Scott of the new Roman

Catholic Church for slanderous journalism. A large crowd travelled from Glasgow to watch, and the jury leaned in favour of the priest, who was awarded damages. In 1822 there was an Orange march in the city, and by 1829 certain societies met to prevent more Catholic concessions coming up from Westminster. In 1830 George IV died and was succeeded by his brother, who became King William IV. With the death of George IV, the government was dissolved by law, and for the last seven years of this Georgian era the Reform Act would come to define it.

Throughout this tumultuous period of political and religious reform the population of Glasgow had breached the 100,000 mark (around 1811). By 1831 that figure had, remarkably, doubled. It is this rate of growth with which we associate Glasgow's strength in numbers. Throughout 1831 around 80,000 people showed up to rally in Glasgow Green in favour of the Reform Act, which was rejected at first attempt by the House of Lords. There were scenes of jubilation throughout the country when the bill was passed on 4 June 1832, signalling one of the most important shifts in Scottish and British history. More people than ever, though not nearly enough, could cast votes in favour of *their* candidate. The next year, the Slavery Abolition Act was passed. Glasgow had long been a participant in the national debate regarding slavery. Many of the city's philanthropists and writers saw it as a clear injustice that slavery was still carried on in their name, while others, worried about the impact of the bill on their estates, maintained their protests against abolition. Of course, trading was kept up and slaves were still kept. Those merchants who were sanctioned with the one hand of the law were compensated with the other. If anything, Glasgow's impact on the world was only deepening. In 1834, the famous cotton merchant Kirkman Finlay sent a ship bearing his name to Canton in China.[35] We might imagine this ship disappearing over the horizon and into the Victorian period itself. It left behind a teeming, flourishing metropolis. This is crucial, because the motifs of Glasgow today are often claimed as purely Victorian.

In Maurice Lindsay's *Illustrated Guide to Glasgow, 1837* (1989) it is said that the Victorian period 'began a reign which was to spread the bounds of the British Empire "wider still and wider" and turn Glasgow into "the workshop of the world"'.[36] But it is the all-too-often overlooked Georgian period in which Glasgow became sure of itself. In the long eighteenth century Glasgow developed from a town, chiefly religious in its culture, to become a major centre of the Scottish Enlightenment, which, in more ways than one, paved the way for the same mechanical and industrial industries that we often exalt as Victorian. Before

1837 Glasgow had played host to many of the great intellectual and commercial achievements in Scotland. Throughout this book, we will explore both the enlightened and the unknown histories of Georgian Glasgow. We will encounter a truly contradictory but fascinating age worth remembering.

NOTES

1. George MacGregor, *The History of Glasgow, from the Earliest Period to the Present Time* (Glasgow: Thomas D. Morison, 1881), 287; George Eyre-Todd, *History of Glasgow, Volume III: From the Revolution to the Passing of the Reform Acts 1832–33* (Glasgow: Jackson, Wylie & Co., 1934), 67.
2. MacGregor, *The History of Glasgow*, 291.
3. This data was obtained from searching *The Trans-Atlantic Slave Trade Database:* <http://www.slavevoyages.org/voyage/26093/variables> (last accessed 30 August 2020).
4. MacGregor, *The History of Glasgow*, 298.
5. Ibid., 300–2.
6. *A vindication of Mr. Hutcheson from the calumnious aspersions of a late pamphlet, by several of his scholars* (1738), 7.
7. Magnus Maclean, ed., *Archaeology, Education, Medical, & Charitable Institutions of Glasgow* (Glasgow: Published by the Local Committee for the Meeting for the British Association, 1901), 92; MacGregor, *The History of Glasgow*, 308.
8. MacGregor, *The History of Glasgow*, 309; James Cleland, Statistical Facts Descriptive of The Former and Present State of Glasgow (Glasgow: Bell and Bain, 1837), 120.
9. See Roger L. Emerson and Paul Wood, 'Science and Enlightenment in Glasgow 1690–1802', in Charles W. J. Withers and Paul Wood, eds, *Science and Medicine in the Scottish Enlightenment* (Phantassie, East Lothian: Tuckwell Press, 2002), 79–142 (88).
10. Already in place were the statues of the brothers Thomas and George Hutcheson, in Hutcheson's Hospital (1639) and the bust of Zachary Boyd in the College.
11. Cf. <http://www.visionofbritain.org.uk/travellers/Defoe/38> (last accessed 30 August 2020).
12. James Oswald Mitchell, 'Table of Dates', *Old Glasgow Essays* (Glasgow: James Maclehose and Sons, 1905), xxxi–xliv.
13. Lithographic reproduction of letter at University of Glasgow, Special Collections: Sp Coll Eph. A/106.
14. MacGregor, *The History of Glasgow*, 322–4.
15. See Alexander Fenton, 'The People Below: Dougal Graham's Chapbooks as a Mirror of the Lower Classes in Eighteenth Century Scotland', Alisoun Gardner-Medwin and Janet Hadley Williams, eds, *A Day Estivall: Essays*

on the *Music, Poetry and History of Scotland and England & Poems Previously Unpublished* (Aberdeen: Aberdeen University Press, 1990), 69–80 (69) and F. W. Freeman, 'Robert Fergusson: Pastoral and Politics at Mid Century', in Andrew Hook, ed., *The History of Scottish Literature Volume 2, 1660–1800* (Aberdeen: Aberdeen University Press, 1987), 141–55 (149)

16. MacGregor, *The History of Glasgow*, 325.
17. Ibid., 337.
18. Maclean, *Archaeology, Education, Medical, & Charitable Institutions of Glasgow*, 95–6.
19. Most prominent among these was the Glasgow Literary Society (founded 1752). See John Strang, *Glasgow and its Clubs: or, glimpses of the condition, manners, characters, and oddities of the city, during the past and present centuries* (London and Glasgow: Richard Griffin & Co., 1855).
20. J. M. Reid, *Glasgow* [British Cities and Towns series] (London: B. T. Batsford, 1956), 70.
21. This will be covered in more detail in Chapter 4.
22. Strang, *Glasgow and its Clubs*, 97.
23. Wallace Harvey, *Chronicles of Saint Mungo; Or, Antiquities and Traditions of Glasgow* (Glasgow: John Smith & Sons, 1843), 98.
24. MacGregor, *The History of Glasgow*, 265.
25. Hugh M. Milne, *Boswell's Edinburgh Journals, 1767–1786* (Edinburgh: John Donald, 2013 [2001]), 333.
26. Reid, *Glasgow*, 80; T. M. Devine, 'The Golden Age of Tobacco', in T. M. Devine and Gordon Jackson, eds, *Glasgow, Volume I: Beginnings to 1830* (Manchester: Manchester University Press, 1995), 139–83 (139).
27. Eyre-Todd, *History of Glasgow*, 43; Reid, *Glasgow*, 84.
28. Jean Jones, 'James Hutton and the Forth and Clyde Canal,' *Annals of Science*, 39:3 (1982), 255–63 (258).
29. Gordon Jackson, 'New Horizons in Trade,' in T. M. Devine and Gordon Jackson, eds, *Glasgow, Volume I: Beginnings to 1830* (Manchester: Manchester University Press, 1995), 214–38 (221).
30. He escaped on board an American trading vessel in January 1796. Interest in Muir is rising: a new book of essays was recently published: Gerard Carruthers and Don Martin, eds, *Thomas Muir of Huntershill: Essays for the Twenty-First Century* (Edinburgh: Humming Earth, 2016).
31. The manuscript is held in the Mitchell Library, Glasgow. This section can be found at MS. 73, f. 27.
32. It was to John Moore that Burns sent his famous autobiographical letter on 2 August 1787. The letter seems to have spent some time in Glasgow, as Burns added a note on 23 September, saying that 'the foregoing letter was unluckily forgot among other papers at Glasgow on my way to Edinr.' (British Library, Egerton MS 1660).
33. There is a good summary of this building, along with many other archi-

tectural gems in Glasgow, in Michael Meighan's *Glasgow in 50 Buildings* (Stroud: Amberley, 2016); for those now lost see Frank Worsdall, *The City that Disappeared: Glasgow's Demolished Architecture* (Glasgow: The Molendinar Press, 1981) and Carol Foreman, *Lost Glasgow: Glasgow's Lost Architectural Heritage* (Edinburgh: Birlinn, 2002).
34. MacGregor, *The History of Glasgow*, 408; Irene Maver, 'The Guardianship of the Community: Civic Authority prior to 1833,' in T. M. Devine and Gordon Jackson, eds, *Glasgow, Volume I: Beginnings to 1830* (Manchester: Manchester University Press, 1995) 239–77 (239).
35. Mitchell, 'Table of Dates'.
36. Maurice Lindsay, *Illustrated Guide to Glasgow, 1837* (1989), 12.

PART II

Remembering the Glasgow Enlightenment

The Glasgow Enlightenment was the collective of intellectual activity and achievement in Glasgow during the Scottish Enlightenment. In its peak years, students of the University could attend the lectures of Adam Smith (1723–90), Joseph Black, John Millar (1735–1801), and John Anderson (1726–96). According to David Steuart Erskine, 11th Earl of Buchan (1742–1829), this was 'a Groupe not equalled in their Departments at that time at any University in the world'.[1] But how is the presence of the Scottish Enlightenment in Glasgow remembered? To answer this we consider the extant architecture and object as well as the layering-up of images, references and commemorations that portray the intellectual side of eighteenth-century Glasgow. In other words, we can review the 'cultural memory' of Georgian Glasgow to see whether or not a strong light has been cast on this history. In the Introduction we looked at the ways memory studies can help us recover lost or forgotten stories such as this one. To recap the core ideas: Maurice Halbwachs's definition of *collective memory* ('the result, or sum, or combination of individual recollections of many members of the same society') has been central to the development of memory theory in many, if not most, fields within the humanities.[2] Since Halbwachs, both Jan Assmann and Aleida Assmann have discussed the nature of collective memory and its adaptability. Theirs is the idea that collective memory is better understood today by bookending the term with two others: 'communicative' and 'cultural' memory. 'Communicative memory' is a living interaction 'which normally reaches no farther back than eighty years, the time span of three interacting generations' while 'cultural memory' can exist in a 'disembodied form', depending on 'institutions of preservation and re-embodiment'.[3] The Scottish Enlightenment in Glasgow is in this sense 'disembodied'. No one alive today was there to literally remember it. But we can, and should, remember it in a cultural sense, and not least of all because there remains a strong tradition of locating the Scottish Enlightenment solely in Edinburgh.

The capital of Scotland was cast as the capital of the Scottish Enlightenment in scholarship of the 1980s. *A Hotbed of Genius: The Scottish Enlightenment* (1986) edited by David Daiches, Jean Jones and Peter Jones was a typical scholarly effort to centralise and, to an extent, sterilise the story.[4] As such it was criticised for its overt tidiness, for being 'uncluttered' with – in the words of one reviewer –

'poverty, Masonry, Jacobitism, or the kirk'.[5] And in spite of references to Glasgow and Aberdeen, and the never-returned-to claim that 'the Scottish Enlightenment can be said to have begun in Glasgow' in the form of Francis Hutcheson, Edinburgh is exalted as the undisputed centre.[6] With an overwhelming preference for Edinburgh-based examples (the index includes four page references for Glasgow and thirty-six for Edinburgh) it is difficult to see those examples from outside the capital as tokenistic. In other words, it was once common to synonymise the Edinburgh Enlightenment and the Scottish Enlightenment. What makes this unusual in *A Hotbed of Genius* is the pretext. First, the cover: an image from the Foulis Academy in Glasgow (see Figure 2). When the text was reprinted in 1996, the cover displayed the famous portrait of David Hume instead, whose statue can be found near that of Adam Smith on the Royal Mile. Second, the title: borrowed from Tobias Smollett's picaresque novel *The Expedition of Humphry Clinker* (1771). The reference to the capital as a 'hotbed of genius' should not be without its context. Smollett's characters are gushing in their praise of various Scottish locales, and this nod to Edinburgh's Enlightenment is followed by a description of Glasgow as 'the pride of Scotland' with its 'fine University, its library, its observatory and its set of instruments'.[7] This list is a description of a local Enlightenment more often forgotten than it is remembered, and which Chapter 2 will go on to discuss.

In the 1990s the focus began to change. Roy Campbell's essay 'Scotland's Neglected Enlightenment' (1990) was the first serious effort to alter the historiographical trajectory of the Scottish Enlightenment. Campbell claims that 'confining the genius of the age geographically' only 'detracts from its influence over the rest of Scotland'. More strikingly, Campbell declares: 'The hotbed of genius which was appropriated by Edinburgh had its intellectual foundations in the work in Glasgow. Glasgow led; Edinburgh followed.'[8] This was a crucial turn, and *The Glasgow Enlightenment* (1995) was soon published. Edited by Andrew Hook and Richard Sher, the volume covered new ground, stressing the importance of the University of Glasgow and the Enlightenment outside the Academy as it abounded in the streets. In the same year, Manchester University Press published *Glasgow, Volume I*. Edited by Tom Devine and Gordon Jackson, this text represents the most comprehensive overview of Glasgow's cultural and social history in the long eighteenth century to date. The Enlightenment is not left behind. In fact, Richard Sher, perhaps for the first time, considers the three principal factors of Georgian Glasgow together in his contribution 'Commerce, Religion and the Enlightenment in Eighteenth-Century Glasgow'. In his co-editorship of *The Glasgow*

Enlightenment almost all of the chief players were accounted for but it is Sher's chapter in the Devine and Jackson work that goes further, portraying a pre-eminent classical Enlightenment which predates Edinburgh and even, in certain respects, London. There were other important works published in the 1990s. The new focus on Aberdeen – see Paul Wood's *The Aberdeen Enlightenment* (1995) – and, to a larger extent, Glasgow, changed the course of Scottish Enlightenment scholarship for the better. But good scholarship was not enough. We can hardly blame the preference for Edinburgh as the centre of the Scottish Enlightenment on academics and art historians. Neither can we ignore the fact that Glasgow boasts other, more dominant features which tower over its Georgian era of Enlightenment, casting a long and stubborn shadow.

The industrial revolution transformed Glasgow completely, encouraging growth away from its historic city centre. It spread west where a new University was built in 1870. The population increased tenfold during the nineteenth century: from 77,000 in 1801 to a staggering 762,000 in 1901.[9] The city became a world leader in shipbuilding, and to this day that civic achievement is revered above all others. Immigration from the Highlands and Ireland during this time rekindled the old flames of prejudice, giving Glasgow an undesirable reputation as a hotbed of sectarianism and intolerance. In the midst of all this, writers were profiting on the rise of razor gangs: McArthur and Long's *No Mean City* (1935) is perhaps the chief example. This explosion of culture forged a split image

Figure 1 Arbuckle Coffee Company card no. 86, *Scotland* (1889).

of Scotland: Edinburgh as the learned and refined Dr Jekyll; Glasgow as the poor and rough Mr Hyde, born in the smog of the new age. In 1889 the Arbuckle Coffee Company produced a 'Scotland' card portraying this exact duality (see Figure 1). When we ultimately go beyond these binaries we find a vivid and largely forgotten culture in Glasgow that bolsters the true story of the Scottish Enlightenment.

NOTES

1. Richard B. Sher, 'Commerce, Religion and the Enlightenment in Eighteenth-Century Glasgow', in T. M. Devine and Gordon Jackson, eds, *Glasgow: Volume 1: Beginnings to 1830* (Manchester: Manchester University Press, 1995), 312–59 (345).
2. Maurice Halbwachs, *On Collective Memory*, ed. Lewis A. Coser (Chicago: University of Chicago Press, 1992 [1941]), 39.
3. Jan Assmann, 'Communicative and Cultural Memory', in Astrid Erll and Ansgar Nünning, eds, *Media and Cultural Memory: An International and Interdisciplinary Handbook* (Berlin: Walter de Gruyter GmbH & Co., 2008), 109–18 (110–11).
4. When a public exhibition sponsored by the University of Edinburgh's Institute for Advanced Studies in the Humanities (IASH), also named *A Hotbed of Genius*, was put on in 1986, it was natural that lectures, seminars and art exhibitions (for instance, on 'The Golden Age of Scottish Painting') focused on Edinburgh.
5. Alan T. McKenzie, '*Robert Burns*' (review) and '*A Hotbed of Genius: The Scottish Enlightenment, 1730–1790*' (review), *Eighteenth-Century Studies*, 22:2 (1988–9), 253–6 (256).
6. David Daiches, Peter Jones, Jean Jones, eds, *A Hotbed of Genius: The Scottish Enlightenment, 1730–1790* (Edinburgh: Edinburgh University Press, 1986), 1.
7. Tobias Smollett, *The Expedition of Humphry Clinker* (London: Penguin, 1985 [1771]), 274.
8. Roy Campbell, 'Scotland's Neglected Enlightenment,' *History Today*, 40:5 (1990) <https://www.historytoday.com/archive/scotlands-neglected-enlightenment> (last accessed 30 August 2020).
9. Population trends for Glasgow 1801–2013, <http://www.understandingglasgow.com/indicators/population/trends/historic_population_trend> (last accessed 30 August 2020).

2

Glasgow as a Centre for the Arts, Science and Medicine

> Here great Buchanan learnt to scan
> The verse that mak's him mair than man.
> Cullen and Hunter here began
> Their first probations,
> And Smith, frae Glasgow, formed his plan—
> 'The Wealth o' Nations'.
>
> John Mayne – 'Glasgow: A Poem' (1803)[1]

Before Glasgow grew in size, it grew intellectually. The city we think of today reaches towards towns like Paisley and Rutherglen at its edges, accounting for over 1.5 million people in what we call Greater Glasgow. In the eighteenth century Glasgow was a self-contained but bustling hive of activity. It grew slowly at first, then more confidently, before stretching out dramatically with each year of the nineteenth century. In the early Georgian period there were only five main roads spreading out from the Mercat Cross: High Street, running north-east toward the medieval cathedral and ancient centre of Glasgow; Saltmarket Street, running south towards the Clyde; Gallowgate Street, taking you out of the city to the east; and Trongate Street which merged with Argyle Street and led to the village of Grahamston (over which Central Station was built) before giving way to the then green and spacious lands we know now as the West End. This brings us to the University of Glasgow: the cradle of the city's Enlightenment and a large player in the Scottish Enlightenment more generally. Today, it sits proudly on Gilmorehill in the West End. The campus as we know it was completed in 1870, but beside this date there are two other important years emblazoned on the University's buildings. Beneath the archway of the main entrance on the south front, in line with the inscription marking the year of the completion of the building – '1870' – a stone plaque bears the year '1451'.

This is when the University itself was founded. A little less obvious is another date which can be seen from University Avenue as you walk towards Kelvin Way. On the back of Pearce Lodge a stone plaque bears the inscription ANNO 1658. This is when the first University campus was complete. Known colloquially as the Old College, the campus once stood proudly on the High Street, about halfway between the Mercat Cross and the cathedral. Its loss was one of the gravest for Glasgow. At an institutional level the University, like many others, retained its history when it moved. While its reputation was not tarnished – indeed it was improved – the cultural memory of Glasgow's Enlightenment suffered greatly. To understand this more fully we must consider the true diversity of the Enlightenment here. What was achieved in Glasgow that would be worth remembering?

The answer takes us through the different branches of eighteenth-century University life. Collaboration was common. Scientists were as involved in the classical world as moral philosophers and the art classes were tailored towards manufacturing as well as honouring the aesthetic grandeur of Rome. Take Alexander Wilson, for instance. Born on the same year the Georgian era commenced, he is known as the first Professor of Astronomy at Glasgow and his discoveries in monitoring sunspot activity have made his name immortal in that field. But he was also a renowned type founder. Coming to Glasgow from St Andrews in the 1740s, he radically improved the printing press of Robert and Andrew Foulis, playing a major role in their becoming a European name in publishing.[2] Such intellectual diversity was the norm during the Enlightenment, and in Glasgow there is no shortage of examples. Tobias Smollett, remembered today as a fine novelist, was also a poet and a long-serving physician. Educated at Glasgow, his connections to the medical literati help us reposition Glasgow as an intrinsic point in the development of the Scottish Enlightenment, constantly bridging professional movement between Edinburgh and London. Two years after Smollett's death the Foulis brothers printed his *Ode to Independence*, followed closely by a new work by James Watt, the chief figure of the Glasgow Enlightenment rivalled only, occasionally, by William Hunter. The list goes on, and so the interweaving connections between the famous names of the Old College comprise a lively web of imagination and invention that outshone Edinburgh.[3] We might think of this network now as a 'living centre', with the University its beating heart. As we proceed, this term should become all the more relevant to the discussion of cultural memory and the inevitable loss of this living centre from the historical image of Glasgow.

A Centre for the Arts, Science and Medicine

The first plaudit Glasgow can claim is that Francis Hutcheson, the so-called 'Father of the Scottish Enlightenment', deployed his brand of humanist moral philosophy at the University of Glasgow, inspiring a new generation of thinkers.[4] His tolerant stoicism was a breath of fresh air in a place that had become known for its devout, and often intolerant, Presbyterianism. It is telling that the first book published in Glasgow was *The Protestation of The Generall Assemblie of the Church of Scotland* (1638), printed to record a period of religious upheaval and set out some new rules. The Covenanters had just excommunicated the Episcopalian bishops at Glasgow Cathedral and were officially posturing, forbidding the printing of religious books without a licence.[5] In Georgian Glasgow books were still mostly religious. The Foulis brothers, however, promoted Hutcheson's ideas through their flourishing press and in their choices as booksellers. Though there has been no stand-alone study of the brothers since 1913 their achievements are well charted in scholarship from recent years.[6] The title page of Foulis's first book – *A Catalogue of Books Imported* (1740) – informs the reader that they should contact Gavin Hamilton, bookseller, in Edinburgh, or Robert Foulis, 'at his Chamber in the College of Glasgow'.[7] The Edinburgh book market would become a vital link in the chain connecting Glasgow to the wider Scottish Enlightenment across all disciplines. This initial, gentle step into the publishing world was followed by thirteen more titles, all printed *for* Robert, 'within the College', and often bearing Hamilton's name.

It was not until June 1742 that Robert began to print for himself. He had just married the sister of the Professor of Greek, James Moor (bap. 1712, d. 1779). Foulis's first book, *The Meditations of the Emperor Marcus Aurelius Antoninus*, was a collaborative effort by Hutcheson and his new brother-in-law Moor, newly translated from the Greek. In a letter from that time Hutcheson reveals that part of the intention in completing this work was to benefit Robert Foulis's career. It went through four editions in Glasgow between 1742 and 1764. The first edition was recently edited and reproduced with an introduction and notes by James Moore and Michael Silverthorne (2008). For them, Hutcheson 'was refashioning Christian doctrine, notably the Presbyterian or Reformed doctrine of original sin, by substituting it' for a classical concept: the 'natural constitution of human nature', containing 'a heart or a soul that is oriented toward affection for others, good offices, benevolence'.[8] This blast of the trumpet from the old world in a city determined to forget it fell on many deaf ears. Most of those who heard it were unhappy. To get a sense of why this would be the case, consider that only twenty years before, a new edition of the story of William Wallace by Hamilton of Gilbertfield (c.1665–1751) was published in Glasgow. In it, the author replaced 'the Old obsolete Words', going as far as to bend the religious tone: swapping the role of the Blessed Virgin Mary for Dame Fortune in the passage where a saltire is painted on Wallace's face.[9] It is said to have been vastly popular in the eighteenth century, second only to the Bible in the bookcases of Scotland's literate populace.

To offer another example, consider Foulis's classical work in another context. Just outside Glasgow in Cambuslang, while the *Meditations* was being published, an unprecedented spiritual revival (or 'Wark') took place.[10] In those days the small town, surrounded by hills and valleys, had only one main road to Glasgow that was often in a treacherous condition.[11] Yet it is said that this awakening 'spread through a fair portion of western and central Scotland, eventually reaching to the far northern shires of Sutherland and Ross'. Afterwards, 'Scottish ministers and laymen kept the Edinburgh and Glasgow presses churning with pamphlets and tracts about the revivals, extending to thousands of pages.'[12] To consider the Cambuslang revival an 'event', though it occurred over three years, in the same way that we might consider the General Assembly of 1638 an 'event' allows for the same theoretical framework to be used.[13] Arthur Fawcett's *The Cambuslang Revival* (1971) provides detailed commentary quoting 'one of the leading Scottish historians in the nineteenth century', Burton J. Hill, who described 'profuse fits of weeping and trembling ... epilepsies and faintings ... contortions and howls ... emitted by old obdurate sinners' suddenly aware of their sins.[14]

T. C. Smout notes that the history of the Covenanters was by then entrenched in the minds of people from these areas, which is in keeping with their united and 'excessive religious zeal'.[15] And so the Cambuslang Revival is particularly interesting here. It gives us an insight into the complex, perhaps oppositional culture in the west of Scotland: on the one hand, well-read and classical, on the other, well-versed and biblical. Two very different histories were being recalled by those eager pupils who read the musings of a Roman emperor and those whose Bible was perhaps their only book, and to two very different effects: the former feeds a small, closed-doors enlightenment in the College while the latter reinscribes a sense of community sewn through religious practice. As such, the Cambuslang Wark tells us more about collective memory than *Meditations*. The presiding minister, William McCulloch, kept a record of 'spiritual narratives of more than a hundred persons from parishes all over western Scotland, from many walks of life'.[16] Fawcett's text gives an adequate overview of these lengthy narratives, the language of which is honest and revelatory about the kind of daily rituals carried out. It is from these first-hand accounts that the transition from orality to manuscript can be perceived. For instance, twenty-year-old Jane Reston told the minister: 'I used all along from a child to pray in secret evening and morning; and if at any time I happened to miss it in the morning, I found something or other go wrong with me that day.' Later in the testimony she says: 'At the entry to public worship I found the words sung powerfully and particularly applied to me, as what was my own case, and I was made to see that I was the most filthy and polluted creature that could be ... and that I was covered all over with wounds and bruises and putrefying sores; and that no soundness remained in me from the crown of my head to the sole of my foot.'[17] This is typical of the secret/public dichotomy found in other narratives: beginning with some account of schooling; the usual method of prayer; sin(s); and reawakening. Jane Reston's account exemplifies the coming to life of the fears accumulated in private prayer when in the company of others. The chorus of voices in the ceremony seems to unleash the idea that she is guilty of a multitude of sins and therefore covered in sores. It is possible to consider this phenomenon in the realm of cultural memory. Mnemonic activities such as learning the catechism become collective when part of the group, and are therefore altered before McCulloch transcribes their testimonies.

In Jan Assmann's *Religion and Cultural Memory* (2006) the author touches on the 'motives' behind our recollections, and how they are inevitably shaped through 'dialogue and intercommunication'.[18] Lynn Abrams' discussion of 'composure' sheds light on the problems of such first-hand accounts. 'The story that a person tells,' she says, 'is just one of many that are possible ... its shape, form and content is determined by the need for the narrator to construct a memory story with which he or she can feel comfortable at that moment. And a comfortable telling is often one in which the story told coheres with larger cultural understandings.'[19] Therefore it is highly likely that there were many exaggerations of emotional states – though this is not to discredit the intensity of the laypeople's emotions – and that the narratives were added to by a Calvinistic God-fearing imagination. It often seems as though the narrators were trying to converse with God, in a way proving their new-found confidence in the established, personal relationship that their religion had promised.

At this, it must be noted that 'Scottish parishioners were, to an unusual extent, a catechized people'.[20] Their ability to read and write (especially among the working classes) was noted in seminal works such as Houston's *Scottish Literacy and the Scottish Identity* (1985). As the narratives show, the Bible is the foremost text used for learning, spiritually and mnemonically. 'And no wonder,' says Fawcett, 'for the Bible was inextricably intertwined with the religious development of the Scottish people from the dawn of the Reformation.'[21] The idea of the book as object is useful here, as 'the Bible was regarded as something in the nature of a talisman'.[22] Landsman reminds us that some of the 'potential converts' were advised by the preachers 'not to rely so much on the words of men (ministers) but to rely instead on the Bible'.[23] In reading their *own* Bible, laypeople's personal relationships with God would inform their collective relationships as well as their conversations with ministers and other powerful men. In *The Printing Press as an Agent of Change* (1979) Elizabeth Eisenstein says that 'Protestantism was above all a "book religion"'.[24] From the oral culture of smaller communities, to the manuscript accounts, the next step was a book culture with a ready market. Following the Cambuslang Wark, Glasgow was increasingly energetic in the publication of religious works, confirming the dominance of the religious identity of the city.

This identity remained strong throughout the eighteenth century despite the work of the Foulis brothers to revive a classical, humanist culture that could fit alongside it. Their so-called 'Glasgow Homer' remains their landmark achievement. Consisting of two folios – *The Iliad*, vols I–II (1756) and *The Odyssey* and *Homeric Hymns*, vols III–IV (1758)[25] – the 'Glasgow Homer' was funded by Glasgow University professors and was 'almost entirely restricted to being an institutional gift'.[26] Different parts of the text were prize-winners in successive years as judged by the Edinburgh Society for the Encouragement of Arts, Sciences, Manufactures and Agriculture. By then the Foulis press had produced the first Greek-language book in Glasgow (1743) and the first work of an English divine translated into Gaelic (1750). Their reputation for fine, simply printed and accurate books was largely due to the arrival of the aforementioned Alexander Wilson, and this success paved the way for their other chief venture. In 1753, the Foulis brothers established their Academy of Fine Arts in the grounds of the University of Glasgow, within the University Library and other buildings.[27] In so doing, they effected an unprecedented joint culture of literature and fine art in Scotland with strong links to France and Italy. In his *Dictionary of Scottish Art and Architecture* (2004) Peter McEwan calls it 'the single most influential factor in the development of eighteenth-century Scottish art'.[28] The origins of the Academy date back to the 1730s, when Robert

Foulis was in Paris, where he witnessed 'the connection and mutual influence of the Arts and Sciences upon one another and upon society' and observed 'the influence of invention in Drawing and Modelling on many manufactures'.[29] The concept of an academy was at the forefront of Robert Foulis's mind long before he became the University printer. And while the French Academy in Paris was 'used as the prototype for art schools throughout the continent' including Florence, Rome, Bologna, Milan and Vienna before 1720,[30] and was undoubtedly the model for the brothers, there was activity in the British Isles before 1753. The first was the short-lived Edinburgh Academy of St Luke, opened by Allan Ramsay senior (1684–1758),[31] the architect William Adam (bap. 1689, d. 1748), and the English engraver Richard Cooper (1701–64) among others in 1729.[32] The other was a school of design in Dublin, opened in 1742.[33]

On top of being short-lived, neither of these had a partner press or an evolved range of arts. Indeed, for all the Scottish Enlightenment publishing that would take place in Edinburgh and London (where the Royal Academy was established in 1768) in later decades, neither city was equipped with a combined culture of print and fine art in the same campus. The Foulis brothers meanwhile had already established a recognisable and prestigious trademark in the classics, and led the way in painting and sculpture as well as drawing and engraving. François Antoine Aveline (1718–62), their choice engraver, would go on to inspire a truly eminent style by, above others, Robert Paul (1739–70), whose topographical views of Glasgow comprise the greater part of the remnants of the Academy. The brothers also hired two painters and a copperplate printer from France and modellers from Italy to initiate their art teaching.[34] Besides Paul's views, the models of James Tassie (1735–99), one of the most famous pupils of the Academy, famously known as 'Tassie medallions' are vital elements in several museum collections in the United Kingdom. They include likenesses of Adam Smith, Joseph Black, Robert Foulis himself and several other players of the Scottish Enlightenment, making Tassie one of the major artists of eighteenth-century Britain. Yet for all the work carried out in the Academy between its opening and its closure in 1775, the venture remains almost extinct in Glasgow's public imagination. Even in most historical and literary scholarship, the Academy is overwhelmed by other, more consistently accepted points, especially Glasgow's commercial and industrial character and Edinburgh's historic nurturing of the arts.[35] Looking back on his time at the Academy, David Steuart Erskine, 11th Earl of Buchan, said that while the University of Edinburgh 'as connected with the Capital' might have been more favourably received, their art school in Glasgow, 'tho in a remote corner, has had the good fortune to awaken the attention of many in different parts of the kingdom'.[36]

It is likely that the brothers' long-standing association with Jacobitism and their seeming fondness of Catholic Europe damaged their reputation in Glasgow and dampened their hopes of obtaining royal patronage. Their lobbying is evident in a few references here and there throughout the surviving letters of Robert Foulis, but can be literally seen in David Allan's 1761 engraving (see Figure 2). As mentioned before, this image was used on the cover of *A Hotbed of Genius* but was subsequently replaced by the Edinburgh Enlightenment face of David Hume. The event portrayed is matched by James MacLehose's description:

> A curious but well vouched-for incident connected with the Academy is that the pictures were exhibited—*sub Jove frigido*—on the walls of the inner

Figure 2 David Allan, *Fine Art Exhibition in the Court of the Old College* (1761). © CSG CIC Glasgow Museums and Libraries Collection: The Mitchell Library, Special Collections.

quadrangle of the University on 22nd September 1761 on the occasion of the coronation of George III; and annually 'upon every return of his Majesty's birthday' till 1775.³⁷

You can hardly imagine an outdoor art exhibition in Glasgow during which the paint stays dry – perhaps the weather in the eighteenth century was fairer than it is today – but there is something about this image we *can* connect to. Not only does it offer us another glimpse into the Scottish Enlightenment, it represents an upheld tradition: a commemorative practice. The combination of commemoration and exhibition is an effective intersection in the formation of cultural memory. The well-known 1896 Burns Exhibition in Glasgow is a good example, and in the centenary years (2014–18) of World War I various events and exhibitions helped us remember it. For any given occasion, marking public engagement with a special date helps instil, in our minds, the very fabric of these memories. That David Allan captured an occurrence of this *in the Georgian period* reveals more than just a high society affair: it captures the layout of the Old College, the styles of dress, the social classes, and (if you can get close enough) the paintings that were on display. All of this pertains to the oft-repeated sentiment that the Academy was 'too far in advance of its time'.³⁸

These social frameworks of collective memory can be utilised in analysing the importance of the image. Following Pierre Nora's symbolic work on the '*lieux*' ('sites') of memory, Jay Winter's theories on the 'sites' of memory have been particularly influential. He says: 'Such sites ... have an initial, creative phase, when they are constructed or adapted to particular commemorative purposes' – the use of the space in the quadrangle in order to exhibit new art. 'Then follows a period of institutionalization and routinization of their use. Such markings of the calendar, indicating moments of remembrance ... can last for decades, or they can be abruptly halted'³⁹ – the repetition of this event to mark the King's birthday served as a method for positioning the new art within the already perceived loyalty of Glasgow to the Hanoverians. However, Winter's estimation that some sites, and the routine practices within them, 'can be abruptly halted' is also true of the Academy and the University following its change of location in 1870. Although the Academy closed in 1775, the potential for a return to this 'site', and the potential to commemorate the commemorators, thus giving us a physical link to the past, was demolished along with the Old College buildings. A more curious effect of this can be observed through the layering of cultural memory. Thankfully, the photographer Thomas Annan captured images of these, and many other, lost buildings. But one of these, rather than 'preserving' the architecture, serves to 'echo' another of David Allan's artworks.

David Allan's *The Foulis Academy of the Fine Arts* (1760) (see Figure 3), which Thomas Annan photographed in the mid-to-late nineteenth century (see Figure 4), takes us inside the brothers' flourishing art venture.[40] The focus is on the large easel, in front of which a student shows his work to Professor James Moor. Just behind them are the Foulis brothers, and all around you get a sense of the different artistic skill being nurtured in the Academy. The importance of these images cannot be overstated. Not only do they offer a view of a lost interior, they give sudden weight to the sense of prestige. It preserves the idea of the Academy for subsequent generations in the same way that the brothers sought to preserve the classics with their celebrated books. Aleida Assmann unravels the relationship between image and memory in her book *Cultural Memory and Western Civilization* (2011). She uses the idea that 'pictures accompanying the biblical tales and the catechisms made a far deeper and more lasting impression on [children's] imagination than any text could have done'.[41] It was perhaps that writing and print represented 'an emanation of the mind and a means of mental reactivation', as stated by Assmann. 'Unlike the image,' she says, writing 'was not the product of a single, irreversible "excarnation", but allowed an unlimited number of repeatable "reincarnations"'.[42] What the Renaissance and Enlightenment scholars could not have anticipated, though, was one of the most important developments in the process, storage, and 'reactivation' of ideas: photography.

Walter Benjamin and Roland Barthes have written on these ideas at length.[43] However, we must consider what effect is made on the presence of an original image by its reproduction in a different medium. It was David Allan who offered us a window into the interior of the Academy. The photograph of the original image by Annan[44] alters the image once more, as does Antonia Reeve with her digital photograph for the National Galleries of Scotland. Annan's new object represents the plethora of reproductions of Allan's image in various books and websites. In the photograph, the image becomes less an 'irreversible "excarnation"', thus representing the 'unlimited "reincarnations"' that are possible. As such, the cultural memory of the image, of the Academy, and of the brothers is repeated, manipulated and dispersed, pertaining to the idea that plurality has complicated rather than unified the cultural memory of their accomplishments. When we also consider the idea that

Figure 3 David Allan, *The Foulis Academy of Fine Arts* (1760). By permission of National Galleries of Scotland (photographed by Antonia Reeve).

Figure 4 Thomas Annan, photographic reproduction of *The Foulis Academy of Fine Arts by David Allan*. Accession number OG. 1947. 84. 1. © CSG CIC Glasgow Museums Collection.

Allan's small oil sketch of the same scene is on display at the Hunterian Art Gallery,[45] the idea of an exhibition within an exhibition becomes a powerful, if disorienting, spatio-cultural metaphor.

But the sociability of these surviving artworks relating to the Foulis press and Academy should not trick us into believing in a simplistic or balanced Enlightenment in Glasgow. Beside the University itself, and a few of the city's wealthiest merchants, there was little support for their plans. Writing to William Hunter in 1766, Robert lamented: 'The Fine Arts do not ripen quickly, especially in a cold climate: but if once brought to maturity it is to be hoped they will naturalize and leave Successors wherever they are blown.'[46] In the same letter, Foulis thanked Hunter for ordering a set of their publications and for supporting a long-intended edition of Plato in Greek (it never came to fruition).[47] Hunter, as we know, was part of a well-connected network of professionals at the cutting edge of their respective fields. But like Smollett he was only active in Glasgow in the 1730s before moving to London. While this may be the case, it is not very well remembered that, for an entire decade the Scottish Enlightenment shone brightest in Glasgow. In the years 1756–66 the Foulis brothers were running a renowned press and a burgeoning art school simultaneously, James Watt had settled and was working in Glasgow, and Joseph Black had succeeded William Cullen in the Chemistry lectureship. Adam Smith and his student John Millar were also active, until Smith was replaced in 1764 by Thomas Reid, who brought from Aberdeen his famous Common Sense strand of philosophy.

Because of the wide-reaching influence of the Scottish Enlightenment, any consideration of the importance of networks or social circles inevitably attracts the most discussion and specialised study. This is evident in the historiographical overview offered at the beginning of *Science and Medicine in the Scottish Enlightenment* (2002) by Charles W. J. Withers and Paul Wood. The excellent chapter on Glasgow in this period by Wood and Emerson (who had both contributed chapters to *The Glasgow Enlightenment*) is one of the few extensive accounts on the city's relationship with medicine in the context of social structures and the literati. Withers and Wood have pointed out that Arthur Donovan's 1975 text *Philosophical Chemistry in the Scottish Enlightenment* was one of the first major works on 'not only the theoretical legacies of earlier chemists and Newtonians, but also their place within the Scottish universities and their engagement with efforts at economic improvement'.[48] Donovan's text is halved, each with its own focus on William Cullen and Joseph Black. Incidentally, the first section is about Glasgow and its placement in the narrative of Scotland's medical development. Geyer-Kordesch and MacDonald (1999) also dedicate a considerable portion of their study of the Faculty of Physicians and Surgeons of Glasgow (FPSG) to this context in their 'Enlightenment' section.

One of the key dates in their discussion can also be found in both Donovan's book and the chapter by Wood and Emerson: the 1690 Parliamentary Commission of Visitation which, to use the words of Wood and Emerson, 'was struck to reform the Scottish universities and to remove those who remained loyal to the Jacobite and Episcopalian cause', bringing about 'the beginning of a new era in Scottish academic and intellectual life'.[49] The impact of this intervention effectively disabled King's College, the older of Aberdeen's institutions, from becoming proactive in the Scottish Enlightenment. As Emerson (1987) points out, the Episcopalian and Jacobite sympathies harboured at King's led to Marischal surpassing it 'in almost every way'.[50] Like the other university cities, Glasgow had no such issues. As we know, Glasgow's Presbyterian activists played a large role outside University grounds. Geyer-Kordesch and MacDonald assert that 'the fertile soil from which [the Enlightenment] *flourished* was not the cleansed one of literati moderation and civic humanism', and that 'the raw body of Scotland's intellectual *industry* was tempered by Calvinism, forged in the truly gruesome trials endured by Covenanters and Presbyterians'. Note the careful use of the language here: the Glasgow words [emphasised] link this argument to the 'images of tall, square-rigged, three-masted ships, with wooden sterns high over the waves and flags flapping briskly in the breeze' which, as Geyer-Kordesch and MacDonald themselves remark, are permanent in the histories of Glasgow.[51] As such, their rejection of 'the notion that Enlightenment was the creation of moderates and *literati*' is in fact a reconstruction; a proclamation that medical advancement in Glasgow was a direct result of religious battles (especially those led by William of Orange), and the lasting impressions of civic pride, family ties and the kirk.

But to subscribe to this bifurcation of the Scottish Enlightenment is to ignore both the achievements of the Foulis brothers and the nuanced methodology in the very text alluded to: Sher's *Church and University in the Scottish Enlightenment* (1985). As Jeffrey Smitten put it, 'Sher chooses a more inclusive, interdisciplinary approach' than his predecessors, looking at the ideas behind the achievements in an attempt to rectify the 'restricted' Scottish Enlightenment image of philosophy and science.[52] As stated in the introduction, Sher's contribution to scholarship on the Scottish Enlightenment seems to have tipped the scales in favour of

Edinburgh over other cities once more. It is this which Geyer-Kordesch and MacDonald seem to focus on; using Glasgow's collective Presbyterianism as a way of discerning a unique Enlightenment. In one sense, they are right to quarrel with Edinburgh's perceived dominance, but in another they fail to take account of Sher's diverse examination of both moderatism and, as he calls it, 'Whig-Presbyterian Conservatism'.[53] Indeed, to cast Edinburgh as the antithesis to Glasgow in terms of its tolerance is to ignore some glaring divisions within the capital itself. We should remember Thomas Aikenhead, the last person to be executed for blasphemy in Britain. His prisoner's march from Edinburgh to Leith 'between a strong Guard of Fuzileers, drawn up in two Lines' is emblematic of the new-found power of the Presbyterian authorities then active in the capital, undoubtedly at their zenith following the Revolution of William of Orange.[54] This lingering atmosphere of religious intolerance – often associated only with Glasgow in the eighteenth century – was the same which blocked David Hume from the Chair in Moral Philosophy in Edinburgh in 1745 (a tense year in its own right).

This is not to say that Sher's text is misleading, but rather that his critics have shown up Glasgow and Edinburgh's most opposing features while ignoring Edinburgh's own brand of intolerance. After all, Sher states that 'it was Adam Ferguson and the Moderate literati of Edinburgh who adopted [Francis] Hutcheson's Christian-Stoic principles most enthusiastically and most completely'.[55] Rather than reading this as Glasgow's failure to do the same we should consider the Scottish Enlightenment as a mobile network of values manifesting itself in various places through various people. Hume's philosophies help us pinpoint the struggle between religion and reason in the Scottish Enlightenment, but what about the unquestionable secularisation that ran alongside the growth of medical practice and teaching in Glasgow via this migrating network? Would the very deep-set, sectarian partialities of traditional communities not be diluted with such movement? As Donovan has said:

> A new generation was coming to maturity during the first third of the eighteenth century, a generation which was unimpressed with the heroics of their fathers. For these young men, at least for those who attended the universities, the opportunities opened by the Union of 1707 were more important than the defence of reformationary truths. [...] Ambitious young Scots could now leave North Britain and seek out the opportunities available in London without surrendering the rights and identity which were theirs by birth.[56]

That William Smellie, William Cullen, William Hunter, Tobias Smollett, John Anderson, John Hunter, John Moore, James Watt and John

Robison (in order of birth) were all born in and around Glasgow is important. Joseph Black, although not born in Scotland, played a vital role in this Glasgow network which is essential to Glasgow's status as a place of medical prominence. Donovan's claim, above, that this new generation was 'unimpressed' contradicts Geyer-Kordesch and MacDonald's staunch defence of Glasgow as having the 'fertile soil' of the Enlightenment as a result of its defiant Presbyterian character, adhering more to the ideas of humanist toleration in Glasgow that we outlined previously. Mike Barfoot (1977) uses the same botanical metaphor in demonstrating Glasgow's importance: 'Cullen and Adam Smith ... moved in the same circle of colleagues, students, and friends. Both were former pupils of the Glasgow Professor of Mathematics, Robert Simson ... Both contributed to the general flowering of the Glasgow Literary Society ... Friendships which grew out of the soil of Glasgow were transplanted to Edinburgh.'[57] This idea of friendship should not be taken lightly. The intolerance of the previous century was changed, if not destroyed, by the rise of polite society. Crucially, though, it was not the stasis of the Scottish Enlightenment that helped change the places in which it developed. Indeed, we should be wary of continuing a discussion which cordons off all of the secular, Enlightenment ideas in one place and all the intolerant, industrial ones in another. The Scottish Enlightenment was not that simple. People moved, and ideas moved with them. Minds were changed, souls stirred. Competition for progress in the sciences became fierce, and the pull of London was always considerable.

It was Cullen's desire 'to articulate and advance the best of modern and natural philosophy and to make it the living centre of the institutions in which he taught'.[58] The concept of 'the living centre' is vital; it represents the medical network as a singular body, intermingling with, but standing aside from, these institutional sites – beginning with the University of Glasgow. Cullen was born in Hamilton, near Glasgow, and even after he was awarded an MD by the University of Glasgow in 1740, he practised as a physician in his hometown. Later, he mentored William Hunter there for a fruitful three years.[59] Before becoming the occupant of the Chair in Medicine at the University of Glasgow in 1751, Cullen was offering lectures 'extra-murally, scheduling them, we may presume, so that students could attend both [Robert] Hamilton's anatomy lectures and his own lectures on medicine'.[60] Before leaving, Cullen was considered 'the most popular lecturer in medical subjects in the United Kingdom',[61] so much so, in fact, that large portions of Cullen's students followed him to the capital.[62] One of his most successful students was also his successor at Glasgow. Joseph Black's paper in *Essays and Observations*

(1756) 'established the separation of carbonic acid, thereby opening up a wide field of research' and built the foundation for his other major achievement: his 'doctrine of Latent Heat' in 1761.[63] Following Black in the chronology of this network are John Robison and James Watt; the three were close friends in Glasgow. The nuances of this relationship are too varied to handle here, and have already been outlined in many of the texts mentioned above. The extensive correspondence between Black and Watt was reproduced by Eric Robinson and Douglas McKie in *Partners in Science* (1970). For Roy Campbell, this relationship is taken up as a symbol of the emergence of a more 'modern' Glasgow, wherein a union was forming between 'its internationally renowned merchants' and 'its scientific and engineering geniuses':

> The classic instance is in the association of James Watt, the mathematical-instrument-maker within the university, with others in the development of the steam engine, particularly with Joseph Black, lecturer in chemistry, whose discovery of the principle of latent heat may be held to have been a prerequisite of Watt's idea of the separate condenser which was fundamental to the later success of his engine.[64]

In terms of cultural memory, Watt's development of the steam engine has surpassed most, if not all, other Georgian-era achievements to have happened in Glasgow. But before we consider this fully we might look beyond the 'living centre' in the University and consider how their work outside the city helped mobilise the principles of the Scottish Enlightenment. Before moving to Glasgow, Alexander Wilson lived in London with the intention of finding work as a medic. It was in London that he become involved with a sort of 'Scottish colony' including Dr Charles Stewart, the private physician of Archibald Campbell, Lord Islay (1682–1761), the soon-to-be Duke of Argyll. After a visit to a type foundry, Wilson decided to move back home in 1739 and set up business with a friend from St Andrews.[65] His achievements, which include his discovery of sunspot activity in 1769 (known as the 'Wilson effect' in science today), would not have occurred without some crucial groundwork further afield.[66] In fact, the professoriate was only established because a former graduate, Alexander Macfarlane, bequeathed the University instruments he had taken on his emigration to Jamaica.[67] This occurred in 1756, and the following year the observatory on the College grounds was built, named after Macfarlane. It is known that the famous telescope maker from Edinburgh, James Short, provided Macfarlane with some of his equipment for his new estate in Jamaica. Before the Observatory was opened it was James Watt who put the instruments and equipment in order for Wilson, illustrating a very intricate and enlightened network of friendships that led to Glasgow's astronomical prominence.[68] As with the book trade, though, London was the centre of a 'global market' of instrument makers, which leads us to the most tangible connection between Glasgow and London in the form of anatomy and midwifery through William Hunter.[69] William and his brother John (1728–93) were born in East Kilbride, near Glasgow. For Roy Porter, who has written extensively on Georgian London's medical environment, the brothers were 'unmatched for anatomical, physiological and obstetrical expertise.'[70] As stated, Cullen, as Hunter's teacher, can be seen as a link in the displacement of the members of the Glasgow medical network. This is because London, where the Hunter brothers lived and worked, was also home to Smollett and John Moore, all of whom were friends. It was also in London that, from 1740, William Hunter learned midwifery from William Smellie.[71] In 1745 Smellie received an honorary MD from the University of Glasgow before his seminal three-volume text, *A Treatise on the Theory and Practice of Midwifery* (1752–64) was printed. Smollett edited large parts of the *Treatise*, a role which 'was responsible in no small degree for the influence which Smellie has had in obstetrics'.[72]

There is a sense of collaboration manifesting as generational progression. Improvements made upon improvements. It is in this argument, in line with Donovan's reflections on an entirely new generation 'coming to maturity', that cities, towns and institutions can be seen to forge connections. For Porter, Hunter's nationality and alignment with fellow Scots in London meant that he had to carry out an 'assault on the social climbers' mountain' lest he 'get bogged down in the morasses of marginality'. Further still, Porter suggests that, as a result of his birth, Hunter was fated for an altogether different life: born in 'the wrong country', into the 'wrong religion – Presbyterianism', matriculating 'at the wrong university – Glasgow', and very nearly making a start in the wrong career as a minister.[73] Porter's dismissal of Scotland, Glasgow, and Presbyterianism as factors of London's Enlightenment unfortunately oversimplifies Glasgow's multifaceted culture and degrades the Scottish Enlightenment with a set of requirements. Rather than considering Hunter's formative education at Glasgow as a factor in his success (which, incidentally, included classes under Hutcheson) he is wrongly portrayed as a heroic exception to the rule. With the centralisation of the Scottish Enlightenment in Edinburgh diluting cultural memory in Glasgow and Aberdeen, speculative arguments such as Porter's are all the more damaging.

Before obtaining his MD from Glasgow University in 1750, Hunter was nothing if not mobile. Beginning with a move to London in 1740, he later travelled to Paris (1743) and Leiden (1748) 'attending anatomical demonstrations and medical lectures'. In 1749 he moved to Covent Garden, London, in 1756 to 42 Jermyn Street, and lastly in 1767 to 'a specially extended house in Great Windmill Street'.[74] This latter property is known to have improved his practical, 'hands-on' teaching style, but becomes more important in the discussion of the Hunterian Museum in Glasgow, later. Several key figures of the Scottish Enlightenment attended his lectures, including Tobias Smollett and Adam Smith. His renown rapidly increased, becoming a Fellow of the Royal Society in 1767, first Professor of Anatomy in the 'newly created Royal Academy of Arts' in 1768, and a Foreign Associate of both the Royal Medical Society (1780) and the Academy of Sciences in Paris (1782).[75] As we know, Hunter also lent financial support to the Foulis brothers. But their relationship is deeper than this. The Foulis Academy pupil James Mitchell also worked on some of the plates for Hunter's renowned medical work, *Anatomy of the Gravid Uterus* (1774),[76] revealing a very intricate and active network of collaboration not just across Britain, but across the parameters of the Enlightenment. That we can locate them more often than not in Glasgow opens up new areas of discussion and future study. Highlighting these friendships and connections also helps 'ground' the messy mobility of this 'living centre'.

Somewhere in this upheaval and overlapping of people and ideas, Tobias Smollett was contributing effervescently to the Scottish Enlightenment. In his novels he was doing much more than satirically crying out for better medical teaching in England: he was applying his ideas on health and medicine into the fabric of his larger-than-life fiction. His only published piece of medical writing, *An Essay on the External Use of Water* (1752), was a precursor to some of his best-known fiction. In the *Essay* he set forth his opinions on normal water in medicine as more effective than mineral water before going on to expose 'the unhygienic conditions which endangered those who sought health at Bath'. His descriptions are vivid and damning, drawing attention to the mixture of healthy with unhealthy skin tissue as promiscuous.[77] In Matthew Bramble, from Smollett's last novel *Humphry Clinker*, we can visualise Smollett's own degenerative health at the end of his life. For instance, beside more scathing accounts of Bath – where he witnesses 'a child full of scrophulous ulcers, carried in the arms of one of the guides, under the very noses of the bathers'[78] – Bramble also refers to his relentless ill health: 'I have had an hospital these fourteen years within myself, and studied my own case with the most painful attention.'[79] The novel itself has been alluded to as 'Dr. Smollett's travelling clinic'.[80] Indeed, Smollett's biographers often refer to his ill health as having an effect on his judgements of French and Italian customs as revealed in *Travels Through France and Italy* (1766). As put by John Ingamells: 'Smollett and his wife were not in the best frame of mind when they set out from Dover . . . their only child had just died,' and, 'Smollett was suffering from the onset of consumption.'[81] In Letter 25 of *Travels*, Smollett complains of 'violent fits of passion' and being 'continually agitated either in mind or body, and very often both at the same time'.[82]

Smollett is believed to have left Glasgow for London in 1739 without completing his apprenticeship.[83] Richard Jones has essayed that Smollett's leaving Glasgow in 1739 'has deflected scholarly attention away from his Scottish origins'.[84] Previously, David Craig remarked: 'J. M. Robertson's idea that "the Scottish polity would die unremembered or but dimly inferred from our idealistic novelists" comes home to us if we think of the realistic impressions of Scottish life that we might have had if Smollett had stayed and written in Scotland'.[85] Such conjecture is reminiscent of David Hamilton's portrayal of a Glasgow enriched by the return of great men of science and medicine: 'William Hunter once proposed to Cullen that they and Black should return to Glasgow and set up a medical faculty which would rival Edinburgh . . . it is interesting to speculate on the fame of a school headed by such a triumvirate.'[86] As we will see in the next section, the curators of the first Hunterian of Glasgow held fast to that same scheme.

One of Smollett's greatest achievements was to capture the incessant sociability of the Scottish Enlightenment in his writing. After all, it was Smollett who enlivened the epistolary mode with the multi-perspective *Humphry Clinker* – a comment on the complexity of Britain with all its competing voices and cultures. Kenneth Simpson has said that 'Smollett's concern with the physical derives jointly from the medieval plenitude of vision and his Enlightenment social concern'. By looking at himself as one in a teeming mass of others, Smollett, 'like a true child of the Enlightenment . . . is committed to the amelioration of the living-conditions of his fellow-men'.[87]

NOTES

1. John Mayne, 'Glasgow', in George Eyre-Todd, ed., *The Glasgow Poets: Their Lives and Poems* (Paisley: Alexander Gardner, 1906 [1903]), 73–87 (74–5).

2. James Boswell dubbed the Foulis brothers 'The Elzevirs of Glasgow', likening them to the famous Dutch family of printers.
3. See Alexander Broadie and Robin Downie, *Glasgow Moral Philosophy in the Enlightenment: Ideas and their International Influence* (Glasgow: College of Arts, 2012).
4. William Robert Scott, *Francis Hutcheson: His Life, Teaching and Position in the History of Philosophy* (Cambridge: Cambridge University Press, 1900), 261.
5. George MacGregor, *The History of Glasgow, from the Earliest Period to the Present Time* (Glasgow: Thomas D. Morison, 1881), 206–9
6. See George Fairfull-Smith, *The Foulis Press and The Foulis Academy: Glasgow's Eighteenth Century School of Art and Design* (Glasgow: The Glasgow Art Index in association with the Friends of Glasgow University Library, 2001) and Thomas F. Bonnell, *The Most Disreputable Trade: Publishing the Classics of English Poetry 1765–1810* (Oxford: Oxford University Press, 2008).
7. Philip Gaskell, *A Bibliography of the Foulis Press* (Dorset: St Paul's Bibliographies, 1986), 65
8. James Moore and Michael Silverthorne, eds, *The Meditations of the Emperor Marcus Aurelius Antoninus*, trans. Francis Hutcheson and James Moor (Indianapolis: Liberty Fund, 2008), xxiii.
9. *A new edition of the life and heroick actions of the renoun'd Sir William Wallace, general and governour of Scotland* (Glasgow: William Duncan, 1722), cf. William Hamilton of Gilbertfield, Blind Harry's Wallace (Edinburgh: Luath Press, 1998 [1722]), 80–1.
10. The word 'wark' is Scots for 'work', being descriptive of the 'work' of the spirit in Cambuslang.
11. Arthur Fawcett, *The Cambuslang Revival: the Scottish Evangelical Revival of the Eighteenth Century* (London: The Banner of Truth Trust, 1971), 32.
12. Ned C. Landsman, 'Presbyterians and Provincial Society: The Evangelical Enlightenment in the West of Scotland, 1740–1775', in John Dwyer and Richard B. Sher, eds, *Sociability and Society in Eighteenth-Century Scotland* (Edinburgh: The Mercat Press, 1993), 194–209 (197).
13. Ned C. Landsman, 'Evangelists and Their Hearers: Popular Interpretation of Revivalist Preaching in Eighteenth-Century Scotland', in *Journal of British Studies*, 28:2 (1989), 120–49 (122).
14. Fawcett, *The Cambuslang Revival*, 4.
15. T. C. Smout, 'Born Again at Cambuslang; New Evidence on Popular Religion and Literacy in Eighteenth-Century Scotland', in *Past & Present*, 97:1 (1982), 114–27 (118).
16. Landsman, 'Evangelists and Their Hearers', 122.
17. *Autobiographical Accounts of Persons Under Spiritual Concern at Cambuslang (Glasgow) during the Revival of 1741–1743, Part One* (Shropshire: Quinta Press, 2008), 342, <http://quintapress.macmate.

me/PDF_Books/Cambuslang_Testimonies_Vol_1.pdf> (last accessed 30 August 2020).
18. Preface to Jan Assmann, *Religion and Cultural Memory: Ten Studies* (Stanford, CA: Stanford University Press, 2006).
19. Lynn Abrams, *Oral History Theory* (London: Routledge, 2010), 66.
20. Landsman, 'Evangelists and Their Hearers', 123.
21. Fawcett, *The Cambuslang Revival*, 80.
22. Ibid., 83.
23. Landsman, 'Evangelists and Their Hearers', 130.
24. Elizabeth L. Eisenstein, *The Printing Press as an Agent of Change* (Cambridge: Cambridge University Press, 1979), 422.
25. Brian Hillyard, 'The Glasgow Homer', in *The Edinburgh History of the Book in Scotland, Volume 2: Enlightenment and Expansion, 1707–1800* (Edinburgh: Edinburgh University Press, 2012), 70–80 (70)
26. Ibid., 76
27. Craig Lamont, 'Cultivating the Classics "in a cold climate": The Foulis Press & Academy in Glasgow', in *Journal of the Edinburgh Bibliographical Society* (2019), 45–66.
28. Peter J. M. McEwan, *The Dictionary of Scottish Art and Architecture* (Ballater: Glengarden Press, 2004), 187.
29. Quoted in George Fairfull-Smith, *The Foulis Press*, 17.
30. Arthur D. Efland, *A History of Art Education: Intellectual and Social Currents in Teaching the Visual Arts* (New York and London: Teachers College Press, 1990), 44.
31. Murray G. H. Pittock, 'Ramsay, Allan (1684–1758)', *Oxford Dictionary of National Biography*, <http://www.oxforddnb.com/view/article/23072> (last accessed 30 August 2020).
32. David Irwin and Francina Irwin, *Scottish Painters: At Home and Abroad, 1700–1900* (London, Faber and Faber, 1975), 83.
33. Anton W. A. Boschloo et al., *Academies of Art Between Renaissance and Romanticism* (The Hague: SDU, 1989), 443.
34. Fairfull-Smith, *The Foulis Press*, 23.
35. All of these points are made in a twentieth-century newspaper clipping describing the Foulis Academy, of an unknown source and date, held in Glasgow University Library's Special Collections: <http://special.lib.gla.ac.uk/manuscripts/search/detail_c.cfm?ID=40391> (last accessed 20 November 2019).
36. 'Memorial of Robert Foulis & Company', Edinburgh University Library, Archives Services: LA. III. 363. 1, ff. 1–47 (f. 8).
37. James McCosh, *The Scottish Philosophy: Bibliographical, Expository, Critical from Hutcheson to Hamilton* (Carlisle, MA: Applewood, 2009 [1875]), 188.
38. Eyre-Todd, *The Glasgow Poets*, 193.
39. Jay Winter, 'Sites of Memory', in Susannah Radstone and Bill Schwarz, eds,

Memory: Histories, Theories, Debates (New York: Fordham University Press, 2010), 312–24 (312).
40. Allan also captured the scene as an oil sketch with minor alterations in 1762. This version is held at the Hunterian Art Gallery, Glasgow.
41. Aleida Assmann, *Cultural Memory and Western Civilization* (Cambridge: Cambridge University Press, 2011), 216.
42. Ibid., 206.
43. See, for example, Benjamin's 'The Work of Art in the Age of Mechanical Reproduction' (1936) and Roland Barthes' *Camera Lucida* (1980).
44. Annan is best remembered for his revelatory photographs of the 'old closes and streets' in Glasgow, captured between 1868 and 1871 as part of a commission from the City of Glasgow Improvements Trust.
45. The placement of this small, unassuming oil-sketch in the Hunterian Art Gallery is a most relevant one indeed. It is placed at the entrance of the gallery, under the title 'An Enlightened Collection'. Nearby, two paintings which were owned by Robert Foulis for the Academy are exhibited, giving a sense of the scale of the ambition of the brothers' venture. They are: a copy of Raphael's *The Entombment* c.1600–50 and Jan Cossiers' *The Martyrdom of St Catherine* (1647).
46. David Murray, 'Some Letters of Robert Foulis (continued)', *The Scottish Historical Review* 14:55 (1917), 249–71 (254).
47. David Murray, 'Some Letters of Robert Foulis', in *The Scottish Historical Review*, 14:54 (1917), 97–115 (109). See also: David Clarke, *Reflections on the Astronomy of Glasgow: A Story of Some 500 Years* (Edinburgh: Edinburgh University Press, 2013).
48. Paul Wood and Charles W. J. Withers, 'Introduction: Science, Medicine and the Scottish Enlightenment: An Historiographical Overview', in Charles W. J. Withers and Paul Wood, eds, *Science and Medicine in the Scottish Enlightenment* (Phantassie, East Lothian: Tuckwell Press, 2002), 1–16 (1–2).
49. Roger L. Emerson and Paul Wood, 'Science and Enlightenment in Glasgow 1690–1802', in Charles W. J. Withers and Paul Wood, eds, *Science and Medicine in the Scottish Enlightenment* (Phantassie, East Lothian: Tuckwell Press, 2002), 79–142 (80).
50. Roger L. Emerson, 'Aberdeen Professors 1690–1800: Two Structures, Two Professoriates, Two Careers', in Jennifer J. Carter and Joan J. Pittock, eds, *Aberdeen and the Enlightenment* (Aberdeen: Aberdeen University Press, 1987), 155–67 (155–6).
51. Johanna Geyer-Kordesch and Fiona MacDonald, *Physicians and Surgeons in Glasgow: The History of the Royal College of Physicians and Surgeons of Glasgow* (London: Hambledon, 1999), 153.
52. Jeffrey Smitten, 'Church and University in the Scottish Enlightenment: The Moderate Literati of Edinburgh (review)', in *Eighteenth-Century Studies*, 19:4 (1986), 580–3 (580).

53. Richard B. Sher, *Church and University in the Scottish Enlightenment: The Moderate Literati of Edinburgh* (Edinburgh: Edinburgh University Press, 1985), 187.
54. Michael Hunter, 'Aikenhead, Thomas (bap. 1676, d. 1697)', *Oxford Dictionary of National Biography*, <http://www.oxforddnb.com/view/article/225> (last accessed 31 August 2020).
55. Roger L. Emerson, *Academic Patronage in the Scottish Enlightenment: Glasgow, Edinburgh and St Andrews Universities* (Edinburgh: Edinburgh University Press, 2008), 341.
56. Arthur Donovan, *Philosophical Chemistry in the Scottish Enlightenment: The Doctrines and Discoveries of William Cullen and Joseph Black* (Edinburgh: Edinburgh University Press, 1975), 11–12.
57. Mike Barfoot, 'Introduction', *An Account of the Life, Lectures, and Writings of William Cullen, vol.1*, ed. John Thomson (Bristol: Thoemmes, 1997), vi; see also Barfoot's diagram in 'Philosophy and method in Cullen's medical teaching', in A. Doig et al., eds, *William Cullen and the Eighteenth-Century Medical World* (Edinburgh: Edinburgh University Press, 1993), 110–32 (115) [many thanks to Jane Corrie for these references].
58. Donovan, *Philosophical Chemistry in the Scottish Enlightenment*, 18.
59. Christopher Lawrence, 'Ornate physicians and learned artisans: Edinburgh medical men, 1726–1776', in W. F. Bynum and Roy Porter, eds, *William Hunter and the Eighteenth-Century Medical World* (Cambridge: Cambridge University Press, 1985), 153–76 (181–2).
60. Donovan, *Philosophical Chemistry in the Scottish Enlightenment*, 50.
61. Henry L. Fulton, 'John Moore, the Medical Profession and the Glasgow Enlightenment', in Andrew Hook and Richard B. Sher, eds, *The Glasgow Enlightenment* (Phantassie, East Lothian: Tuckwell Press, 1995), 176–89 (179).
62. Lawrence, 'Ornate physicians and learned artisans', 169.
63. Alexander Duncan, *Memorials of the Faculty of Physicians and Surgeons of Glasgow* (Glasgow: James MacLehose & Sons, 1896), 258–9. The full title of Black's paper was 'Experiments upon magnesia alba, quicklime, and some other alcaline [sic] substances', *Essays and Observations, Physical and Literary. Read before a Society in Edinburgh, and published by them. Volume II* (Edinburgh: G. Hamilton and J. Balfour, 1756), 157–225.
64. Campbell, 'Scotland's Neglected Enlightenment'.
65. Clarke, *Reflections on the Astronomy of Glasgow*, 79.
66. George Stronach, 'Wilson, Alexander (1714–1786)', rev. Roger Hutchins, *Oxford Dictionary of National Biography*, <http://www.oxforddnb.com/view/article/29633> (last accessed 30 August 2020).
67. A. D. Morrison-Low, '"Feasting my eyes with the view of fine instruments": Scientific Instruments in Enlightenment Scotland, 1680–1820', in Charles W. J. Withers and Paul Wood, eds, *Science and Medicine in the*

Scottish Enlightenment (Phantassie, East Lothian: Tuckwell Press, 2002), 17–53 (38).
68. Clarke, *Reflections on the Astronomy of Glasgow*, 51–5.
69. Morrison-Low, '"Feasting my eyes with the view of fine instruments"', 36.
70. Roy Porter, 'Medical Lecturing in Georgian London', in *The British Journal for the History of Science*, 28:1 (1995), 91–9 (94).
71. Helen Brock, 'Hunter, William (1718–1783)', *Oxford Dictionary of National Biography*, <http://www.oxforddnb.com/view/article/14234> (last accessed 30 August 2020).
72. Paul Harper, 'Tobias Smollett and the Practice of Medicine', in *Yale Journal of Biology and Medicine*, 2:6 (1930), 408–16 (415).
73. Ibid.
74. Lawrence Keppie, *William Hunter and the Hunterian Museum in Glasgow, 1807–2007* (Edinburgh: Edinburgh University Press, 2007), 3–5.
75. C. H. Brock, 'Dr William Hunter's Museum, Glasgow University', in *Journal of the Society for the Bibliography of Natural History*, 9:4 (1980), 403–12 (403).
76. Though the work contained Latin and English, its full title was *Anatomia uteri humani gravidi tabulis illustrata, auctore Gulielmo Hunter, serenissimae Reginae Charlottae medico extraordinario, in Academia Regali anatomiae professore, et Societatum Regiae et Antiquariae, socio* [*The anatomy of the human gravid uterus exhibited in figures, by William Hunter, physician extraordinary to the Queen, professor of anatomy in the Royal Academy, and fellow of the Royal and Antiquarian Societies*] (Birmingham: John Baskerville, 1774). It consisted chiefly of engravings. The full 'text', intended to accompany these plates, was not published until 1794, eleven years after Hunter's death, by which point it had been edited and expanded upon by Matthew Baillie.
77. Lewis M. Knapp, *Tobias Smollett: Doctor of Men and Manners* (Princeton, NJ: Princeton University Press, 1949), 146.
78. Smollett, *The Expedition of Humphry Clinker*, 75.
79. Ibid., 53.
80. Geyer-Kordesch and MacDonald, *Physicians and Surgeons in Glasgow*, 186.
81. John Ingamells, 'Tobias Smollett', *A Dictionary of British and Irish Travellers in Italy 1701–1800* (New Haven: Yale University Press, 1997), 873.
82. Tobias Smollett, *Travels Through France and Italy* (London: The Folio Society, 1979 [1766]), 244.
83. Henry L. Fulton, 'Smollett's Apprenticeship in Glasgow, 1736–1739', in *Studies in Scottish Literature*, 15:1 (1980), 175–86 (178–9).
84. Richard Jones, *Tobias Smollett in the Enlightenment: Travels Through France, Italy and Scotland* (Lewisburg, PA: Buckness University Press, 2011), 4.

85. David Craig, *Scottish Literature and the Scottish People, 1680–1830* (London: Chatto & Windus, 1961), 279.
86. David Hamilton, *The Healers: A History of Medicine in Scotland* (Edinburgh: Mercat, 2003), 126.
87. Kenneth Simpson, *The Protean Scot: The Crisis of Identity in Eighteenth-Century Scottish Literature* (Aberdeen: Aberdeen University Press, 1988), 18.

3

'Unimpaired remembrance reigns'

Like many of his contemporaries, Tobias Smollett's connections with Glasgow have not fared very well. His memory is most stable in the canon of English Literature, and in the Scottish Enlightenment his reputation is more international than local. Two of the known monuments erected in memory of Smollett survive. The first is in Renton, his birthplace, the second in Livorno, Italy, where he died. The 60-foot Scottish monument was erected in 1774. The Latin inscription by Samuel Johnson at the base declares:

> In testimony of his many great virtues, this empty monument, the only pledge, alas, of his affection, is erected on the banks of the Leven, the scene of his birth and of his latest poetry, by James Smollett of Bonhill, his cousin, who should rather have expected this last tribute from him. Try to remember: this honour was not given alone to the memory of the deceased, but for the encouragement of others; deserve like him, and be alike rewarded.

There is much to pick apart here, not least of all the nod to Smollett's manifold career. Obviously the location is suitable and the style reflects a very Georgian, classical mode of remembrance. There is also a performative modesty in the 'empty' remark, redolent of these times. But it is quite possible that Smollett was too many things to be remembered more simply at this local level. He was in many ways an overflowing, rather than empty, vessel. You can see this easily in the frontispiece to James Browne's *Works of Tobias Smollett* (1872): he is youthful, wearing his wig, presiding above the devil, a picaresque hero, a mask, a trumpet, and the medical symbol of the staff entwined by the snake. It begs the question: how do we begin to remember such a complicated character? Dramatist, artist, biographer, scholar; not one of these aspects of Smollett's career survives well on its own. How many of those who admire Smollett's monument, for instance, will know that the pro-Union stance he solidified in *Humphry Clinker* is juxtaposed by his youthful rile against the Hanoverians in the wake of Culloden? In his poem 'The Tears of Scotland' he lamented for the slain Jacobites, promising that:

> While the warm blood bedews my veins,
> And unimpair'd remembrance reigns,
> Resentment of my country's fate,
> Within my filial breast shall beat;
> And, spite of her insulting foe,
> My sympathizing verse shall flow:
> 'Mourn, hapless Caledonia, mourn
> Thy banish'd peace, thy laurels torn.'[1]

Smollett and his many masks help us come to terms with the Enlightenment as a period that proved difficult to characterise concisely. This is true of so many of the figures who make up the Glasgow Enlightenment. Part of the problem is that we are unable to visualise the Enlightenment as a singularity. Perhaps the closest thing to a unifying cultural memory of it is Joseph Wright of Derby's famous painting *An Experiment on a Bird in the Air Pump* (1786). Images like this capture that sense of awe in the secular, scientific world: a moment of light surrounded by centuries of darkness. But they, too, tell only part of the story.

We have seen some of the ways Glasgow inspired a culture of Enlightenment which transformed the Georgian period. But to comprehend the full extent to which we have *remembered* the Glasgow Enlightenment, we have to consider the extant institutions, monuments, and other markers that have shaped cultural memory. The Smollett Monument, above, is one such example, though its location in Renton, some eighteen miles from Glasgow city centre, means it lies outside the catchment zone of association. In an East Kilbride Morrisons supermarket, the entrance foyer proudly displays a mural of Scottish history, at the heart of which is the double portrait of two locals: William Hunter and John Hunter. Both born in East Kilbride, this mural, like Smollett's monument, re-emphasises the important of the 'local' and the 'place of birth' in the process of remembrance. In many ways, the East Kilbride mural is more effective than the Renton monument: more people, surely, see the mural when they enter the supermarket than those who stop and take the time to read the inscription to the classical monument. The monument, superior in terms of history, construction and survivability, is arguably inferior in terms of effectiveness.

We can apply the same deliberation on a larger scale, plotting the different sites of interest across Glasgow with a view to visualising a topography of cultural memory. There are several such sites, the most significant of which is the University of Glasgow itself. The 'here' in John Mayne's poem on Glasgow (see Chapter 2) is long gone. Its site is covered by a car park, student flats, and a Glasgow City Council building. For us, in cultural memory terms, the University of the Georgian period is a 'there', with an arrow pointing to the past. The Old College is preserved and enshrined in writings, etchings and photographs. These memories are archival, dormant. But parts of the old campus remain intact. In 1887, a large section of the main entrance of the Old College was dismantled and carted over to the new campus. Erected at the foot of University Avenue, it was named Pearce Lodge in memory of Sir William Pearce, of the famous Fairfield Shipbuilding and Engineering Company. This is a common Glasgow story: the elite men of shipbuilding supplanting the memories of the past in an effort to preserve them. Curiously, an inscription reads: 'By moving these buildings from the ancient seat of the University, William Pearce again united with the past.'[2] There is an attempt to rekindle a connection with, or a memory of, that past which has been physically lost. Another extant feature from the Old College is the Lion and Unicorn Staircase. Now built onto the Victorian campus, in the square just west of the Gilbert Scott Building, or Main Building, these heraldic beasts from the seventeenth century once stood in the inner court of the Old College. These are important remnants, serving as a reminder of the culture of the seventeenth and eighteenth centuries that grew up around distinguished alumni. But these markers are also 'anonymous'. They are important only in the process of understanding what 'remains' from the Georgian period. To the untrained eye, these buildings are part of the one unified campus, built together to last together. To go deeper into the formation of cultural memory we should review the individuals who are commemorated around the campus.

In 1952 the Memorial Gates of the University were unveiled to honour the outstanding individuals in its 500 years. The names appear in rows, with the top row commemorating the figures of the nineteenth century, the second bearing the names of the eighteenth century, the third the seventeenth, the fourth the sixteenth century, and the fifth and final row the fifteenth century (though Donald Dewar and John Smith were later added to either side of the fourth row). It is no surprise, then, to find the key figures of the Glasgow Enlightenment all in one place: William Hunter, William Cullen, John Millar, James Watt, Adam Smith, Thomas Campbell, Thomas Reid and Robert Foulis are all immortalised in this quincentenary cast. Reid's tombstone is built into the wall of the entrance of the Gilbert Scott (main) building, while most of the others have been remembered fairly well in various different ways. The Foulis brothers, however, have not been as fortunate. The first attempt to do so was an unsuccessful call for subscriptions in 1866 to establish a Foulis Library in the city. It declared: 'While Glasgow has great reason to be proud of being the birth-place and scene of labours of printers who rival Aldus and the Stephani brothers, it is scarcely creditable to her sons that no complete Collection of the Foulis Works are in existence.'[3] While speculation should be limited, it is arguable that such a library may have served as a solid reminder of the brothers' contribution to Glasgow's print culture, and of their 'non-sectarian Christianity' which was unique in the city.

There were also exhibitions. The first took place in the University of Glasgow's Examination Hall in April 1913. The five components of the exhibition were: an overview of the printing history of Glasgow from 1638 to 1742 (the date at which Robert Foulis commenced University Printer); the Foulis Press; examples of the typefaces of Alexander Wilson; personalia, such as private possessions and relics held by the family; and examples from the Academy.[4] The second exhibition was dedicated to the Academy itself, held at the Mitchell Library from April through September in 2001. It was advertised as 'the first major exhibition devoted to the history of the school.'[5]

There is a commemorative paving stone outside the Ramshorn Church in Glasgow's Ingram Street, bearing the inscription: 'FOULIS BROTHERS: PRINTERS AND BOOKSELLERS', followed by their dates. This new stone cleverly resembles a book, slotted in among the other paving stones. It replaces the previous stone which contained a simple cross, and the brothers' initials on either side. While their cultural memory was further impaired with the loss of Foulis Building in the Glasgow School of Art Campus and the closure of the Art School's honorary Foulis Press, there is another lasting tribute to their efforts.[6] In St Nicholas Garden, near Glasgow Cathedral, there are eight semi-abstract figures made from steel (1995) depicting the different people associated with Provand's Lordship, the oldest surviving house in the city. Robert Foulis is depicted with a book and quill pen as part of the 'mercantile and cultural' set of figures.[7] But for all this, the brothers are only a minor part of Glasgow's cultural memory. Not, it should be said, because they are ignored by scholars, but because the milieu in which they flourished has been left out of Glasgow's mainstream image. Their Glasgow University contemporaries have fared much better in the mind, with sculptures commemorating Adam Smith (Gasser, *c.*1867) and Joseph Black (Schotz,

1952–4) elsewhere on the University campus. There is also the Joseph Black Building, the Adam Smith Business School, and the Adam Smith Building and Library. But it is common practice in University campuses to name buildings and libraries after famous alumni, and while Universities are an important part of tourism, we should be careful whether the 'public domain' should mean simply 'free', no matter where, or 'free and easy-to-find' in busy, public spaces. The James Watt statue in the Hunterian Museum, for instance, and the Hunterian Museum itself demand a closer look. They bring us out of the here and now and back across Glasgow to the Old College, the 'there' that is the University of the Georgian period.

Before we arrive at this point we should stop at the important arenas of cultural memory en route. George Square may not look very Georgian today, but despite its Victorian appearance, the clue is in the name. It began to take shape in the early Georgian era and grew from a private space to a public zone of commemoration.[8] The City Chambers (1887) now dominates the once modest-looking space, and the U-shaped Cenotaph (1924) erected in honour of those lost in World War I has been the chief location for public remembrance in the city since those first commemorations. The square itself is distinguished by its twelve statues, all bronze with the exception of Sir Walter Scott, who towers 24 feet above the rest in yellow freestone. They are:

Sir John Moore (1761–1809)*	1810–19
James Watt (1736–1819)*	1830
Sir Walter Scott (1771–1832)*	1834–8
Queen Victoria (1819–1901)	1854
James Oswald (1779–1853)	1856
Sir Robert Peel (1788–1850)	1859
Prince Albert (1819–61)	1863–6
Colin Campbell, Lord Clyde (1792–1863)	1867
Thomas Graham (1805–69)	1871
Thomas Campbell (1777–1844)*	1875–7
Robert Burns (1759–96)*	1876–7
William Ewart Gladstone (1809–98)	1899–1902

The names marked *, above, represent those Georgian figures who contributed in one way or another to the Scottish Enlightenment. John Moore is best remembered for his war heroics in Corunna, where he died, but is included here because of his direct association with the Glasgow Enlightenment. His father, also John Moore, took him on his Grand Tour of Europe when he was a private physician to Douglas, the 8th Duke of Hamilton. The three have been the subject of paintings by

Jean Preudhomme and Gavin Hamilton. So, the representation of the Glasgow Enlightenment in the city's chief square is arguably strong. Yes, we might weigh up the literal overshadowing of Scott, and his Edinburgh, over these venerable figures. We might also consider that the equestrian royals and the politicians on show offer an overwhelmingly imperial site, ousting from our minds the deeds of the Scottish Enlightenment. But there is much more to the story of Glasgow's cultural memory than this one square.

Surrounding Glasgow's twelfth-century cathedral and ancient centre is the Necropolis. Glasgow's City of the Dead came into being in the 1830s, partly inspired by the Père Lachaise Cemetery in Paris and generally in line with the increasing taste for mass commemoration. Graveyards are unlike any other public realm in that they are generally silent, respectful places. Unlike the city streets, the very purpose of a graveyard creates an atmosphere, a sense of an unspoken remembrance that is imbued upon its visitors. The tallest statue in the Necropolis is also the highest in the city. The John Knox Monument (1825), though not as tall as the Scott Monument in George Square, sits on higher ground (approximately eighty-seven metres above the level of the River Clyde).[9] Knox's influence in the rise of Protestantism in Scotland remains strong in the public imagination, but in many ways it is deeply ironic. Without a doubt, the statue has aided the survival of Knox's cultural memory. It was erected a mere forty-six years after the same anti-Catholic riots which saw religious statues destroyed in the city. The time span between these events falls within the remit of collective, generational memory. The same generation tearing down the idols of one religion were exalting another in stone. Thus we may ask, is the famous monument of Knox not a religious statue, too? Unlike statues of the Virgin Mary, Knox in the Glasgow Necropolis does not form part of religious ceremony, but his towering presence over city graves *does* suggest something 'special', for Knox was not buried in Glasgow. It is a kind of memory secularisation. Murray Pittock and Christopher Whatley have outlined how the statues of Burns created the image of the poet as 'a secular saint', reinforcing 'the concrete dimensions of Scottish national memory as Scotland engaged more widely with a British and imperial history increasingly remote from the *loci memoriae* of its national poet.'[10] In James Coleman's *Remembering the Past in Nineteenth-Century Scotland* (2014) even more of these fascinating issues are teased out.

If the multitude of memorials in the Necropolis are somewhat off limits in the review of Glasgow's cultural memory then so, too, are those inside the cathedral itself. The site, however, is another matter. St Mungo's or, simply, Glasgow Cathedral, survived the Protestant Reformation intact when few Catholic buildings managed to survive at all in Scotland. Its roof has protected its centuries of ceremony from the skies since consecration in 1197. Unlike designated spaces like George Square, where the public stop to interact or simply rest, there is an extra emphasis on religious ritual here. We can glean this from the semantics of memory in describing the General Assembly of 1638, one of the major shifts in Glasgow's history. In one historic passage the cathedral is described as 'that noble pile,' standing 'then' (1638) as it stands 'now' (1881), and 'as it had stood for centuries before'.[11] This convergence of the present, the past, and the ancient are crucial to our understanding of cultural memory. Not only does it bear historiographical importance, it reveals layers of topography that are crucial to obtaining an 'image' of the city, such as the one we see building as the passage continues:

> [The cathedral] rose solemnly there amid the gravestones of many generations, pointing back to the time when good Bishop Jocelyn laid the foundations of its peerless crypt. Beyond the Molendinar Burn, so famous in ancient story, the rocky eminence was covered with scraggy firs, which is now the thickly peopled 'city of the dead'.[12]

We should take the chance to juxtapose the above discussion of cultural memory with the recollections of someone with a closer view. Robert Fleming, minister from Cambuslang, remembered 'a remarkable time', he wrote, 'wherein the Lord did let forth much of the Spirit on his people, in the year 1638, when this nation did solemnly enter in covenant, which *many yet alive* [emphasis added] at this day do know how the spirits of men were raised ...'.[13] There is a confidence here that surpasses the usual historical distance of describing these events. Subsequent historians relate to different aspects of the story, including memories of their own to make the story read as liveable as their memory permits. But these lived memories are those which shape cultural memory for future generations to consume. For the latter part of the twentieth century, writers would talk about 'where they were' when Kennedy was assassinated. The twenty-first century had only just begun when the World Trade Centre was attacked, and we live in a time when '9/11' is a byword for not only the event, but for the images that repeat on a loop in our minds.[14] Halbwachs was one of the first to put these quirks of memory into a social context, claiming that his memory of certain events do not depend on him being there, but of an amalgamation of information cobbled together and obscured, as 'scant of meaning as most tombstone inscriptions'. Coming to a conclusion, he remarks that history 'resembles a crowded cemetery, where room must constantly be made for new tombstones'.[15] When we liken Halbwachs' history-as-cemetery metaphor to the specific, Glaswegian 'city of the dead', new meanings are built up around this site. In this sense, Halbwachs' example becomes Glasgow's, and the histories which have 'crowded' the 'city of the dead' have done so through the use of other cultural objects; to use Halbwachs' terms: 'symbols passed down through time . . . occasional anecdotes or quotations'. It is as though the further one moves away from the event in time, the more one depends on the complex layers of what we call cultural memory.

Outside the cathedral we find ourselves in Cathedral Square. Home to several bronze statues, this space takes us even further into Glasgow's past. On the outer reaches of the square, in the gardens, you can visit the equestrian, lead statue of William of Orange. It is the only statue of its kind from eighteenth-century Glasgow to survive. The sculptor is not known, but its original position in 1735 was in the heart of the city, in the Trongate. We know that Glasgow's Presbyterian, anti-Jacobite character welcomed this political expression of loyalty with open arms. Just as the High Street lost its prestige with the movement of the University, so too did the old city centre, and the statue fell into disrepair. But the memory of 'Protestant Willie' was deemed too sacred, and the statue was moved in line with improvements to the area. It was moved again to its present location in 1926.[16] The statue to David Livingstone will be discussed in the next chapter, but it is worth mentioning the 2-metre-high pillar in the centre of the square. The Bishop's Palace Memorial Pillar was erected in 1915, bringing us to another one of the large bumps in Glasgow's cultural memory. Francis Henderson, who commissioned the pillar, wanted to remind his fellow citizens about 'the older life of Glasgow'.[17] This desire to remember the distant past was relatively new. In George MacGregor's *History of Glasgow* (1881) it is noted that the Palace had long been in a 'ruinous condition', as 'the spirit of the times did not favour the preservation of such a venerable relic, for it brought to the Presbyterian mind memories of Papal supremacy'.[18] It is therefore quite appropriate that William's equestrian statue landed so close to this symbolic site with all its imperial pomp.

The crumbling remains of the old Palace were eventually cleared when the city gained a Royal Charter in 1791 for a new Infirmary. Glasgow's first hospital was situated on Clyde Street near the present St Andrew's Roman Catholic Church but it has not survived. The Royal Infirmary opened its doors in 1794, and its close proximity to the Old College was beneficial for the new generation of medics and physicians. More to the point here, its physical presence also became symbolic. As with many other new buildings, the alteration of the topography of Glasgow offered a chance for ceremony. Previously, the Foulis brothers' *Glasgow Courant* reported on the ceremony of the laying of the foundation stone for the Macfarlane Observatory (the same used by Alexander Wilson). Medals with Latin inscriptions were placed at the four corners of the foundation, but these did not survive demolition in 1856.[19]

As the century progressed, ceremonies like this were more common and more public. Philanthropists would literally have their memory paraded after their death, such was the case with the merchant George Wilson. When he died on 26 April 1778 it was decided that the children in Glasgow who benefited from his charity would carry out an annual procession pageant on the anniversary of his death, taking them across the old city centre and into a church service, followed by the reward of a roast beef dinner and plum pudding. As you might have guessed, a toast 'to the memory' of their benefactor was part of this tradition.[20] Ceremonies surrounding the laying of the foundation stones for the Trade's Hall (1791), Hutcheson's Bridge (1794), Assembly Rooms (1796), York Street Riding School (1796), and Nelson's Monument (1806) were typically very busy affairs, attended to by the governing bodies and officials in their finest garb, drawing crowds for the moment of initiation. It became common practice to place a glass jar beneath the stone, containing coins and copies of local newspapers.[21] Whether or not they survive, the intention of planting these 'time capsules' reveals a clear attempt to *inhabit* cultural memory. The laying of the foundation stone for the Royal Infirmary in 1792 was captured in verse by the Glasgow poet William Campbell,[22] a work not at all unlike John Home's 1753 poem detailing 'laying the foundation stone of the new Edinburgh exchange'.[23] Campbell's civic pride is in full form, as he declares:

> No more th' impending wall offends our eyes
> A nobler happier dome is seen to rise
> Whose milder aspect bids contention cease
> And sooths the mind to harmony and peace . . .[24]

Unlike the other sites, this one seems to have been a symbolic opportunity for the cleansing of cultural memory. There is a definite sense of Glasgow being 'cured' from 'memories of Papal supremacy' (MacGregor, above) in this new age. The Royal Infirmary was better regulated than its predecessor and enjoyed a beneficial relationship with the FPSG, another historic institution which preserves centuries of history. The nearby Physic Garden belonging to the University added to this new collaborative centre of medical development. It was in this building that Joseph Lister worked, following his appointment to the Chair of Surgery in the University in 1860.[25] The Royal is still in use to this day, although the original building designed by Robert Adam – who also designed the Trades Hall, one of Glasgow's finest remaining Georgian buildings – was replaced and expanded in the early twentieth century.

The symbolic importance of the dome built into the Royal Infirmary (see Figure 5) essentially leads us towards the discussion of the original Hunterian Museum (see Figure 6). For Thomas Markus, these domes were classical expressions of the Age of Reason.[26] Geyer-Kordesch and MacDonald have picked up on this, summarising these sites as 'architectural paeans to the need to classify and understand the natural order'.[27] The portrayal of these late Georgian buildings as a meeting point of natural and moral philosophy, of science and art, is firmly established in

Figure 5 James Fittler, *Glasgow Infirmary* (1804). Reproduced with the permission of the National Library of Scotland.

Figure 6 Joseph Swan, *View of the Hunterian Museum, &c. from the West*, (1829). © CSG CIC Glasgow Museums and Libraries Collection: The Mitchell Library, Special Collections.

Markus' article: both in the excellent reading of William Hunter's movements in London, with particular focus on his house in Great Windmill Street which 'incorporated' his 'mature ideas on the physical framework needed for medical practice, teaching and dissection, and the housing of anatomical, natural history, coin, art and book collections'; and in the study of Anderson's Museum which formed 'part of the late eighteenth century westward development' of Glasgow.[28] One of the most intriguing insights in this reading is Markus' comparison of structure with natural order: 'The development of anatomy can be seen as an analogy which in an interesting way anticipates the relationship of form, function and space in architecture.'[29] In this we can come to terms with the impact of 'the living centre' upon location and cultural memory. Unlike the functional designation of buildings such as hospitals (treatment and teaching), the Museum can effectively become the very 'image' of a place via its collections. That Hunter's work in London began to combine teaching with exhibition is a very interesting notion indeed, leaving us to consider the effect of the overlap of the individual and the place in the figuration of cultural memory.

Heading back to the site of the Old College allows us to consider James Watt and the Hunterian Museum more fully. First established on the original University Campus in 1807, the Hunterian was Scotland's first public museum. But unlike the Foulis brothers, Alexander Wilson, Joseph Black and Adam Smith, Hunter's 'Glasgow-ness' has seemingly always been uncertain. Having only spent the years 1731–6 in the city proper, Hunter is an example of the Scottish Enlightenment at home in London. Yes, he had mused on a latter-day School of Anatomy for Glasgow, but we must consider the true effect of that dormant period between his death in 1783 and the completion of his museum in 1807. It was set so that 'for 30 years' Hunter's vast collections 'would remain in London, and continue to be used for teaching and demonstration'.[30] During the wait, Cullen, Black, Smollett and John Moore all died, rendering the opening of the Museum a sort of delayed-reaction, dampening Glasgow's ability to crystalise its scientific and medical achievements. London – as valid a site of the Scottish Enlightenment as any other city – has been said to have suffered greatly when his collections were uprooted.[31] We should not ignore the idea that, when Hunter's legacy collection found itself in Glasgow in the form of a repackaged cultural memory, there was a sort of double dilution of what Markus and Rolfe see as a living, breathing connection between Hunter's ideas and his displays. We may still, of course, rightly praise the immediate effect of the Hunterian on the Old College: forming a new quadrangle with the building that once housed this Academy of Fine Arts and the professors' houses, 'known as Museum Square'.[32] But with the effect of cultural memory in mind, we should also practice caution and ask: to what extent had Glasgow already moved on from the 'heyday' of the Enlightenment in the latter part of the Georgian era?

We can glimpse the answer in Thomas Hamilton's 1827 novel *Cyril Thornton*. Coming back to Glasgow after his youthful student days, Cyril described the Hunterian as: 'barbarously discordant with the prevailing character of the place [. . .] It almost seemed to have dropped from the clouds, and stood staring on the dark and time-honoured masses, by which it was surrounded, as if wondering by what extraordinary chance, it had been thrown into such company.'[33] The Londoners who expected Hunter's collections to remain in place probably felt equally bewildered that their beloved collection had vanished.[34] But at least we can discern in Glasgow a sense of the Scottish Enlightenment the people there wished to capture. The posthumous portrait of Hunter (1787) by Sir Joshua

Reynolds (1723–92) commissioned by the University of Glasgow tells us that they were making an effort to promote the forgotten connections between the city and the mobile Scottish Enlightenment. Crucially, we can add into this a completely overlooked facet of Glasgow's civic awareness, within the museum itself. As Thomas Hastie Bryce (1862–1946), Regius Professor of Anatomy at Glasgow and curator of the archaeological and anatomical specimens at the Hunterian Museum, tells us, the museum housed many paintings of all kinds brought from Hunter's house in London, 'with three exceptions. These are the portraits of Cullen, his master; of Tobias Smollett, his friend – both by Cochrane,[35] the Scottish portrait painter; and of Francis Hutcheson, whose teaching of Moral Philosophy helped to mould Hunter's character as a young student.'[36] These paintings surely represent a Glaswegian triumvirate of the Scottish Enlightenment. That they were the 'exceptions' to Hunter's paintings tell us that they were put there for contextual purposes by the University. Together with the painting of Hunter and the statue of James Watt (Chantrey, 1830), there is little doubt that 'the living centre' was entirely represented here under one roof.

But what about Watt? His presence in the Hunterian Museum symbolises the tension at the heart of the Glasgow Enlightenment and the sticking point in remembering it. He steals the show quite literally in a mid-nineteenth-century painting entitled *The Interior of the First Hunterian Museum with the Statue of James Watt*.[37] In this work the statue is illuminated and his world-famous steam engine rests behind a curtain: a suitable portrayal of the man eclipsing his work. Indeed, this painting represents the point of departure from the local: in statue form Watt not only eclipses the Hunterian and the invention for which he is recognised, but also William Hunter himself. (Watt is even known to have designed the heating system for the building.) In MacLeod's excellent study *Heroes of Invention* (2007) she states that while the scene may very well be imaginary, 'proposing Watt as an exemplar for artisans to emulate,' it is just as likely that we are glimpsing 'a real occurrence – even a regular one'.[38] In either scenario, the painting remains an interesting piece of cultural memory evoking an unusual sense of immediacy in the space. And why not? Watt was Glasgow's chosen son of the Enlightenment.

His first statue, by John Greenshields, was sculpted in 1823–4, predating both the George Square and Hunterian statues by Francis Leggatt Chantrey (both 1830). There had been 'agitation' for a statue to commemorate Watt for some time, and this inaugural effort was placed 'on the attic' of the Mechanics' Institute and Technical College of Science in Bath Street.[39] Following the Chantrey statues, the next likeness of Watt was erected in McPhun Park, Bridgeton, around 1864. Like the Greenshields statue, this one by Charles Benham Grassby has Watt leaning on a steam cylinder: his mnemonic symbol and 'invention'. Although this statue has been in a very sorry state (chipped, worn and headless) for some time, its survival draws us closer still to a *lieu de mémoire*. Bridgeton rests on the boundary of Glasgow Green where, it is famously believed, Watt had his moment of enlightenment, his breakthrough thought on how to improve the steam engine that would soon change the world. In Glasgow Green there is a round granite stone bearing the message: 'NEAR THIS SPOT IN 1765 JAMES WATT CONCEIVED THE IDEA OF THE SEPARATE CONDENSER FOR THE STEAM ENGINE PATENTED 1769.' It was placed there on 2 September 1969, the bicentennial year of the patent. The consecration of this spot in Glasgow's chief green place was the result of the reinscription of his achievement throughout the nineteenth century.

On what was once Strathclyde House, in Elmbank Street, statues of Cicero, Galileo, Watt, and Homer flank the façade (Mossman, c.1878). In Nelson Mandela Place, Watt is one of the key figures in the 'Scientific Education' sculptural group, also by Mossman (c.1886). In both instances Watt is depicted with the centrifugal governor (see Figure 7), a crucial part in the improved engine. David Philip Miller's book on Watt (2009)[40] links these Glasgow statues to their counterparts in England, where Watt was being valorised as a hero of the British nation. By the turn of the twentieth century, Watt had been removed from the classical contexts set by Mossman and was placed in the company of other famous engineers, as we see in Albert Hemstock Hodge's full portrait sculpture of Watt on the Clydeport Building in Robertson Street (1906–8). Rather than grouping Watt with the likes of Galileo and Homer, Watt is found between the Scottish engineers Thomas Telford and Henry Bell. His condenser remains, and so he becomes synonymous with that object regardless of the context. The potency of the steam engine motif is why Grassby's statue in Bridgeton could still be identified without Watt's head. But this may just have been a harbinger for the forgetting of the Glasgow Enlightenment: the loss of memory, if you will, in the form of Watt losing his head.[41]

Miller, above, has written extensively on the history and legacy of Watt, but one argument bears particular relevance here. His inquiry into 'why it was important for various historical actors that Watt be constructed as a philosophical inventor' actually helps us discover why the Glasgow Enlightenment has been so poorly remembered.[42] In raising Watt higher

Figure 7 John Mossman, sculpture of James Watt and Youth, Nelson Mandela Place, Glasgow (1886). Photo: the author.

than his contemporaries and inscribing Watt The Philosopher for the majority of the nineteenth century forced the likes of William Cullen and Joseph Black into competition with Watt in the public imagination.[43] Watt is the inevitable winner, and Glasgow's Enlightenment gradually begins to resemble *Watt's* Enlightenment, though the recent spotlight on Watt's complicity with slavery has brought his heroic status into some scrutiny.[44] All told, Watt's enduring popularity is part of the reason why Glasgow's cultural memory is overburdened with images of Victorian progress.

These images often eclipse other locations, sites and symbols through which we can recall the Enlightenment. The allegorical sculptures in the Kelvingrove area – such as John Mossman's frieze depicting the Smithian progression from barbarism to enlightenment on La Belle Place (1858), or Paul Montford's old, bearded philosopher complete with skull on the Kelvin Way Bridge (1926) – could not stack up against the incessant reinscription of the new commercial and industrial Glasgow. Excluding the historical portraits above, there is no 'personification' of the Enlightenment in Glasgow's proud tradition of sculpture. In contrast, there are four to Abundance, five to Britannia, thirteen to

Commerce, and eighteen personifications of Industry, bringing us back to the common image of Glasgow as a smoggy city of bustle and heavy lifting (as seen in Figure 1).[45] You can almost feel the ground shake with the progress of the industrial world here, the same which ultimately forced the University to move from the old city centre.

Indeed it is hard to disagree with Maurice Lindsay's notion that the demolition of the Old College buildings 'was probably the City's greatest ever loss'.[46] The land owned by the University on which the old campus stood was sold to the City of Glasgow Union Railway Company 'for a goods station serviced by steam engines'.[47] It is the ultimate irony. The steamrolling over of the Glasgow Enlightenment in the cityscape a century after the idea that made it possible. The point is not lost to David Clarke, who quotes the following passage from *The Herald* in full:

> Deep-brooding Watt, sitting in his academic shop, studying great physical powers, evoked from his brain the very spirit ... which is about to lay the walls of his student's cell in ruins. It is to the railway that the University is about to yield up its ancient dwelling-place, and, in a few months, there will sweep over the spot where the great philosopher sat the very spirit which he was then chaining to the car of civilisation.[48]

Perhaps these words deserve more attention for their incredible relevance to the understanding of memorialisation. Even if we are being ironic, blaming Watt for the demolition of the old Hunterian and the College in the background of his portrait (see Figure 8), where the open-air Foulis exhibition was held, is probably excessive.[49] It would also be necessary to blame Cullen, Black, and their colleagues across Britain. Instead we should continue to reconnect these narratives into some sort of order and remember the extent of the Glasgow Enlightenment. This has been achieved for other places through studies such as Jenny Uglow's *Lunar Men* (2002). Uglow's astute metaphor regarding the enlightened friends whose paths 'crossed like cotton threaded between pins on a map' is indicative of the difficulty in harnessing cultural memory.[50] But we should continue to challenge our own impressions of city 'images'. We should look behind the metaphorical curtain that has been draped over these histories, as we might imagine the two artisans in the first Hunterian doing as they considered that statue of Watt by Chantrey. Only then can we begin to ask the more difficult questions, those which transcend the physical boundaries of Glasgow but which make it complicit nonetheless. As we look towards another major theme in the next chapter, it will be shown that Glasgow's sites of slavery and empire are

Figure 8 John Blake MacDonald, *James Watt* (1858). © The Hunterian, University of Glasgow.

as unevenly remembered as we have seen them to be here. With slavery comes the dilemma of remembering a transatlantic mass-movement of people, thus pushing the theories of cultural memory to the limit.

NOTES

1. *The Miscellaneous Works of Tobias Smollett, M.D. with a Life of the Author in Twelve Volumes, Volume 4* (London: Otridge and Rackham et al., 1824), 268.
2. Ray McKenzie et al., *Public Sculpture of Glasgow: Public Sculpture of Britain, Vol. 5* (Liverpool: Liverpool University Press, 2002), 388.
3. University of Glasgow Library Special Collections, Call Number: Mu2-x.9/13c.
4. *Catalogue of the Foulis Exhibition Held in the University of Glasgow April 1913* (Glasgow: James MacLehose and Sons, 1913).
5. For the digital exhibition and details from the 2001 exhibition, see <http://special.lib.gla.ac.uk/exhibns/foulis/index.htm> (last accessed 30 August 2020).
6. Hugh Ferguson, *Glasgow School of Art: The History* (Glasgow: The Foulis Press of Glasgow School of Art, 1995), 14.
7. McKenzie et al., *Public Sculpture of Glasgow*, 57–8.
8. Ibid., 114–15.
9. Ibid., 294.
10. Murray Pittock and Christopher A. Whatley, 'Poems and Festivals, Art and Artefact and the Commemoration of Robert Burns, c.1844–c.1896', *The Scottish Historical Review*, Volume XCIII, 1: No. 236 (2014), 56–79 (58).
11. George MacGregor, *The History of Glasgow: From the Earliest Period to the Present Time* (Glasgow: Thomas D. Morison, 1881), 204.
12. Ibid.
13. John Gillies, *Historical Collections Relating to Remarkable Periods of The Success of The Gospel and Eminent Instruments Employed in Promoting It, Volume I* (Glasgow: Robert and Andrew Foulis, 1754), 315
14. See also Andreas Huyssen, *Twilight Memories: Marking Time in a Culture of Amnesia* (New York: Routledge, 1995).
15. Maurice Halbwachs, *The Collective Memory* (New York: Harper & Row, 1980), 52.
16. McKenzie et al., *Public Sculpture of Glasgow*, 67.
17. Ibid.
18. MacGregor, *The History of Glasgow*, 363
19. David Clarke, *Reflections on the Astronomy of Glasgow: A Story of Some 500 Years* (Edinburgh: Edinburgh University Press, 2013), 64.
20. Robert Chambers, *The Gazetteer of Scotland* (Edinburgh: Balfour & Jack, 1836), 481–2.

21. James Cleland, *Enumeration of the Inhabitants of Scotland taken from the Government Abstracts of 1801, 1811, 1821; containing a particular account of every parish in Scotland and many useful details respecting England, Wales and Ireland* (Glasgow: James Lumsden & Son, 1823), 193.
22. Little is known about this particular poet, beside a collection of his poems held in the Mitchell Library, with much material on Glasgow, political reform, and the French Revolution.
23. Richard B. Sher, *Church and University in the Scottish Enlightenment: The Moderate Literati of Edinburgh* (Edinburgh: Edinburgh University Press, 1985), 188.
24. William Campbell, 'On laying the foundation stone of the infirmary on the ruins of the old castle', Mitchell Library, MS. 73, f. 5.
25. Christopher Lawrence, 'Lister, Joseph, Baron Lister (1827–1912)', *Oxford Dictionary of National Biography*, <http://www.oxforddnb.com/view/article/34553> (last accessed 30 August 2020).
26. Thomas A. Markus, 'Domes of Enlightenment: Two Scottish University Museums', *The International Journal of Museum Management and Curatorship*, 4:3 (1985), 215–42.
27. Johanna Geyer-Kordesch and Fiona MacDonald, *Physicians and Surgeons in Glasgow: The History of the Royal College of Physicians and Surgeons of Glasgow* (London: Hambledon, 1999), 186.
28. Markus, 'Domes of Enlightenment', 221.
29. Ibid., 224.
30. Ibid., 223–47.
31. W. D. Ian Rolfe, 'William and John Hunter: breaking the Great Chain of Being', in W. F. Bynum and Roy Porter, eds, *William Hunter and the Eighteenth-Century Medical World* (Cambridge: Cambridge University Press, 1985), 297–319 (299)
32. Lawrence Keppie, *William Hunter and the Hunterian Museum in Glasgow, 1807–2007* (Edinburgh: Edinburgh University Press, 2007), 51.
33. Thomas Hamilton, *The Youth and Manhood of Cyril Thornton* ed. Maurice Lindsay (Aberdeen: The Association for Scottish Literary Studies, 1990 [1827]), 426.
34. Keppie, *William Hunter and the Hunterian Museum in Glasgow*, 36–7.
35. The named artist is the same William Cochrane (1738–85) from the Foulis Academy. His portrait of Cullen is well known (*c.*1765), but his Smollett portrait less so. In fact, to attribute this to Cochrane may help clarify the murkiness surrounding another portrait of 'A Gentleman', believed to be Smollett, painted by another pupil of the Academy: Archibald McLauchlan (*fl.* 1752–70).
36. T. H. Bryce, 'The Hunterian Museum', *Glasgow University Students' Handbook* (Glasgow; Glasgow University, 1935), 50–2 (51).
37. Christine MacLeod, *Heroes of Invention: Technology, Liberalism and*

British Identity, 1750–1914 (Cambridge: Cambridge University Press, 2007), 292–3.
38. Ibid., 293. MacLeod also outlines the cult of Watt that grew up in the west of Scotland to great effect.
39. Alexander Humboldt Sexton, *The First Technical College: A Sketch of the History of 'The Andersonian', and the Institutions Descended from It, 1796–1894* (London: Chapman & Hall, 1894), 73.
40. David Philip Miller, *James Watt, Chemist: Understanding the Origins of the Steam Age* (London: Pickering & Chatto, 2009).
41. All of the dates and background information for the Watt statues derived from McKenzie et al., 2002,
42. David Philip Miller, '"Puffing Jamie": The commercial and ideological importance of being a "Philosopher" in the case of the reputation of James Watt (1736–1819)', *History of Science*, 38:119 (2000), 1–24 (3).
43. Ibid.
44. As the recent University of Glasgow report by Stephen Mullen and Simon Newman – *Slavery, Abolition and the University of Glasgow* (Glasgow: University of Glasgow, 2018) <https://www.gla.ac.uk/media/media_607547_en.pdf> (last accessed 30 August 2020) – highlights, Watt's father was a West India merchant and slave-trader, and Watt himself profited from the slave trade. This report is highlighted again in Chapter 4.
45. Abstracted from the Index in McKenzie et al., 2002. Industry number taken as (12) Industry (4) Shipbuilding, (2) Engineering.
46. Hamilton, *Cyril Thornton*, 458.
47. Quoted in Clarke, *Reflections on the Astronomy of Glasgow*, 59.
48. Ibid.
49. This point was made first in Craig Lamont, 'Cultivating the Classics "in a cold climate"': The Foulis Press & Academy in Glasgow', *Journal of the Edinburgh Bibliographical Society*, (2019), 61.
50. Jenny Uglow, *The Lunar Men: The Friends Who Made the Future, 1730–1810* (London: Faber and Faber, 2002), 35.

PART III

Empire and the Displacement of Memory

In 1929 the English travel writer H. V. Morton said, 'there is a transatlantic alertness about Glasgow which no city in England possesses'.[1] For all that Glasgow's Enlightenment narrative has been neglected, Glasgow's commercial canniness has driven its self-perception in modern times, feeding directly into the image of the city as an industrial force and entrepôt of global trade. When it comes to using the North Atlantic as a trading route Glasgow has a clear geographic advantage over Edinburgh on the east of Scotland and to a lesser extent the chief port cities in England outside London. Despite this, Edinburgh led the charge for commercial growth in the first half of the Georgian period in Scotland. Cultural innovation and the compact shape of the Scottish capital made it cosmopolitan in character.[2] Glasgow's growth was slower. But with an increasing amount of its mercantile stock across the Atlantic, and with most of it concerning only a small community of wealthy merchants, it makes sense that the city was in relative stasis for longer. As Chapter 4 will show, one of the largest barriers in remembering Georgian Glasgow is the sudden insecurity of our imperial and colonial history whenever issues like slavery are raised. Who does this memory belong to? Who portrays it, and with what motivations in mind? We can ask the same questions in the context of the Scottish diaspora, looking at some of the Glaswegian emigrants who planted the cultural memories of their home into foreign soils. With this we can gain a new perspective of Glasgow beyond its boundaries, with a view to understanding how it shaped the Georgian era *elsewhere* for better and for worse. In *The Scottish Diaspora* (2013), authors Bueltmann, Hinson and Morton reflect on the transmission of 'remembered connections', or cultural memory, 'through our own lives and more widely through the lives of others across land and ocean'.[3] Mass migration of any kind shifts the dynamic of memory and alters our vocabulary. We are no longer looking at one site, one object, and saying 'this is it'. When people and things move we are asked to consider multiple spatial references, each of them positioned within their own – and often unlikely – cultural contexts. Old and new worlds collide. And when migration is forced, as in the case of the slave trade, our discussion of memory is bound to a new set of terms. The language becomes heavier, perhaps more morally responsible. Issues of ownership and justice are woven into our understanding of what *should* be remembered, preserved and analysed. As we will see with Glasgow's

'Merchant City' district, sites of memory can assume new symbolic meanings during political and cultural disputes. When sites become contested, the fabric of cultural memory is stretched, but without the debate we might never glimpse the true fabric of the past. In other words, by looking at Glasgow's issues with memory where movement and displacement are concerned we have a new opportunity to reconcile the histories that have been obscured over time.

NOTES

1. H. V. Morton, *In Search of Scotland* (London: Methuen, 2000 [1929]), 293.
2. Morton, writing in 1929, actually describes Glasgow as the more cosmopolitan of the two chief Scottish cities. Undoubtedly he writes with Victorian Glasgow and, arguably, a disdain for the over-sentimentalised image of Edinburgh in mind. New studies like Murray Pittock's *Enlightenment in a Smart City* (2018) shed light on the unique trading and early enlightenment in the capital.
3. Tanja Bueltmann, Andrew Hinson and Graeme Morton, *The Scottish Diaspora* (Edinburgh: Edinburgh University Press, 2013), 37.

4

'That barbarous traffic'

> See what a change trade's golden wand can do!
> As if by magic make a village spring
> To all the glories of a capital.
> Her towers rise high in heaven, while far around
> The hum of nations, gather'd like stray'd bees
> By blooming commerce, to one busy spot,
> Rolls like low thunder o'er the settled scene.
>
> Dugald Moore, *The Bard of the North* (1833)[1]

Glasgow's relationship with slavery is far from straightforward. The myth that Scotland only became imperial after the Union with England in 1707 was dispelled long ago, not least of all thanks to books by Fry (2001) and Devine (2003) on Scotland and Empire.[2] But myths die hard, and the *Britishness* of Empire may explain why Glasgow and Scotland escaped the spotlight of complicity for so long. As Duffill (2004) has shown, the Darien scheme (1698–1700) was a more logical starting gun for Scots merchants to begin slaving, with further evidence suggesting that Scotland's trade on the slave coasts began as early as the 1630s.[3] But this is not the prevailing legacy. As we will see in the next chapter the Darien 'scheme' or 'plan' has become the Darien 'disaster' in our minds, invoking a very specific cultural memory wherein the loss of Scottish lives and capital crystallised as the final straw that led to the Union. It is the ultimate Scots Tragedy, and a much more compelling narrative for the nation than slave trading and the evils of empire more generally.

Indeed, the big success story of Georgian Glasgow became the antidote to the ills of post-Darien life. This is the story of the first wave of merchants during the golden years of the tobacco trade. The so-called 'Tobacco Lords' included John Glassford (one-time owner of the Shawfield Mansion) and William Cunninghame (whose mansion is now Glasgow's Gallery of Modern Art). These merchants helped boost Glasgow's economy while increasing Scotland's share in the British tobacco trade from 10 per cent in 1738 to over 50 per cent by 1769.[4] The surviving images of these merchants are of them peacocking their wealth in the city's coffee houses and clacking their canes on the 'plainstanes' of Glasgow Cross. Elisabeth Kyle's *The Tontine Belle* (1951) portrays this world, drawn from scores of historical accounts vying to characterise Glasgow's famous merchant class.[5] On the other hand, the enslaved people toiling on Virginia's plantations are not present enough as to affect cultural memory. There are, however, moves within the University of Glasgow to acknowledge and commemorate its own ties to the slave trade.[6] As the first university in the UK to do so, these new plans will help improve public knowledge of slavery in the city. In November 2019 civic leaders in Glasgow followed this example by launching an in-depth investigation into the ties between the city's built heritage and the gains of chattel slavery. Monuments, street names, civic buildings and bequests to the town council will be examined in this keen and searching light.[7]

This momentum for reparation – whether culturally symbolic or financial – has been building in the past few years thanks to a swathe of studies and public events, but it follows a long-term dissociation with the subject. It was not until the Black Lives Matter movement gained popularity across Europe and the UK in 2020 that these issues became national headline news. The murder of George Floyd (b. 1973) on 25 May 2020 by a police officer in Minneapolis sparked new marches and rallies against police brutality and institutional racism. Suddenly the debate on how to exhibit awareness of historic slavery in public spaces was thrust to the fore. This will undoubtedly be the case in scholarly discussion too, which has really only dealt with the *invisible* economy of slavery in the past twenty years. James Walvin has made the point that British historians tend to write about slavery as something that happened mostly in the Americas. 'Who,' he asks, 'when they looked the expansive and prospering face of late eighteenth-century Liverpool or Glasgow, saw that behind their handsome new buildings was the misery of African slaves?'[8] Time and again his book (2000) takes Glasgow in the same hand as Liverpool and Bristol, effectively setting up the three cities as a British triumvirate (outside London) of complicity: a rhetoric long absent from Scottish scholarship.

Fortunately a new wave of academic and public engagement with Scotland's links to slavery has been gaining momentum. Three edited collections in particular have established the debate at the forefront of literary, historical and sociological studies: *Invoking Slavery in the Eighteenth-Century British Imagination* (Swaminathan and Beach, eds, 2013), *Recovering Scotland's Slavery Past* (Devine, ed., 2015), and *Britain's History and Memory of Transatlantic Slavery* (Donington et al., eds, 2016). Memory plays a major role as scholars seek not only to outline the facts, but to illustrate subsequent attempts to commemorate the slave trade. As we know, Maurice Halbwachs' term 'collective memory' marks the beginning of this theoretical framework. In its widest sense, it refers to the memories of events and ideas shared by small groups (i.e. witnesses of an event) and/or large groups (i.e. members of the same city or country). Therefore, historical events might be actively 'remembered' only by a small group while impressions of these events may be generally 'remembered' later by large groups. As such, the term 'collective' has been appropriately recast as either 'communicative' (short-term, generational) or 'cultural' (long-term, transgenerational) memory.[9]

With a focus on the Georgian era, the majority of this book has an obvious dependence on 'cultural' memory. However, the rejuvenation of slavery discourse in recent years has brought about a unique situation, drawing issues of 'trauma memory' and 'sites of memory' into the same framework.[10] These terminologies are always in danger of becoming transient and interchangeable. For instance Tom Devine's use of the word 'amnesia' regarding Scotland's memory of slavery is effective, but misleading.[11] The term 'amnesia' implies that people have gradually 'forgotten' something about their history. If the 'forgetting group' here are Glaswegians, or Scots, then the deeper implication with 'amnesia' is that we are talking about a single generation. But we cannot make the case that Glasgow's pedestrians in 1950 had the same opportunity to remember the origins of the names of Virginia Street and Jamaica Street – the city's most tangible links to plantation slavery – as those walking through them in 1850. This assumption confuses 'cultural' with 'collective memory.'

Mnemonic terms require careful handling. For instance, Jan Assmann offers an alternate to Pierre Nora's famous essay in which he sets 'history' and 'memory' on opposite sides. As one of the leading thinkers in the field of cultural memory Assmann describes it as 'that body of reusable texts, images and rituals specific to each society in each epoch, whose "cultivation" serves to stabilise and convey that society's self-image'.[12] Thus, rather than setting memory and history in direct opposition, Assmann underlines the importance of a variety of cultural memories (and their reuse within history) which offer a view particular to the present day. But because of its international connections, there is a significant volume of interdisciplinary scholarship on slavery, such as that found within the journal *Slavery & Abolition* (1980–present). 'Memory' in slavery has therefore been subject to a variety of claims. For instance, the case studies in *Slavery in Africa* (2011) demand a wide-reaching consideration of 'place' that goes beyond the national levels found, for example, in Nora's study of France. Lane and MacDonald state that 'the trend across the [African] continent has been to focus only on the localities and material remains which are linked in some way with European involvement in slavery', effectively restricting 'indigenous systems and eras of slavery'.[13] In other words, the very definition of slavery has become narrowed both geographically and chronologically: a sort of scholarly colonisation in itself.

Furthermore, the slavery system is often referred to as the 'Triangular Trade', in which you encounter the concept of 'the middle passage'. In and of themselves, these spatio-cultural terms should point to the difficulty of locating the memory of slavery in one place rather than the other. There is perhaps no symbol more powerful in conveying this than Jason Taylor's *Molinere Bay Underwater Sculpture Park* (2006). The submerged concrete figures off the coast of Grenada tell the stories of slaves cast overboard, either with the realistic depiction of their cruel fate or with the fantasy notion that they survive in defiance. This unanchored, movable sense of memory has resulted in scholarly comparisons to the Holocaust and 'trauma' discourse. Following Peter Meusburger's terms, the 'trauma' subset of memory studies goes beyond the typical conditions laid out above. 'The traumata of slavery, colonialism, Gulag, Auschwitz, forced expulsions,' he explains, 'do not disappear with the death of the last witness.'[14] The nature and size of global atrocities therefore displaces and disturbs memory as society acts upon it. This is a growing field of concern, but as early as 1993 Charles Maier asked the still-valid question 'can there be too much memory?'[15] Maier proposed that 'former perpetrators and victims – pre-eminently, though not exclusively, Germans and Jews – have been locked into a special relationship. No matter what material or other public debts are paid, confessional memory is demanded as the only valid reparation'.[16] As the host of the Commonwealth Games in 2014, Glasgow's dormant connections with slavery were roused, becoming engaged in a similarly 'special' dialogue wherein memories of Empire and the associated guilt were brought to the fore.[17] As we will see in the Conclusion, these connections were not always as implied as we might think. That we have redacted the word 'Empire' from the title of the

Commonwealth events since 1970 tells us something about the effect of language on memory.

But while these histories were teased out, Glasgow did not suffer too glaring a spotlight because of its relatively invisible plantation economy. Both Liverpool and Bristol saw the growth of a black community at home as a result of their imperial efforts: Glasgow did not. But as the recent *Runaway Slaves in Britain* project has shown, the deployment of slaves as servants in Scotland was not exactly rare in the eighteenth century. From 1719 throughout almost every decade of the century the Scottish newspapers advertised notices of runaways. Readers were asked to give notice to the slave-owning merchant if the runaway was spotted, almost always with the offer of a reward. To help identify the slaves, details of their appearance and their attire were given. Sometimes they escaped in the trappings of their owners' wealth while others ran barefoot, cold and unwell. Some runaways were described by the tone of their skin – 'not a good black, but a little on the yellow' – and others were given names like Cupid, London and Neptune. Christian names were also popular, and in one case the name Roderic [sic] Random was given to a runaway from Bellfield, near Hamilton in 1773.[18] Curiously, this slave was named after the titular picaro from *The Adventures of Roderick Random* (1743) by the same Enlightenment-era Tobias Smollett of the last chapter. It is deeply ironic that in said novel, Roderick Random is a sojourning Scot who witnesses slaving on the coast of Guinea and the outbreak of a fever epidemic on a cargo ship. This fictional scene was informed by what would have been common knowledge amongst educated Scots.

With resources like the *Slave Voyages* database we can go further and pinpoint Glasgow's stake in the trade and transport of slaves. As we know from Chapter 1 there were slave ships named after King George or his royal house in the early decades of the century. During the height of the tobacco trade, ships left mostly from Greenock and, in the 1760s especially, Glasgow merchants were directly involved in slave transportation. Such was the civic pride in the transatlantic empire that a ship named *Glasgow* was registered in London and set sail from Leith in May 1764. Only 93 of the 114 Gambian slaves survived the journey. The ship *Juba* left Greenock on 5 July 1765, picking up 110 slaves in Casamance, Senegal, before landing in Barbados on 17 November the next year with only 98.[19] The loss of life en route is its own tragic story and the numbers are often much higher. In name and all, Scottish ports were very much involved in this imperial network. But the city that flourished whether or not as a direct result of this trade should be put into full view.

The extant letters of Glasgow merchants gives us a further insight into the thoughts on the trade and its purposes. On 5 April 1746 the merchant Claud Alexander of Newton (1724–72) received a letter from his contact in Barbados, where the slave ships would often land. It read:

> One trade by much the most beneficial of any carried on ... to the British West Indies which the People of Glasgow seems to take no Notice of and that is the Trade to the coast of Africa for slaves by which the people of Liverpool and co have enrich'd themselves and I can see no advantage that they have superior to you.[20]

The letter is unique in its starkness: such a direct statement made about Glasgow's patronage of slavery is rarely found elsewhere. And we might ascribe the dormancy of cultural memory regarding this issue to the fact that letters like this have simply not been made public enough. Text from the archive needs to be retrieved, digested and displayed before we can understand its impact on the public. Yet there are more striking visual examples. The *Portrait of Claud Alexander and his Brother Boyd with an Indian Servant* (1784) – the sons of Claud Alexander of Newton – by Johann Zoffany (1733–1810) was commissioned as a status symbol. In the painting Claud (1752–1809) is holding a letter telling him that he has acquired the Ayrshire estate of Ballochmyle. Incidentally, Robert Burns's song 'The Bonnie Lass o' Ballochmyle' was addressed to Wilhelmina, Claud and Boyd's sister. Most striking of all is the placid Indian servant, gazing through time at us while the brothers stand frozen in their moment of success.[21]

In recent years Stephen Mullen has been the lead interrogator on the issue of transatlantic chattel slavery. His essays and book chapters have pushed Glasgow into the centre of the colonial image of British slavery, with a particular focus on the latter end of the eighteenth and the beginning of the nineteenth century. Mullen's PhD thesis (2015) takes this further, offering a holistic view of the second wave of Glasgow's mercantile story.[22] The tobacco trade was all but lost following the American War of Independence (1775–83) while sugar trading funded much of Glasgow's expansion. But Glasgow was much more than its merchants. After all, the key players of the neglected Glasgow Enlightenment were neighbours with these shrewd men of business.

It was during his Lectures on Jurisprudence (1762) at the University of Glasgow that Adam Smith set out a Four-Stage Theory of Development from 'warlike aristocracy' to 'a society pursuing personal betterment in a commercial environment'.[23] In other words, successful commerce in a city provides opportunities for a metropolis to grow. It is no surprise that Smith is featured so prominently in Christopher Berry's *The Idea of Commercial Society in the Scottish Enlightenment* (2013), so much so that Smith's assertion ('slavery is a bad institution') is said to be 'without exception the position of the Scots and the rest of the Enlightenment'.[24] Alexander Broadie has also pointed to Smith's successor, Thomas Reid (1710–96), who wrote to his cousin James Gregory from Glasgow in 1788 saying: 'Our University has sent a petition to the House of Commons, in favour of the African slaves. I hope yours will not be the last in this humane design; and that the Clergy of Scotland will likewise join in it.'[25] Far from being an annexe of Glasgow's cultural history, the Scottish Enlightenment gives us access to a narrative where philosophical and commercial improvement are intertwined. Preceding *The Wealth of Nations*, Smith's *Theory of Moral Sentiments* (1759) contains what Swaminathan calls his 'cornerstone of morality':[26]

> There is not a negro from the coast of Africa who does not ... possess a degree of magnanimity which the soul of his sordid master is scarce capable of conceiving. Fortune never exerted more cruelly her empire over mankind, than when she subjected those nations of heroes to the refuse of the jails of Europe, to wretches who possess the virtues neither of the countries which they come from, nor of those which they go, and whose levity, brutality and baseness, so justly expose them to the contempt of the vanquished.[27]

The American diplomat Arthur Lee made use of this 'extraordinary' passage as the lead for his examination of Africans and their masters in his *Essay in Vindication of the Continental Colonies of America* (1764) – a sign of Smith's early influence on abolitionists. But for many modern scholars such as John Cairns, Smith's running 'imagery of noble African savages and decadent Europeans is undoubtedly too strong', in the end detracting from what is otherwise a clear statement to be made in the case against slavery. Cairns also notes that by the sixth edition of *Moral Sentiments* Smith had added a passage on domestic slavery, portraying this 'vilest of all states': the sales of 'man, woman and child', rendering them cattle in a market.[28] When one considers the legacy of *The Wealth of Nations*, the succession of images from heroic savages to marketable cattle becomes increasingly interesting, as Smith by then focused less on the moral abhorrence of slavery than the economically founded reasons to abolish it. Between these key texts of Smith's there exists, in his *Lectures on Jurisprudence*, the discussion of colonial slavery as comparable to slavery in ancient times. At one point the wretched conditions of slaves as servants and within households is elucidated, with Smith stressing the point that 'their lives were taken away on the slightest occasion'.[29]

The economic concern of the debate is at its foremost in *The Wealth of Nations*, in which Smith states that 'the work done by freemen comes cheaper in the end than that performed by slaves'.[30] The point being made is that money spent by masters on their slaves is too costly, for, while they benefit from *forced* and unpaid labour, they are responsible for the continued care of the slaves to ensure they are fit to work. This sentiment is extended: 'A person who can acquire no property, can have no other interest but to eat as much, and to labour as little as possible. Whatever work he does beyond what is sufficient to purchase his own maintenance can be squeezed out of him by violence only.'[31] Although 'violence' is mentioned, the lamenting tone found in Smith's 'sympathetic' morals had somewhat faded. Nonetheless, Smith's popularity was secured with this work, and its memory was manipulated to suit both sides of the slavery debate. As Swaminathan says, Smith's influential works 'put forth ideas that abolitionists appropriated, and this appropriation forced slavery apologists to question and reappropriate or counter Smith to serve their own ends.'[32] Craig Smith, the current Adam Smith Lecturer in the Scottish Enlightenment at the University of Glasgow is among the authorities to consider this problem most recently. His article 'Adam Smith: Left or Right?' (2013) challenges the attempts made by the 'political left' to 'rescue [Smith] from his admirers on the free market "right"'.[33] In the end, the tug-of-war over Smith's legacy effectively diminishes the authority of all cultural claimants. One can, however, make an initial attempt to 'locate' Smith by tracing his legacy in the direct context of philosophies coming from the University both before and after his time there.

John Millar's seminal work *Observations Concerning the Distinction of Ranks in Society* (1771) is a descendant of the theories laid out by Smith in his *Lectures on Jurisprudence*.[34] Like Smith, Millar describes systems of slavery in ancient times before putting forward sentiments concomitant with the anti-slavery movement. One such example comes to the conclusion that 'It is difficult to ascertain the degree of authority which, from the principles of justice and humanity, we are, in any situation, permitted to assume over our fellow-creatures'.[35] The language here, specifically 'fellow-creatures', is telling of a then-engrained ideology of the moral framework deployed by scholars at the heart of the debate. Cairns outlines the source of Millar's *Ranks*, again comparable to Smith, being his series of lectures at the university as well his 'Discourse on the Conditions of Servants in different ages and Countries' given before the Glasgow Literary Society in 1770.[36] Millar also composed both University of Glasgow anti-slave trade petitions to Parliament in 1788 and 1792.[37] With all this considered it is unfortunate that his legacy is not as represented in recent literature as Smith's.

It is suggested by Cairns that both David Brion Davis and C. Duncan Rice have placed Millar's *Ranks* at the heart of the Scottish Enlightenment, which is often the starting point for those studying slavery in Scotland.[38] Nonetheless, there exists little to the memory of Millar outside the prestigious John Millar Chair of Law established in 1985 at the University of Glasgow.[39] Smith might be a colossal figure by comparison but his legacy is complex. At the tip of the iceberg is Smith's reception as 'the patron saint of free market capitalism'.[40] While it is one thing to consider Smith in the parameters of the *Scottish* Enlightenment, it is another to place him in the heart of Glasgow. As Berry reminds us, Smith was part of the diverse community in Glasgow in which merchants and philosophers met and shared ideas. It was in conversations with Andrew Cochrane (1693–1777) that Smith gained ideas for his *Wealth of Nations*. Additionally, Smith's text worked its way into 'the Glasgow merchant rhetoric . . . in favour of Smithian free trade in cotton' following the decline of profits from West India colonies in the nineteenth century.[41] This is an interesting light to see Glasgow in, but where is Adam Smith in the cultural memory of the city?

The only likeness of Smith rendered during his lifetime was in 1787 (three years before his death) by James Tassie, once pupil of the Foulis Academy. A similar image of Smith was used on the Kirkcaldy Penny, a token from 1797 which bears on the reverse side an imperial scene and the title 'WEALTH OF NATIONS'. In the nineteenth century Smith's cultural memory grew considerably. Two plaster busts created in the 1840s can be found in Scotland: one in the Adam Smith Theatre in his home town, Kirkcaldy; the other in Glasgow's Kelvingrove Museum. Before the pairing of Smith and Hume on the north-west tower of the Scottish National Portrait Gallery, Edinburgh (1890), there were three statues of Smith made in the 1860s. The first (1860–2) was erected at the entrance to the Vienna Business School; the second was created between 1866 and 1869 and was situated alongside figures such as Newton, Milton and Locke on the façade of 6 Burlington Gardens, London; and the third, dating from 1867, is situated beneath Randolph Hall in the Main Building of the University of Glasgow. However, Glasgow's civic appreciation of Smith outside the University is extremely underwhelming. As of 1967 the University campus housed the Adam Smith Building, but, besides Smith's name on the University Memorial Gate, he has been largely ignored. What better example of this cultural disembodiment than the 10-foot bronze statue of Smith being unveiled in 2008 in

Figure 9 Adam Smith statue, Royal Mile, Edinburgh. Photo: the author.

Edinburgh's Royal Mile (see Figure 9), 'within the view' of the statue of 'Smith's friend David Hume'.[42]

By cementing Smith's official Scottish Enlightenment context in Edinburgh his time in Glasgow is essentially circumscribed. The other major monuments to Smith are chiefly in remembrance of his economic importance – again, prolonging his legacy as 'the patron saint of free market capitalism'. These are a series of sculptures, created by American artist Jim Sanborn (b. 1945) between 1997 and 2001 in North Carolina, Cleveland and Connecticut. They feature Smith's writings within, and projected from, cylindrical forms known as 'spinning tops' and 'circulating capital'.[43] Should it come as a surprise at all that the 2007 decision for Smith's figure to appear on the Bank of England £20 note was based entirely on the legacy of his political economy and not, as one might presume – given Smith's influence on anti-slavery discourse – to coincide with the Bicentenary of the Abolition of the Slave Trade?[44] The case can be made that Smith's legacy, like so many Glaswegian figures of the Georgian era, has been made complicated by subsequent scholarship, journalistic feuds and political movements. In this case it is ironic that Smith, the first Scot to grace a Bank of England note, belonged to a particularly Glasgow Enlightenment, yet is best remembered for his most famous text which has time and again taken him *out of* Glasgow in the public imagination.

The city's links with socialism have made Smith's position even less tenable. The Calton Weavers' strike in 1787 and the 1820 Radical Rising are popular narratives in the city's history while the Red Clydeside movement in the early twentieth century continued this tradition of working class uprisings against unjust social systems. Edward Gaitens's *Dance of the Apprentices* (1948) addressed this. For Gaitens's protagonist Eddy Macdonnel the 'Capitalists' are 'others', they are 'contented wage-slaves' yet to 'see the light'.[45] And although Burns's poetry and impressions of eighteenth-century Glasgow are handled rather well, Gaitens later juxtaposes 'a massive volume of Karl Marx' with 'a tiny volume' by Joseph Conrad, quipping: 'What's the use o' literature an' poetry an' art anyway? They're all right for rich an' middle-class people wi' plenty o' leezure but nut for us workin' men!'[46] The speaker here, Donald, serves as an emblem for the active, masculine, working-class Glaswegian whose taste for 'useful' political literature eradicates the place of ballad poetry in Glasgow which, as portrayed earlier by Eddy, 'seemed to come out of the heart of young Scotland, out of the childhood of his country's life'.[47] The implication that Glasgow's coming of age, socially speaking, brought about the death of old 'literature an' poetry an' art' is a powerful one, explaining, at least in part, the impaired cultural memory of Georgian Glasgow.

Adam Smith may have *belonged* to Glasgow in more than one sense, but it seems that his legacy was simply incompatible with the city's working-class development. Glasgow's socialist appearance became so recognisable that the evident prosperity of the eighteenth-century men and women was cut off, in a sense, from a more comfortable left-wing image. Smith became a representative of the elite, and his diverse contributions to Glasgow's literary and philosophical history were elided. There is historic precedence for Glasgow's self-reflexive commercial character which can be gleaned, for instance, in a pamphlet by the Rev. William Thom, of Govan, entitled *The Defects of an University Education, and its Unsuitableness to a Commercial People* (1762). When John Anderson died, his Institution was opened by command of his will, serving to compete with the University of Glasgow. Anderson's became the University of Strathclyde, whose motto ('The place of useful learning'), reveals this split in late Enlightenment discourse: the traditional versus the practical.[48] In the process of this cultural displacement the city essentially lost a tangible connection to slavery discourse. The fame of the Tobacco Lords has outweighed the fame of Smith in Glasgow just as the fame of the Clyde's shipbuilding scene has outweighed the same river's implications with transatlantic slavery. What any place needs in order to be associated with certain historical narratives, it seems, is a recognisable and enduring figure.

Enter David Livingstone. John Mossman's statue (1875–9) of Livingstone can be found in Glasgow's Cathedral Square (see Figure 10). Around the plinth of the statue are different scenes including toiling

Figure 10 David Livingstone statue, Cathedral Square, Glasgow. Photo: the author.

slaves and African natives gathered around Livingstone with an open Bible. The statue itself features abolitionist iconography in the form of a sextant, an astrolabe and an ankle shackle. Nearby, on the University of Strathclyde's campus you can find the Livingstone tower, inside which there is a second portrait statue of Livingstone. This concentration of Livingstone in Glasgow's older district ousts Smith further from Glasgow's cultural memory. As we know, some of the Old College's buildings moved west with the new campus in 1870 and, as a result, the legacies of key eighteenth-century figures such as Smith, Millar and Reid were displaced. The statue of Lincoln and the freed slave in Edinburgh's Old Calton Burial Ground similarly disorients Edinburgh's own men and women who fought for emancipation. In these examples and more, the heroic character overwhelms the narrative. These figureheads are, in a sense, lightning rods for memories. Without a strong and identifiable focal point, the subtler points might be non-existent rather than simply overshadowed. The monumentality of these men, however contrived certain aspects of their legacy may be, is not something shared by Adam Smith: the names Livingstone and Lincoln conjure certain ideas that remain popular while Adam Smith, although familiar in Enlightenment and economic contexts, simply does not have the same universal presence.

According to C. Duncan Rice (1981) it was probable that, unlike the 'enlightened views [...] expressed in the salons of Edinburgh and Glasgow, most normal Scots probably shared James Boswell's response to the evangelical campaign'.[49] Boswell, the famed biographer of Samuel Johnson and shining light of the Scottish Enlightenment in Edinburgh was in fact taught by Smith during his brief spell at the University of Glasgow. By any account Boswell is a contradictory figure. In his *Tour of Corsica* (1768) his language seems to align with the anti-slavery movement: 'He who is in chains cannot move either easily or gracefully.'[50] Boswell also helped the indentured servant Joseph Knight in his case against his owner John Wedderburn in the famous trial of 1778, and is said to have helped found the same abolition movement of which Thomas Clarkson was a part.[51] Despite all this he penned a very unusual poem in 1791, titled *No Abolition of Slavery; or, the Universal Empire of Love*. It was printed (anonymously) as an attack on the abolitionists just before their bill was put forward in Parliament.

Suffice to say even Glasgow's neglected Enlightenment was not straightforward. And in the same way that Glasgow's proud era of industrialisation outstrips its literary past, the abolitionists are usually given more precedence in public discourse than pro-slavery voices (Boswell's included). In the last decade of the eighteenth century it was the oldest society – the Edinburgh Committee for the Abolition of the Slave Trade – that was also the strongest in Scotland.[52] However in 1791, months before Boswell's poem was printed and Wilberforce's initial bill had been rejected in Parliament, the Glasgow Committee added its voice to the debate with a pamphlet entitled *An Address to the Inhabitants of Glasgow, Paisley, and the Neighbourhood, Concerning the African Slave Trade*. The importance of this publication should not be understated. It represents one of the first explicit denunciations of slavery coming from within Glasgow in a non-academic context. Troy Bickham notes that while Smith's *Moral Sentiments* was among the cheapest work available (six shillings), many works of Scottish philosophy on the subject were beyond the grasp of the poorer literate public, such as Kames's *Sketches of the History of Man* (1774) which cost £2 2s.[53] Pamphlets like this from the Glasgow Committee brought the debate to a new audience. Within the pamphlet, the language is clear in its disapproval of the trade:

> It would be endless, to enumerate all the facts, by which the iniquity of that barbarous traffic, has been proved in the fullest manner . . . There is likewise much reason to believe, that those Europeans employed in the trade, not only give encouragement to those shocking measures, but sometimes take an active part in the execution of them.[54]

Several incidents of disaster in 'the middle passage', of disease spreading on board, and one incident of a slave being beheaded in front of the crew are recounted in the hope of sparking public outrage. This all suggests that, beforehand, the true horrors of the trade were in fact *not* so well known. There may have been the occasional runaway in Glasgow, but again we return to a predominantly invisible economy: the trade *outside* Glasgow across the seas.

This began to change when an infamous illustration was printed in the pamphlet, 'between two pages of the text'.[55] The diagram of the Liverpool slave ship *Brooks* (see Figure 11) is an image which displays the painful conditions endured by captured slaves during their transportation to plantations (where they were made to labour) or to mansions (where they became servants). At a glance, the proximity of the slaves makes them appear as one with the ship, such is the lack of space between them. It is only when one studies the image at length that the detail is revealed: most of the slaves have their arms at their sides or over their crotch while others, at the bow of the ship, take advantage of their extra space by outstretching an arm or bending a leg. The diagram was included in many anti-slavery publications following its creation in 1788

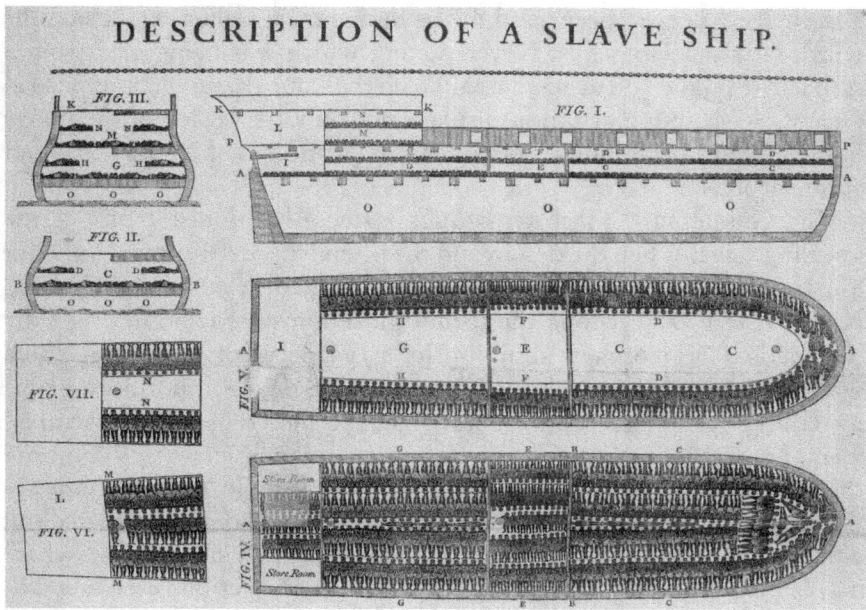

Figure 11 Cropped section from *Description of a Slave Ship* (London: James Phillips, 1789). © The British Library Board, 522.f.23, p. 46.

in Plymouth and must have had a monumental effect on the public. The power of this striking image, reproduced on the cover of various books, displayed in museums, and found infinitely online, is a direct link to the past. Images like *Brooks*, although politically motivated, contain a different kind of cultural memory from those found in literary works. Their reappearance over time carries an enduring intellectual charge more effectively than, say, a famous text like *The Wealth of Nations* or a famous person like David Livingstone. This is because the image of *Brooks* becomes the object, albeit malleable and transmittable across different media. With books and with people we have more than one way to remember them. The art historian Aby Warburg (1866–1924) showed this with his *Mnemosyne Atlas*: a series of panels on which he mapped out images from the Renaissance to explore their aesthetic afterlife. As Aleida Assmann said: 'Warburg did not take the existence of images for granted, but instead inquired into the conditions that underlay their origin and their survival.'[56] The emotive response intended in the society's inclusion of the *Brooks* diagram is the same, for example, as is intended in its multi-media projection onto the contemporary public via model reproductions of the ship, as well as stamps and artworks.

The image has even been used in the design of a T-shirt, alongside the words 'African Holocaust Never Again', which was being sold from a stall to the public and academics alike on the same day as a conference in Ghana.[57] This popularisation displays not only the legacy of the image but also its translatability to the memorialisation of the plight of other ethnic groups.

The counterpart image to *Brooks* is the Abolitionist motif of the kneeling slave. When the design and the often recycled motto – 'Am I not a man and a brother?' – were first implemented by Josiah Wedgwood (1730–95) in 1787 it took the form of a ceramic medallion: 'originally intended to be worn by abolitionists as a means of identifying them with the cause'.[58] Mary Guyatt's examination of the importance of the medallion (see Figure 12), from its origin as a piece of jewellery worn by men and women to its current usage as a museum piece helps delineate the effect it can have in various contexts. For example, Guyatt compares the Victoria and Albert Museum's choice of displaying the medallion amongst similar Wedgwood miniatures with the British Museum, where it was 'displayed in a thematic case housing a collection of eighteenth-

Figure 12 Medallion by Josiah Wedgwood, *Am I Not a Man and a Brother?*
© Wedgwood Museum/WWRD.

century political ephemera [. . .] the sole attempt yet made to contextualize the medallion in terms of both its status as fashionable jewellery and influential political tool'.[59] As with the *Brooks* diagram, the medallion was adopted, altered, added to, and therefore impressed upon many different communities. James Walvin notes that these images in particular have left a 'permanent mark on the collective British memory'.[60]

As Scotland headed toward abolition there was fierce debate. Rice (1981) and Whyte (2006) have outlined the formation and influence of the Glasgow Anti-Slavery Society (later the Glasgow Emancipation Society), the Glasgow Ladies' Auxiliary Society, the (Pro-Slavery) Glasgow West India Association, and the various presses associated. The passing of the Slavery Abolition Act in 1833 can be seen as the key date in these interrelations rather than the 1807 Slave Trade Act. In the build-up to and in the aftermath of the parliamentary debates which would eventually outlaw slavery completely, activity was at an all-time high in Glasgow. Anthony Cooke notes that 'after emancipation, the Glasgow West India Association made donations to the Anti-Slavery Society', effectively taking the 'moral high-ground' in their preference 'for British West Indian sugar grown by free labour, as opposed to slave-grown sugar from Cuba or Brazil'.[61] But, as is often the case in Glasgow's historiography, an effort was often made to portray these complicit merchants in a less glaring light:

> Nineteenth-century accounts of the merchant elite in Glasgow were generally reticent about the links between Caribbean wealth and slavery. They preferred to focus on their subjects' cultural, charitable or religious activities, or the academic, medical, legal, sporting or military distinction achieved by their descendants.[62]

We might go even further to say that this nineteenth-century condition of cultural memory was predominant throughout the twentieth century also. In fact, for many British cities the first real attempt to publicly engage with the issue was in 2007 during nationwide events to mark the bicentenary of the aforementioned Slave Trade Act. The opening of Liverpool's International Slavery Museum in that year was perhaps the most resounding civic attempt to affect change in the public imagination. A gesture of that size made sense in a city where the cultural memory of slavery was more vibrant. As Jeremy Paxman says in *Empire* (2012) 'you would have to be wilfully deaf and blind to remain ignorant of the profound change the slave trade was working in England during the seventeenth and eighteenth centuries'. Liverpool, he says, 'was *the* slave city'.[63]

Madge Dresser has noted that the then Deputy Prime Minister John Prescott 'originally envisaged Hull, Liverpool, London and Bristol as the port cities that should spearhead commemorations' and had 'began meeting with Bristol people to this end in 2005'.[64] As the largest city and centre of the British Empire, London had an obvious obligation here, while Hull went on to reopen Wilberforce House: the museum in memory of Britain's leading abolitionist. Yet the politics of these commemorations, with all due credit to their thoroughness and use of local objects, are also conflicted by competition and are to a certain extent guilty of distorting historical narratives to focus on themselves. The rhetoric connected to Liverpool and Bristol's events – 'We Are Setting the Truth Free' and 'Breaking the Chains' – often portray the city as the present-day liberator, effectively subverting their shared role as historic oppressor. This brings us back to Maier's 'perpetrator and victim' dialogue which has, in this case, been successfully dissolved. If everyone shares in the history, then the attention can be solely on the 'victim'.

The engagement with slavery, however, was not always confined to these exhibition spaces. Dresser draws our attention to the statue of Edward Colston (1636–1721), a Bristol-born merchant with ties to slavery.[65] Dresser describes how 'the public remembrance of slavery in Bristol is uniquely informed by its "cult" of Colston' and how 'since the late 1990s, when Colston's involvement in the slave trade became more widely known ... his statue [became] a symbolic lightning rod for highly charged attitudes about race, history and public memory'.[66] What is so crucial about the Colston example for us is that it reveals Glasgow's underwhelming ability to channel these public opinions about British imperialism. Moreover, a popular shopping area in Bristol, Broadmead, was the centre of controversy in 2006 when 'Merchants Quarter' was chosen as its new name, but this was forced to change due to an uproar about Bristol merchants' involvement with slavery.[67] In Glasgow there was a similar furore around the Merchant City region of the city centre. Unlike Bristol, the connection between merchants and slavery was not a strong aspect of Glasgow's cultural memory. There were voices of disapproval, most notably in the Workers City movement. James Kelman featured in Farquhar McLay's Workers City book *The Reckoning: Beyond the Culture City Rip Off* (1990). Glasgow had just been granted the title City of Culture for the year and the Merchant City region was part of a new series of urban development projects. The shame of eighteenth-century slavery in building the city is mentioned in McLay's book, but the tone and the content bring us back to a predominantly class-driven political debate here. It is also problematic that the term

'Merchant City' does not have a clear lineage. It seems to have appeared for the first time in Gomme and Walker's *Architecture of Glasgow* (1968), in a chapter titled 'The Reformation and the Merchant City, 1560–1800'. The term may well have been in architectural or social discourse beforehand, but following this book its usage certainly increased. At the *Remaking Cities* Conference in Pittsburgh (1988), Stuart Gulliver of the Scottish Development Agency offered his paper 'Merchant City: the Recolonization of Central Glasgow', an outline of the development of the SDA from 1975 and the rigorous regeneration process led by the city council in the 1980s to revive the so-called Merchant City.[68]

Despite the rise of this term from an architectural descriptor to an official governmental region there has never been enough public awareness of the involvement of these celebrated merchants and the ills of empire. Guided tours of Glasgow's old streets and the merchants' nefarious trade helps inform and spread the word, but a plaque, a monument, or a renamed street might well enhance Glasgow's cultural memory. In the USA these sort of symbolic gestures are becoming more common. Theirs, however, is a culture of reparation dating back to the nation's foundations on slavery, whereas in Scotland we are constantly negotiating images that span millennia and shifting the emphasis from one history to another. From *Braveheart* (1995) to *Outlander* (2014–present) and *Mary, Queen of Scots* (2019), Scotland's already-popular cultural selling points become reinforced and deeper entrenched in our minds. Our medievally skewed national imagination seems to be the excuse (albeit a poor one) for our lack of knowledge when it comes to transatlantic slavery.

The Scots Makar Jackie Kay wrote about these issues in March 2007 in her excellent article 'Missing faces'. She discusses the lack of public awareness regarding Scotland's role in slavery, confirming the idea in the previous chapter that James Watt and his industrial revolution were the more popular stories in cultural memory: 'I was proud of Watt's steam engine, but I was not taught that money from a slave trader financed his invention. [. . .] I learnt that Glasgow was a great merchant city. I learnt about the shipping industry, but not about the slave ship *Neptune* . . .'[69] In his most recent reflections on the subject Devine cites Kay's article before lamenting an issue of the *Historical Review* that never made it to the press and other 'academic neglect'.[70] But Glasgow's engagement with the issue in 2007 was not as muted as we have always made it out to be. There *were* exhibitions and events in Scotland, and Glasgow did not hide from view. Glasgow Built Preservation Trust launched Stephen Mullen's heritage trail *It Wisnae Us*. A pamphlet published by

Glasgow Museums and City Council, *Towards Understanding Slavery – Past and Present*, outlined the city's official approaches and the Burrell Collection exhibited *Mind-Forg'd Manacles: William Blake and Slavery*, utilising art and writing by Blake as provided by the British Museum, thus placing Glasgow in a British context with slavery. The Gallery of Modern Art (GoMA) took an expectedly contemporary approach. *Downpresser* by Graham Fagen featured photographs, screen prints of modernised versions of eighteenth-century posters for voyages across the Atlantic and DVD projections (including 'an impromptu performance of Burns's 'Slave's Lament' ... sung on a beach'.)[71] There were talks and workshops held in Kelvingrove Museum, Provand's Lordship, and the St Mungo Museum of Religious Life and Art, all with the aim of positioning Glasgow within the nationwide discussion of slavery. The National Trust for Scotland also held events in the west of Scotland, including a travelling display named *This is Our Story*, stopping at Culzean Castle, Brodick Castle and Greenbank House (in the Clarkston area of Glasgow) – all three of which were deemed suitable buildings in which to connect Scotland's links with slavery with a further emphasis on David Livingstone. A commemoration service was held at the David Livingstone Centre in Blantyre, while community workshops incorporating drama, music, song, film and performance took place in Pollok House.[72]

More than most, the Glasgow object with the most relevance to slavery was, and remains, *The Glassford Family Portrait* (c.1767) by Archibald McLauchlan (see Figure 13). Whether or not as a reaction to Kay's article, it went on display in the People's Palace in Glasgow's East End as part of an exhibition. *The Glassford Family Portrait: A Hidden Legacy* ran from August 2007 to March 2008 and the portrait was advertised as 'the starting point' of the examination 'of Glasgow's involvement in the tobacco and slave trades'. To complement the portrait, Glasgow Museums displayed other objects including two emancipation medals from 1807, a black figure advertising tobacco, and a donation box used by the Glasgow Ladies' Emancipation Society in the early nineteenth century featuring an illustration of slaves being beaten with a whip by their master and a line from the Book of Samuel on the lid. By enveloping these objects into the 'hidden' narrative, the curation of this exhibition is arguably more Glasgow-centric than most of the other West of Scotland events.

The main focus of the McLauchlan painting has been the faded outline of a young black servant. The boy was once a more prominent feature of the painting, perhaps, as Stephen Mullen has suggested, as a

Figure 13 Archibald McLauchlan, *John Glassford and his Family* (c.1767) with servant figure highlighted. Accession number 2887. © CSG CIC Glasgow Museums Collection.

'symbol of wealth'.[73] The long-standing myth attached to this painting is that Glassford's descendants were ashamed of their ancestral ties with slavery and so painted over it. A letter from Elspeth King of the People's Palace to a descendant of the merchant living in Cheshire in 1979 makes it clear that, at the time, this is what people believed.[74] This was repeated in Mary Edward's *Who Belongs to Glasgow?* (1993) and Iain Whyte's *Scotland and the Abolition of Black Slavery, 1756–1838* (2006). It was not until restoration work was carried out in 2007 on the portrait that it was discovered the figure 'had faded only as a result of discolouration of the pigment'.[75] Amazingly, some journalists who had visited the exhibition continued to speculate that the servant was painted over.[76]

This is the issue with cultural memory. Myth is often more powerful than facts and more convincing than evidence. Studying the Scottish diaspora teaches us the same thing: memories of the Old World are uprooted, transplanted, revived, recycled and adapted over time in the New World. And to an infinite array of effects.

NOTES

1. Dugald Moore, The Bard of the North: A Series of Poetical Tales, Illustrative of Highland Scenery and Character (Glasgow: David Robertson, 1833), 164–5.
2. Michael Fry, *Scottish Empire* (Phantassie, East Lothian: Tuckwell Press, 2001); T. M. Devine, *Scotland's Empire: 1600–1815* (London: Allen Lane, 2003).
3. Mark Duffill, 'The Africa trade from the ports of Scotland, 1706–66', *Slavery & Abolition*, 25:3 (2004), 102–22 (114, n. 1).
4. J. H. Soltow, 'Scottish Traders in Virginia, 1750–1775', *The Economic History Review*, 12:1 (1959), 83–98 (85).
5. Elizabeth Kyle, *The Tontine Belle* (London: Peter Davies, 1951).
6. For the full report cf. Stephen Mullen and Simon Newman, *Slavery, Abolition and the University of Glasgow* (Glasgow: University of Glasgow, 2018): <https://www.gla.ac.uk/media/media_607547_en.pdf> (last accessed 30 August 2020). Some of the recommendations include reparative gestures such as student scholarships and visiting fellowships from the University of the West Indies, as well as commemorations in the form of a new building being named after James McCune Smith and a plaque explaining the accumulation of the University's estate through slave-trade activities.
7. Dr Stephen Mullen, co-author of the University of Glasgow's report on slavery, will lead the investigation. The plans were formally launched in Glasgow's City Chambers on 7 November 2019: cf. 'Glasgow launches detailed study of its historical links with transatlantic slavery', *Evening*

Times 10 November 2019, <https://www.eveningtimes.co.uk/news/18026972.glasgow-launches-detailed-study-historical-links-transatlantic-slavery/> (last accessed 30 August 2020).
8. James Walvin, *Britain's Slave Empire* (Stroud: Tempus, 2000), 32.
9. For more, see Jan Assmann, 'Communicative and Cultural Memory', in Astrid Erll and Ansgar Nünning, eds, *Media and Cultural Memory: An International and Interdisciplinary Handbook* (Berlin: Walter de Gruyter GmbH & Co., 2008), 109–18 (110); Christina West, 'Memory—Recollection—Culture—Identity—Space: Social Context, Identity Formation, and Self-construction of the Calé (Gitanos) in Spain', in Peter Meusburger, Michael Heffernan and Edgar Wunder, eds, *Cultural Memories: The Geographical Point of View* (London: Springer, 2011), 101–19 (104).
10. Pierre Nora, *Realms of Memory: Rethinking the French Past* ed. Lawrence D. Kritzman (New York: Columbia University Press, 1989 [1984–1992]).
11. See <http://www.heraldscotland.com/comment/letters/the-lessons-of-slavery-must-be-taught-in-the-proper-context.23149105> (last accessed 20 November 2019); T. M. Devine, 'Lost to History', in T. M. Devine, ed., *Recovering Scotland's Slavery Past: The Caribbean Connection* (Edinburgh: Edinburgh University Press, 2015), 21.
12. Jan Assmann, 'Collective Memory and Cultural Identity' from *New German Critique*, 56 (Durham: Duke University Press, 1995), 125–33 (132).
13. Paul J. Lane and Kevin C. MacDonald, 'Introduction: Slavery, Social Revolutions and Enduring Memories', Lane and MacDonald, eds, *Slavery in Africa: Archaeology and Memory* (Oxford: Published for the British Academy by Oxford University Press, 2011), 1–22 (12).
14. Peter Meusburger, 'Knowledge, Cultural Memory, and Politics', in Peter Meusburger, Michael Heffernan and Edgar Wunder, eds, *Cultural Memories: The Geographical Point of View* (London: Springer, 2011), 51–69 (54).
15. Charles S. Maier, 'A Surfeit of Memory? Reflections on History, Melancholy and Denial', *History & Memory*, 5:2 (1993), 136–52 (152).
16. Ibid.
17. See, for example, the following article: <http://www.heraldscotland.com/news/home-news/city-urged-to-apologise-for-connections-with-slavery.20883245> (last accessed 20 November 2019).
18. For more examples, see <https://www.runaways.gla.ac.uk/> (last accessed 30 August 2020).
19. This data was obtained from searching the Trans-Atlantic Slave Trade Database: <http://www.slavevoyages.org/voyage/26093/variables> (last accessed 30 August 2020).
20. Thanks to Dr Anthony Lewis for sharing this source, held in the National Records of Scotland, GD393/91, f. 10.
21. For a comparative analysis on the role of servants and slaves in visual

culture, see Agnes Lugo-Ortiz and Angela Rosenthal, eds, *Slave Portraiture in the Atlantic World* (Cambridge: Cambridge University Press, 2013).
22. Stephen Mullen's published work in this field began with It Wisnae Us: The Truth About Glasgow and Slavery (Edinburgh: The Royal Incorporation of Architects in Scotland, 2009). His PhD thesis The 'Glasgow West India interest': integration, collaboration and exploitation in the British Atlantic World, 1776–1846 (University of Glasgow, 2015) was the catalyst for much of the recent debate, which will be developed in the forthcoming monograph, provisionally titled The Sugar Aristocracy of Glasgow in the British-Atlantic World.
23. Murray Pittock, 'Historiography', in Alexander Broadie, ed., *The Cambridge Companion to The Scottish Enlightenment* (Cambridge: Cambridge University Press, 2003), 258–79 (262).
24. Christopher J. Berry, *The Idea of Commercial Society in the Scottish Enlightenment* (Edinburgh: Edinburgh University Press, 2013), 125.
25. Quoted in Alexander Broadie, *A History of Scottish Philosophy* (Edinburgh: Edinburgh University Press, 2009), 242.
26. Srividhya Swaminathan, 'Adam Smith's Moral Economy and the Debate to Abolish the Slave Trade', *Rhetoric Society Quarterly*, 37:4 (2007), 481–507 (482).
27. Adam Smith, *The Theory of Moral Sentiments*, second edition (London: A. Millar, 1761), 316.
28. John W. Cairns, 'John Millar and Slavery', in Neil Walker, ed., *MacCormick's Scotland* (Edinburgh: Edinburgh University Press, 2012), 103.
29. Adam Smith, *Glasgow Edition of the Works and Correspondence*, Vol. 5, *Lectures On Jurisprudence* (Oxford: Oxford University Press, 1976 [1762]).
30. Adam Smith, *The Wealth of Nations, Books I–III* (London: Penguin, 1986 [1776]), 184.
31. Smith, *Wealth of Nations* (1986 [1776]), 488–9.
32. Swaminathan, 'Adam Smith's Moral Economy', 483.
33. Craig Smith, 'Adam Smith: Left or Right?', *Political Studies*, vol. 61 (2012) 784–9 (784).
34. Cairns, 'John Millar and Slavery', 87.
35. John Millar, *Observations Concerning the Distinction of Ranks in Society*, second edition (London: J. Murray, 1773), 254–5.
36. Quoted in Cairns, 'John Millar and Slavery', 77.
37. Stephen Mullen and Simon Newman, *Slavery, Abolition and the University of Glasgow* (Glasgow: University of Glasgow, 2018), 5, <https://www.gla.ac.uk/media/media_607547_en.pdf> (last accessed 30 August 2020).
38. Cairns, 'John Millar and Slavery', 105.

39. See <http://www.universitystory.gla.ac.uk/chair-and-lectureship/?id=67> (last accessed 20 November 2019).
40. Donald Winch, 'Smith, Adam (bap. 1723, d. 1790)', *Oxford Dictionary of National Biography*, <http://www.oxforddnb.com/view/article/25767> (last accessed 30 August 2020).
41. Stephen Mullen, 'A Glasgow-West India Merchant House and the Imperial Dividend, 1779–1867', *Journal of Scottish Historical Studies*, 33:2 (2013), 196–233 (196, 205).
42. For more information, see <http://www.adamsmith.org/the-adam-smith-statue/> (last accessed 30 August 2020).
43. See <http://elonka.com/kryptos/sanborn-new.html> (last accessed 20 November 2019).
44. See Mervyn King's speech on 29 October 2006, 'Trusting in Money: From Kirkcaldy to the MPC', <https://www.bankofengland.co.uk/speech/2006/trusting-in-money-from-kirkcaldy-to-the-mpc> (last accessed 20 November 2019).
45. Edward Gaitens, *Dance of the Apprentices* (Edinburgh: Canongate Classics, 2001 [1948]), 41.
46. Ibid., 202.
47. Ibid., 23
48. Paul Wood, 'Anderson, John (1726–1796)', *Oxford Dictionary of National Biography*, <http://www.oxforddnb.com/view/article/481> (last accessed 20 November 2019).
49. C. Duncan Rice, *The Scots Abolitionists, 1833–1861* (Baton Rouge: Louisiana State University Press, 1981), 21.
50. James Boswell, *An Account of Corsica* (London: Edward and Charles Dilly, 1769), 33.
51. Michael Morris, 'Joseph Knight: Scotland and the Black Atlantic', *International Journal of Scottish Literature*, 4 (Glasgow: Association for Scottish Literary Studies, 2008), 3; also James Robertson's novel *Joseph Knight* (2003) in which Boswell is portrayed.
52. Iain Whyte, *Scotland and the Abolition of Black Slavery* (Edinburgh: Edinburgh University Press, 2006), 87.
53. Troy O. Bickham, *Savages within the Empire: Representations of American Indians in Eighteenth-Century Britain* (Oxford: Clarendon Press, 2005), 201.
54. A Society in Glasgow, *An Address to the Inhabitants of Glasgow, Paisley, and the Neighbourhood, Concerning the African Slave Trade, 1791, from The Slave Trade Debate: contemporary writings for and against* (Oxford: Bodleian Library, 2007), 314.
55. Whyte, *Scotland and the Abolition of Black Slavery*, 90.
56. Aleida Assmann, *Cultural Memory and Western Civilization: Functions, Media, Archive* (Cambridge: Cambridge University Press, 2011), 214.
57. Marcus Wood, 'Significant Silence: Where was Slave Agency in the Popular

Imagery of 2007?', in Cora Kaplan and John Oldfield, eds, *Imagining Transatlantic Slavery* (New York: Palgrave Macmillan, 2010), 162–90 (166–7).
58. Mary Guyatt, 'The Wedgwood Slave Medallion: Values in Eighteenth-Century Design', *Journal of Design History*, 13:2 (2000), 93–105 (93).
59. Ibid., 93–105 (94–5).
60. Reyahn King et al., *Ignatius Sancho: An African Man of Letters* (London: National Portrait Gallery Publications, 1997), 109.
61. Anthony Cooke, 'An Elite Revisited: Glasgow West India Merchants, 1783–1877', *Journal of Historical Studies*, 32:2 (2012), 127–65 (152).
62. Ibid.
63. Jeremy Paxman, *Empire: What Ruling the World Did to the British* (London: Penguin, 2011).
64. Madge Dresser, 'Remembering Slavery and Abolition in Bristol', *Slavery & Abolition*, 30:2 (2009), 223–46 (231).
65. The Colston statue was often targeted by protestors, and it was eventually removed on 7 June 2020. The statue was pulled down, dragged to the harbour and thrown into the water. It has since been recovered, and plans to display the statue in an appropriate museum – with the protestors' ropes and graffiti possibly left on – are underway.
66. Dresser, 'Remembering Slavery and Abolition in Bristol', 225.
67. See <http://www.bbc.co.uk/bristol/content/articles/2006/09/04/broadmead_feature.shtml> (last accessed 30 August 2020).
68. Barbara Davis, ed., *Remaking Cities: Proceedings of the 1988 International Conference in Pittsburgh* (Pittsburgh, PA: University of Pittsburgh Press, 1988), 78–80.
69. Jackie Kay, 'Missing faces', *The Guardian*, 24 March 2007.
70. Devine, 'Lost to History', 21–2.
71. Cf. <http://www.list.co.uk/article/1779-graham-fagen-downpresser/> (last accessed 20 November 2019).
72. See <www.scotlandandslavery.org.uk/Resources/This_isOurStory_leaflet.pdf> [Accessed 11/03/19].
73. Mullen, *It Wisnae Us*, 56.
74. Letter retrieved from object file, Glasgow Museums Resource Centre. Many thanks to Fiona Hayes for allowing access.
75. Mullen, *It Wisnae Us*, 56.
76. In Ben Riley-Smith's 'Call for memorial to Glasgow slave trade' (*Sunday Herald* 17 March 2013) <http://www.heraldscotland.com/news/home-news/call-for-memorial-to-glasgow-slave-trade.20523508> (last accessed 30 August 2020) the painting over of the servant is given a renewed, albeit cautious, legitimacy. The captioned image helps imply this cover-up, clearly confusing the lingering likeness of Glassford's ex-wife (removed) for the servant, who occupies a different section of the painting entirely. A recent

BBC video also claims that the servant was painted out: 'Glasgow's slave trade past is all around us' (25 October 2018) <https://www.bbc.co.uk/news/av/uk-scotland-45978791/glasgow-s-slave-trade-past-is-all-around-us> (last accessed 30 August 2020).

5

'Then went forth our Scots'

While some Scots were probing the coasts of Africa for gold and trading links in the early seventeenth century, others were looking toward the climes of North America for new colonies. Long before the word 'Darien' became part of the national vocabulary it was Sir Robert Gordon of Lochinvar and Sir William Alexander, Earl of Stirling, who set the wheels of emigration in motion. Alexander, a poet and courtier of James I and VI, obtained a Royal Charter in 1621 and went on to establish Nova Scotia: New Scotland. In deconstructing the 'Myth of Scotch Canada' (1999) Edward J. Cowan outlines the criss-crossing paths of these Scots pioneers, asking important questions about our nation's independent, pre-Union imperialism. But where does Glasgow fit into all this?

Compared to the eighteenth and nineteenth centuries we have less documentary evidence regarding this period, but we can infer a reasonable amount by looking at Glasgow itself. For instance we have the four sugar refineries constructed between 1667 and 1700, a sign of a new and prospering system of commerce.[1] We also know from Privy Council records that a 'Memorial concerning the Scottish plantation to be erected in some place in America' (1681) that Scots wanted to colonise a new settlement in either Cape Florida or Carolina, where English plantations already existed.[2] In the same year as this proposal, Glasgow University appointed a Professor of Navigation and by 1695 a navigation school had opened in the city.[3] In 1684 there were two separate attempts by Scots to colonise parts of America. True to the 'Memorial' of 1681, these were both on the fringes of English colonies. The first was in East New Jersey, as directed by 'the celebrated Quaker apologist' Robert Barclay of Ury.[4] The second was Stuarts Town near the English settlement of Charles Town in Southern Carolina.[5]

What connects these colonial schemes is religious persecution at home, a theme later iterated by John Galt and his contemporaries. Robert Barclay stated the case for Quakerism with his *Apology for the True Christian Divinity* (1678)[6] at a time when Aberdeen's Episcopalian authorities often imprisoned religious dissenters. By the time Barclay left for Carolina in 1684 however, Quakers were not as harshly persecuted as they had been before, and while his idea for a colonial venture was perhaps influenced by an intolerant atmosphere, his was a national rather than a sectarian scheme.[7] As a result it became a Scottish rather than a Quaker colony. Sowerby's reading of the civic language established by the settlers implies the translation of cultural memory from one place to another [emphasis added]:

> Indeed the general tenor of one of the acts passed by the East Jersey Assembly in 1686, by which time Scottish settlers were established in considerable numbers in the colony, implies that the newcomers had *carried across the Atlantic certain well-marked tendencies characteristic of Scottish life* in the unquiet days of the seventeenth century.[8]

Glasgow and Aberdeen were among the port towns from which the journey was made, transporting distinctive provincial identities and creating a microcosm of Scotland's religious make-up in the New World. In the case of Stuarts Town, we can gain further insight into Glasgow's place in pre-Union imperialism. More so than the Quaker influence on East New Jersey the journey to Carolina from Glasgow was based on ideas of religious freedom. George Pratt Insh says that 'a proposal of carrying over a plantation to Carolina had been put before the Covenanters' as early as 1672.[9] Chief among the Presbyterian exiles who established the short-lived colony of Stuarts Town were William Dunlop and Henry Erskine (Lord Cardross). Like Barclay of Ury, Dunlop 'had grown to manhood in an atmosphere of religious persecution and civil strife'.[10] As we will see shortly, John Galt went on to portray the Covenanters in *Ringan Gilhaize* (1823), a work which, like Sir Walter Scott's *Old Mortality* (1816), sought to chronicle and analyse the Covenanting story of Scottish religious history. Taken together, these novels represent a crucial intersection of Scottish literary history, a pivotal moment in which the cultural memory of the Covenanters was etched deeper into the imagination of their readers.

It was Walter Gibson, a Glasgow merchant and ship-owner, who transported the exiles on the *Carolina Merchant*. In 1682 the plan for what would become the Carolina Company began to take form when Gibson met with the prospective colonists.[11] That his ship was already named after Dunlop's and Cardross's destination informs us that Gibson had made this journey before.[12] Besides offering to take persecuted Scots from Glasgow and Edinburgh to Carolina for a set fee, Gibson was also 'commissioned by the privy council to transport banished criminals and Covenanters to America'.[13] Stuarts Town promised much but the 'political relationship' between the Scots and the English was 'too ambiguous' and the site was eventually destroyed when the Spanish, who had occupied the area previously, attacked the colony: plundering houses, killing livestock and burning down the settlements.[14] This took place in September 1686, and those who survived ended up in neighbouring colonies including Charles Town (now Charleston).[15] The Seal of the House of Cardross belonging to Lord Cardross is the only artefact that remains of the Scottish colony.[16] It is therefore understandable that the colony, and Glasgow's part in its establishment, is not well known. In the same way that a forgotten writer can no longer play a part in the public's perception of the past, an object cannot contribute to the public's understanding of its provenance if it is never seen.

While the abrupt end to Stuarts Town might account for its lack of representation, there remain tangible, even successful, links. Cardross, Dunlop and Gibson were not among those to lose their lives in the raids: Gibson went on to become the Glasgow city provost in 1688 while Dunlop was voted into office as Principal of Glasgow University in 1690. Their roles in the history of the Covenanters as holders of high office following the Revolution of 1688 are essential in that they involve an unsuccessful colonial scheme in America which anticipated the much more adventurous Darien plan. For Michael Fry the initially antagonistic role of the English in Charles Town represented a wider dichotomy of English imposition on Scotland's independent imperial efforts, affecting the Anglophobic sentiment that would arise in the fallout of Darien.[17] Again we come back to popular writers and mnemonic language. Just as slavery is one of Scotland's 'amnesiac' sins for Devine et al., Darien is described as 'a scar on the memory of the Scots' by John Prebble.[18] These terms are what bind historical events to national and political identities.

The chief instigator of Darien was one William Paterson (1658–1719). He was born in Skipmyre, Dumfriesshire, but was raised for much of his youth in England.[19] And while we still consider Darien as Scotland's final, futile independent frontier, it should be remembered that Paterson did not always envisage the Darien Company (or, the Company of Scotland Trading to Africa and the Indies) as a Scottish scheme in the first place. It was only after 'opposition from the English East India Company' that Paterson had to 'withdraw the original plan and propose a solely Scottish venture'.[20] It seems Paterson was more an entrepreneur with few options than a Scottish visionary. Recent scholarship by Julie Orr (2018) has helped expand our understanding of the misadventure.[21] By examining the archives in England, Spain, Jamaica and the USA,[22] Orr takes us beyond the Scottish and British view to reveal an entire map of dangers and antagonists that had the scheme marked from the outset. For those unfamiliar with the course of events, T. C. Smout offers one of the best summaries:

> The Company, ill-led and undercapitalized, rashly staked everything on a settlement at Darien in Central America, [. . .] they were driven out by disease and the Spaniards whose territory they had annexed, and [. . .] the English government of William III, determined at all costs to avoid antagonizing Spain, refused to allow the settlers the least assistance even in their last extremity.[23]

In 1700 an anonymous pamphlet was printed in Glasgow titled *Certain Propositions Relating to the Scots Plantation of Caledonia*. Several defensive points are made, including the Scots' 'right' to colonise Darien, 'confirmed by Invitation from, and League with the original free Natives of that Country'. France's 'Persecution' of 'the poor Remnant of Protestants' throughout Europe is also invoked.[24] These were the sentiments and the struggles that Scottish authors of the early nineteenth century sought to revive in their sketches of older Scottish life while cities like Glasgow and Edinburgh grew in population and wealth as part of a more secure Britain.

In 1700 another pamphlet was printed in London: an anonymous attack on the Scots and the Presbyterian religion, titled *Caledonia; or, the Pedlar turn'd Merchant: A Tragi-comedy, as it was acted by His Majesty's Subjects of Scotland, in the King of Spain's Province of Darien*. The Scots are openly mocked for believing in the 'fly' men of the Kirk who promised them 'a large piece of ground, where gold was as plenty as sand'.[25] The final stanzas, concerning the total failure of the scheme, are as crude as they are remorseless:

> Two thirds being *dead*, and another made *Slaves*
>   By the Spaniard for fear of his Oar,
> They left *felling Trees* and ceas'd *digging Graves*,
>   And *crawl'd* to their Ships from the Shore.
>
> The first Time a Scot ever wished himself *home*,
>   For want of *good Air* or of *Bread*,

And the last (if he's wise) that he from it will *come*
On such a *Fool's Errand* as Trade.[26]

These remarks help us identify the heightened tensions that were central to the pamphleteering that would bring about the Union of 1707. These tensions were long-lasting, and the definition of 'Britain' was put to the test constantly during the century. Just as John Wilkes and the radical journal *The North Briton* vilified the Scots for their roles in the government, Tobias Smollett made the cultural case for the Union in his *Expedition of Humphry Clinker*. Smollett had lived through the second Jacobite rising and switched his stance from an anti-Hanoverian – his poem 'The Tears of Scotland' was written immediately after Culloden – to a cautiously optimistic pro-Unionist one towards the end of his life. In many ways Smollett is the precursor here to Walter Scott's *Waverley*, the great novel of the nineteenth century. Scott's clever 'Postscript, which should have been a Preface' stakes the innocent claim that for 'older persons' *Waverley* 'will recall scenes and characters familiar to their youth; and to the rising generation the tale may present some idea of the manners of their forefathers'.[27] This sense of time and distance was key to his ability to convey the strongest lesson of the work which, as Gifford, Dunnigan and McGillivray put it, was 'to fashion a new mythology, which would give dignity to the story and support that side of the Union arch which was Scotland'.[28] To some extent this argument had already been won in Smollett's *Humphry Clinker*, through the incessant references to the topography of the Scottish Enlightenment in Glasgow and Edinburgh, as witnessed by the Welsh squire Matthew Bramble in his journey through Britain.

As the eighteenth century came to a close Glasgow's population was still below 80,000. By 1831 it had swelled to 202,000: the first period of rapid growth in its history. Glasgow's stake in the slave trade was at its height and manufacturing was on the rise. This time of unprecedented change was reflected time and again by Scotland's leading writers. No writer could surpass Scott in terms of popularising a Scottish tradition of historical writing, as Paul Barnaby's 'Timeline of European Reception' has shown.[29] But Scott was not alone in his day. And when we go looking for Georgian Glasgow in this genre, no writer tells us more about the period than Galt. Just as Smollett captured the essence of his age in the eighteenth century, Galt did the same – if not more – for the early nineteenth century. The lives of these writers often run parallel with the worlds they fictionalise, making for an interesting comparative study between the patriotic and imperial characters they invent and their own shifting allegiances. In the wake of the French Revolution writers like Galt, Scott and Hogg worked in an unusual situation which questioned the status of the British Empire, calling forth their sentimental patriotism for Scotland's past. These generational narratives were, for Galt, not fictional novels but 'Theoretical Histories'.[30] Many of these concerned Glasgow.

As we know, the increasingly specialised and place-specific uses of memory terminology have encouraged discourse globally, often resulting in competing definitions coexisting across the field. To be clear, it should be stated again here that our interpretation of memory involves the progression of collective memory, i.e. the collected memories of a single generation in witness of an event become cultural memory: the multifaceted, layered and contradictory impressions passed down the ages. This progression is what makes Galt such an interesting cultural witness, weaving his experiences into increasingly experimental modes of fiction. For instance, his use of 'found' narratives, a phenomenon made popular by Hogg's *Private Memoirs and Confessions of a Justified Sinner* (1824), create a fictional distance between the author and the subject, in a way enshrining the story as something antiquated and romantic. Like Hogg, Galt frequently gave us unreliable and satirical narrators. In spite of this we can sift for the common ideas particular to the generation of these characters. These common ideas, habits and fashions are essentially cultural memories. They become as relevant to our understanding of a topic as museum objects or documentary films. To use Aleida Assmann's metaphor they are 'like tools and utensils that have lost their original function and links with daily life and have been collected as relics'.[31] Texts like Galt's most famous work *Annals of the Parish* (1821), which initially spoke to readers in the Georgian era, now speak to us as 'relics'. *Annals*, in fact, was said to be 'so accurate' in its 'account of social change' that historians used and relied upon it for their research.[32] This was no ordinary writer who happened to visit and write about Glasgow. Galt was a match for Scott in many ways, and his preservation of manners specific to the west of Scotland helped engender a 'Glasgow School' of fiction which produced both local and colonial stories. Included in this school we can count the aforementioned Thomas Hamilton (1789–1842), whose *Cyril Thornton* offers several sketches of Georgian Glasgow. For more examples of Scots abroad we have *Tom Cringle's Log* (1829–34) by Michael Scott (1789–1835), in which the author chronicles often harrowing events during his role as a planter in Jamaica.[33]

On top of this Bruce Lenman claims that Galt was 'the best example of linkages between literary and pictorial artists in the common endeavor to preserve lively images of a way of life clearly threatened with extinction'.[34] For example, Galt's connection with the renowned painter David Wilkie helps us visualise the workings of cultural memory as a resistance to the vanishing world of Scottish peasantry, as we can see in Wilkie's *The Penny Wedding* (1818), which some say depicts an account by Galt.[35] Indeed, the painting does seem a close match with Galt's account of the penny-wedding scene in *Annals*, which he began writing in parts in 1813.[36] Although we cannot be sure, the painting and text may have been informed by a real-life experience. But they are both cultural memories in their own right and their value as cultural memories, when combined, is increased by the intersection of more than one point of view. Such connections between different media suggest the materiality of cultural memory with which we can engage. Looking back over Galt's oeuvre we can see an impressive range of subjects and an ambitious range of time, though perhaps not matching Scott's larger geographical terrain. Nonetheless Galt does three crucial things for Glasgow's cultural memory across his work: he creates one of the best prose topographies of the city; he focuses the reader's understanding of national narratives such as Darien onto this topography; and he puts Glasgow in a new context through the prism of emigration to North America. In other words, his work becomes a point of access in our reading of not only the Georgian period in which he lived and recalled, but the period before.

In *The Entail* (1823), for instance, Galt's main character Claud Walkinshaw is introduced as 'the sole surviving male heir of the Walkinshaws of Kittlestonheugh', and his grandfather is said to have been 'deluded by the golden visions that allured so many of the Scottish gentry to embark their fortunes in the Darien Expedition'.[37] As such, Galt's novel revives the rhetoric and, indeed, the cultural memories of the Darien disaster, repackaging them alongside an array of Jacobite and Hanoverian allusions. Where this differs from Scott's *Waverley* (1814) is that nobody during the Darien scheme was alive to read *The Entail*. By contrast *Waverley* was a deliberate play on collective memory, in which people could read a fantastical account of the Jacobite rising they lived through as children, or maybe were told about by their parents or grandparents. The subtitle – *'Tis Sixty Years Since* – even advertises its intentions of looking back *within a single generation*. This might explain its impact on Scott's fame and on Scotland's fate. George IV's visit to Edinburgh in 1822 becomes a sort of afterlife to Scott's writing, inventing a new Scotland based on the transference of loyalties and, arguably, the popularisation of *story* over *history*. The Jacobite story was as vibrant as it was malleable. Darien, on the other hand, lay mouldering in the cultural memory of the nation as a national tragedy worth forgetting.

The nation has been called 'the main mnemonic community' in times when information and political opinions are accessible, if unequally distributed, to the majority of the population.[38] If 9/11 represents the dawning of globalised instantaneous video news, therefore effecting an incalculable series of collective memories, then the Darien expedition at the opposite end of the spectrum is better perceived through the literature of its time – and better still through the literature of subsequent epochs, during which the sectarian tensions that pervaded the fallout were substantially weakened. To put it another way, the speed at which collective memory is transmitted depends on the technologies through which to share information. Barbara Misztal uses the term 'global simultaneity' to describe this. For instance we have the *Titanic* disaster (1912) of which 'people in various countries could read in the morning news'.[39] By contrast, in 1699 a second fleet had already left port in Scotland for Darien before news reached home about the fate of the first, resulting in further loss of life and capital. With the distance of time and the advantage of technology we can access cultural memories and in some cases flatten them out for comparison. We can read the London-based tirade *Caledonia; or, the Pedlar turn'd Merchant* (1700) but we can also read *Darien; or, The Merchant Prince. A Historical Romance* (1852) by the Irish writer Eliot Warburton. Over time a natural elision of the defensive/attacking binary takes place. Even more interesting is the invented patriotic voice in Warburton's *Darien*:

> Then went forth our Scots,—pioneers of a new power, that, though quelled for the time, will yet rule those glorious countries wi' righteous justice and gospel law [. . .] I can imagine my auld kinsman Paterson, standing upon a peak of Darien, e'en as we stand now upon Ben Laighal [. . .] And a' thae braes, and glens, and steepy hills, wad be the backbone itsel' o' the isthmus, trampled doon into roads fit for leddie's powny, by the million feet o' prosperous wayfayers, to and fro travellin', circulatin' the gifts o' heaven from the Auld warld to the New.[40]

The speaker is Highland soldier McGregor, who we are told keeps an old musket and claymore ('with which his grandfather had hewn his way through Sassenachs from the battle of Culloden') over the fireplace. As with Scott's works, Warburton drapes Jacobite colours over a specifically Scottish-looking yet British imperial character: 'The [sword] tells its ain story; tho' dinna doot but it wad strike for our bonny Queen this day, as truly and stoutly as ever it focth again' her great grandfather a hundred years gane by.'[41] McGregor also has a 'kist' of papers relating to the Darien scheme, and the rest of the novel is a romantic history of the venture based loosely on William Paterson's experiences. Warburton's is therefore a diverse cultural interpretation of an historical event. An invention. His blending of generational memories and sentiments is not at all unlike Galt's or Scott's in execution. In *The Literary Life*, Galt wrote:

> I considered the discovery of America as equivalent to the creation of another continent, purposely to relieve the oppressed of the old, and to afford an asylum to those who were inclined to the moderation of that way of life, which derives its comforts from other employments than the glories of our hemisphere.[42]

Galt's colonial travels commenced in the 1820s, by which point America had declared its independence from the British Empire and the focus of colonial activity had changed. Yet in Glasgow religion was still at the centre of overseas expeditions, concomitant with the expectation of further colonisation. The Glasgow Colonial Society (or, The Society for Promoting the Religious Interests of Scottish Settlers in British North America), in operation 1825–41, sought to fulfil the need for religious correspondence between the growing number of emigrants and the doctrine of their homeland.[43] In terms of collective identity, these missionaries can be seen as influential to the Presbyterian essence of North America today. In Galt's time the Glasgow Colonial Society extended its influence to Canada and New South Wales.[44] Most of all, petitioners to the society seemed to value 'the capacity of ministers from home to recreate the ritual and intellectual conditions that were the distinctive mark of Presbyterian religious practice in Scotland'.[45] In terms of memory, these ideas can be linked to Halbwachs' definitions of a collective memory. More specifically, a 'religious collective memory':

> Every religion ... reproduces in more or less symbolic forms the history of migrations and fusions of races and tribes, of great events, wars, establishments, discoveries, and reforms that we can find at the origin of the societies that practice them.[46]

In the case of the Scottish diaspora there were acts of religious repetition, conversion and church-building, sometimes to an extent which might now seem like the creation of an idyllic version of home on foreign soil. Even when colonial schemes are unsuccessful we can trace some to the present day. The Glasgow Ohio Company was established in 1824 by wealthy Glasgow merchants. It lasted no more than eleven years, yet Ohio is peppered with streets named after Scotland: in Madison, Glasgow Street runs parallel to Dundee Street, Douglas Drive and Kelso Street, and also nearby are Inverness Drive, Campbell Drive, and Orkney Road. These streets are the stories of movement and connection, in the same way that Jamaica Street and Virginia Street in Glasgow tell us something (though not enough) about Glasgow's links with those places. As we will see, Galt played an important role in the transportation of symbolic cultural markers in new towns. Held together, his impressions of Georgian Glasgow evoked in his novels comprise one of the most valuable archives of memory we have today.

Liam McIlvanney first made the claim that Galt's *Annals of the Parish* (1821) can be read as a 'Glasgow Novel'.[47] The novel, set in the fictional parish of Dalmailing between 1760 and 1810, is narrated by The Reverend Micah Balwhidder. Nearby Glasgow is ever-present, effecting much change throughout the fifty-year period. Indeed, the novelties of material goods in Dalmailing, often introduced with awe and excitement, become problematic or divisive over time. Each new building and imported fabric is like a pin on Galt's map of the encroachment of Empire on the natural landscape and local traditions. Beside the wealth that Empire allows (such as that represented through Girzie Gilchrist's brother: a nabob from India), Galt portrays the ills of slavery through Mr Cayenne's relentlessly harsh treatment of his 'blackamoor servant'. Galt is further critical of Glasgow's burgeoning imperialism in the way that he reveals the social issues behind large-scale change. As McIlvanney puts it: 'It is the very inability of Balwhidder's parish chronicle to contain and make sense of its 'global' material that lends the novel its power and point.'[48] Whisky distilleries, coal-heughs and cotton mills transform the landscape of the area, and Balwhidder admits that 'we had intromitted so much with concerns of trade, that we were become a part of the great web of commercial reciprocities, and felt in our corner and extremity, every touch or stir that was made on any part of the texture'.[49]

The destructive quality of Empire is clear in this development, aided in part by Galt's clever semantic field of weaving. A similar image is used to describe Glasgow's westward spread in *The Ayrshire Legatees* (1821), when Zachariah Pringle writes about the changes he observes: 'at Greenock I saw nothing but shipping and building; at Glasgow, streets spreading as if they were one of the branches of cotton spinning.'[50] Such an effective image calls to mind the Victorian attitude of Improvement or 'Creative Destruction'. The Glasgow City Improvements Act was passed in 1866 (four years before the original University was levelled), effectively 'erasing' the 'old secondary street pattern', making way for 'new, ventilated thorough-fares'.[51] In Peter Mandler's 2012 paper '"Faust comes to town": "Creative Destruction" in the Victorian City', the influence of Georges-Eugène Haussmann on British cities including Glasgow is elucidated, and his point that the development of the railway system was the most destructive on the medieval and early modern townscapes certainly speaks to the points raised in Chapter 2 about James Watt and issues of memory in Glasgow's Enlightenment.[52]

In *The Entail* Galt leaves behind the 'single-volume fictional memoir for the full-length novel, which he makes the vehicle for a critical argument with the genre of national historical romance practiced by Scott'.[53] The story, set mostly in Glasgow in the eighteenth century, revolves around the Walkinshaw family, of which Claud Walkinshaw (orphaned, as we have noted, as a result of the Darien disaster) grows up in poverty. The three-volume generational family history that ensues is a fascinating insight into the Georgian era in Glasgow, beginning with Claud's return to the city as a successful merchant. We are told that Claud 'settled himself as a cloth-merchant, in a shop under the piazza of a house which occupied part of the ground where the Exchange now stands'.[54] Galt therefore places him near Glasgow Cross, the intersection of Glasgow's four principal streets which Daniel Defoe had described as part of his campaign to bring about the Union as 'the finest built that I have ever seen in one city together'.[55] After purchasing a farm Claud 'entails it, ruthlessly manipulating his family in his mad need to pass on his property intact'.[56] Morally, *The Entail* exemplifies the corruptive power of fiscal improvement: a slant perhaps on Glasgow's proud self-image at the time.

In *Ringan Gilhaize* Galt compounded yet another multi-generational tale (from the 1550s to 1690), therefore localising the ideas of Scottish identity through religious history. Patricia Wilson has said that Galt preferred his readers to believe more in his imagination than his skills at turning history into fiction, but that a level of research was undertaken to aid his own knowledge of the subjects in question. In this case, the Covenanters and religious identity in Scotland.[57] Wilson's assertion 'that there can be no doubt that memory played a large part' in Galt's reconstruction of this epoch of the Reformation brings us to another theory. It was Hans Robert Jauss who stated that:

> a literary work, even when it appears to be new, does not present itself as something absolutely new in an informational vacuum, but predisposes its audience to a very specific kind of reception by announcements, overt and covert signals, familiar characteristics, or implicit allusions.[58]

In other words, every work of literature is a product of its time, however subtly the presence of that time might appear. This also works the other way, as Astrid Erll explains in her discussion of 'collective texts': works like *Pride and Prejudice* (1813) are almost inextricably bound to a score of other media and mnemonic markers.[59] *Old Mortality* had already been printed across Europe by the time Galt's *Ringan Gilhaize* was first published, so it is safe to say that the 'germ' – to borrow Wilson's phrase – of Scott's tale had 'lain some time in Galt's mind'.[60] But this need not diminish the originality of Galt's fiction. Quite the opposite, for it is important to note that *Ringan Gilhaize* was by all accounts an attempt to reconstruct rather than reinscribe that period from the Covenanting point of view.[61] It is in this reconstruction that Galt also saw fit to connect 'the Covenanting struggle for religious freedom with the earlier struggle for national independence', as is evident in Galt's attachment of the *Declaration of Arbroath* (1320) as a postscript.[62] Having already mocked the 'pomp and hollow pageantry' of the 1822 royal visit in Edinburgh in *The Entail*, Galt seems to be challenging the uses of Scottish cultural identity in his own time, choosing to reinforce the longevity of religious identity as being the 'true' Scottish marker.[63]

To this day Galt's reputation as a Scottish novelist is at odds with his reputation as an agent of Empire in Canada. Before the renewed scholarly interest in Galt's life and works had reached its peak in the 1970s, Charles Shain lamented that 'none of Galt's biographers and none of the recent investigators of British-American cultural relations in the nineteenth century have noticed that Galt was the first well-known British novelist to write an American novel'.[64] He is speaking of *Lawrie Todd* (1830), a tale of the founding of Rochester, New York, which looks forward to Galt's *Bogle Corbet* a year later. The latter is much more significant where Glasgow is concerned. Rarely cited among Galt's best works, Katie Trumpener has noted how few others connect 'British North America' with 'other parts of the empire' quite as firmly as *Bogle Corbet*.[65]

The tale begins with his recollections of childhood in a Jamaica plantation, followed by Corbet's time in Glasgow during the late eighteenth century. In a letter to D. M. Moir, Galt described the novel as 'a Glasgow story' and, in comparison to his earlier work, said: 'The object of the work is a view of society generally, as the "Provost" was of burgh incidents simply.'[66] Galt's reliance on the success of his West of Scotland-based work is evident here as well as the preface to the novel, where it is stated: 'Information given as incidents of personal experience is more instructive than opinion.'[67] This indicates a continuation of Galt's emphasis on the familiarity which permeates throughout his works, thus creating a symbol in Corbet of Galt's own literary emigration from Glasgow to Canada. In terms of style, it can be argued that Galt's major achievement in *Bogle Corbet* is in fact a failure of sorts. Unlike his Scottish novels, in which the growth of towns consistently revealed the manners, unity and shortcomings of characters, *Bogle Corbet* offered 'a random sequence of scenes', which, for Elizabeth Waterston, was Galt's comment on the 'wilderness' of Canada and the initially 'disunified unharmonious small-town life of Canadian communities'.[68] Waterston saw this as the precursor for the Canadian novel. But in establishing Galt as pioneer of a North American literary tradition, with the obvious parallel of Galt as colonist, she effectively altered the legacy of *Bogle Corbet* altogether.

In 1977 the text was given 'its first modern and first Canadian printing, in the canon-forming New Canadian Library of McClelland and Stewart, "the Canadian Publishers"'.[69] In the same year, the same publishers printed *The Galts: A Canadian Odyssey, John Galt 1779–1839* by H. B. Timothy. In Kenneth McNeil's study of *Bogle Corbet* he recalls being 'surprised to discover that [Elizabeth Waterston's] edition contains not quite half of the original 1831 three-volume version', thus creating a new impression on readers: that Galt's narrative actually starts *after* Corbet's emigration experience.[70] This, says McNeil, is done to keep the work parallel to the 'national impetus', that which Trumpener explained as being 'a period of intense anti-American sentiment and equally intense literary nationalism in Canada'.[71] There are already parallels between the cultural context of this specific text and that of Scotland in the same decade. As Pittock elaborates, the 1970s saw the rise of Scottish publishing houses which rejuvenated interest in Scottish literatures, modern and classic, predating the flurry of Scottish texts that came about after the Hollywood favourites *Rob Roy* (1994) and *Braveheart* (1995).[72] Wulf Kansteiner, in his historiographical essay on memory studies (2002), updated some of the terminology often used: first of all 'memory makers' were outlined as those who 'selectively adopt and manipulate' the 'cultural traditions that frame all our representations of the past'; and secondly the 'memory consumers' who 'use, ignore, or transform' objects of the past, such as texts and images, 'according to their own interests'.[73] While New Canadian Library might be seen to have 'made' memories in the sense that they were affecting the interpretation of the historic object (Galt's original text), the publisher's actions pertain more to the 'memory consumers' category for their selectivity based on their own interests. Therefore, *Bogle Corbet* is symbolic of Galt's dual identity as a town-builder in Canada (and in North American academia as a literary pioneer) and a relatively minor Scottish novelist in the age of Sir Walter Scott. And so this inquiry of Georgian Glasgow in literature must ask: what is lost in Waterston's erasure of Corbet's earlier life?

As we know from *The Entail*, Galt carefully rendered Glasgow's cityscape and speech patterns. In *Bogle Corbet*, Galt offers several accounts of Glasgow's city centre in 1789, which accompanies his various portrayals of the Trongate found in *Annals of the Parish* and *The Steam-Boat* (where Duffle is 'convened to the Cross' like cattle 'upon entering the multitude'.)[74] We can compare these scenes to those provided by the various artists who depicted Glasgow Cross at its busiest, such as *Old Glasgow Cross or The Trongate* (1826) see Figure 14) by John Knox (1778–1845).[75]

Crucially, because Bogle was not raised in the city, his observations retain the 'awe' that we find in eighteenth-century civic poetry, as in the early drafts of John Mayne's poem 'Glasgow' (1783) which we will come back to in the next chapter. In addition, there is more attention drawn to the confluence of accents, revealing the influence of Empire on everyday life in Glasgow: the 'almost English tongue of Mr. Macindoe' from his years in the West Indies; the English-American 'decisive and energetic

Figure 14 John Knox, *Old Glasgow Cross or The Trongate* (1826). Accession number 2887. © CSG CIC Glasgow Museums Collection.

vernacular' of Dr. Leach; and the 'genuine Trongate' of Mr. Aird.[76] As Bogle comes to work in Mr. Aird's weaving workshop, there are signs of radicalisation among the weavers who, in the spirit of the French Revolution, transform the shop into a Jacobine club. Furthermore, the Revolution's interference with Glasgow's trade is said to 'thin' the 'canopy of smoke that overhung its spires and chimney-tops'.[77] In this particularly topographical chapter Corbet describes the cathedral and the Molendinar Burn before commenting on the characteristics that distinguish the young men who attend 'the College' from those who visit 'the Exchange', and the spoils of Empire that he finds in the Tontine coffee-room.

The abundance of detail tells us that Bogle Corbet had Glasgow's metropolitan social structure in mind when he moved to Canada. Gilbert Stelter has outlined Galt's fascination with Glasgow, Edinburgh and London and how they 'formed' his 'conception of cities' and, eventually, led to his interest in the foundation of towns like Ardrossan in 1805.[78] Therefore, Galt's line of thought between his impressions of Glasgow and his founding of Guelph in 1827 seems clear. Moreover, the founding of Guelph was fictionalised in *Bogle Corbet*, when the narrator describes the felling of the first tree, and the subsequent naming of the town:

> I left the name to be given by the settlers themselves, and in the course of the day heard that they had fixed on one; both appropriate, as it referred to themselves, and agreeable to me, as applied to a new place. In Glasgow there is an old well-known street called "The Stockwell", and . . . Several of the Glasgow men being artisans and crafts' men, Stockwell was intended chiefly for them, and those who might come after of the same kind.[79]

This event, being fundamental to Waterston's shortened text, seems isolated from any sense of the Old World city (Glasgow) that would be gained in a full reading. Not only do we find Glasgow missing, we also find a restricted cultural memory. Dislocating the Glasgow section from the Canada section is to cut off what Kenneth McNeil has called a 'debilitating persistence of memory', calling forth 'the debasing horrors of transatlantic slavery, of economic collapse . . . financial ruin . . . constant dislocation and uprootedness'.[80] Such emphases on the negative aspects of emigration are not entirely unjustified, as we have seen with the religious exiles and naval disasters in the late seventeenth century. After all, as Jennie Aberdein has noted, the aim of the novel was 'to warn and inform the would-be emigrant'.[81] This follows on from *Statistical Sketches of Upper Canada* (1832) by Galt's friend William Dunlop (1792–1848), intended 'for the use of immigrants'.

Above all, Galt's work for the Canada Company encapsulates the role of transatlantic imperialism and the formation of national identity. Although his *Autobiography* contains information about the breakdown of trust between the company and himself, it would be inconsequential to collate merely these; instead the achievements themselves should be illuminated. Working on behalf of the company, Galt opened the Huron Tract with permission to build on and turn profit from an area of one million acres.[82] In this vicinity Canada received a great influx of British idealism. As soon as 1896, almost fifty years after the company was closed, a book entitled *In The Days of the Canada Company* brought to light the seeds of the British that were laid and left to grow. The geographical importance of Upper Canada is not the sole focus, for it is stated that 'into the depths of the Huron Tract ... Galt, Dunlop, Strickland, Don ... carried their tastes, their habits, and their enthusiasms.'[83] There is suggestion, then, of an intellectual colonisation. Katie Trumpener describes Galt as the Canadian Christopher Columbus, and notes *Bogle Corbet* as being 'overtly concerned with imperialism's historical meaning and psychic consequences'. Going further, she ties the naming of the town of Guelph in 1827 as an origin myth creation.[84] As we know, Galt recalled Glasgow's artisan community in the naming of the fictional "Stockwell". But across the Huron Tract, the legacy of town names recalls many British noblemen and leaders, which, in a sense, connects only the official state memories of Britain with Canada, rather than the close-knit communities who would go on to expand the area. The original name of Guelph, as it appeared on its first map (see Figure 15), was 'Guelf' – a tribute to the House of Hanover, descendants of the House of Guelf. What is more, the chosen date for the foundation and naming ceremony was St George's Day, another clear homage to the Anglo-Britishness that permeated imperial activities of this kind.

We should clarify the opposing opinions surrounding Guelph's name. Stelter has suggested that Galt sought 'publicity and prestige' in his choice of name, 'for he had no great respect for the Hanoverians as a dynasty ("no usurpation was ever achieved with greater treachery ... than the Hanoverian acquisition of the British throne.")'[85] Jeffrey Cass, however, has said that 'the moral ambiguities attending colonialism' – that is, that 'European involvement in the cultures of others may result in unthinking destruction' – simply 'don't bother [Galt]'.[85] And indeed, when we recall Galt's dismay at the King's visit to Edinburgh in 1822, his apparently loyal officiating in Canada is highly ironic. After all, Guelph's links to the Hanoverian dynasty led to its nickname 'the Royal City'. In *Bogle Corbet*, Glasgow is frequently referred to as 'the Royal

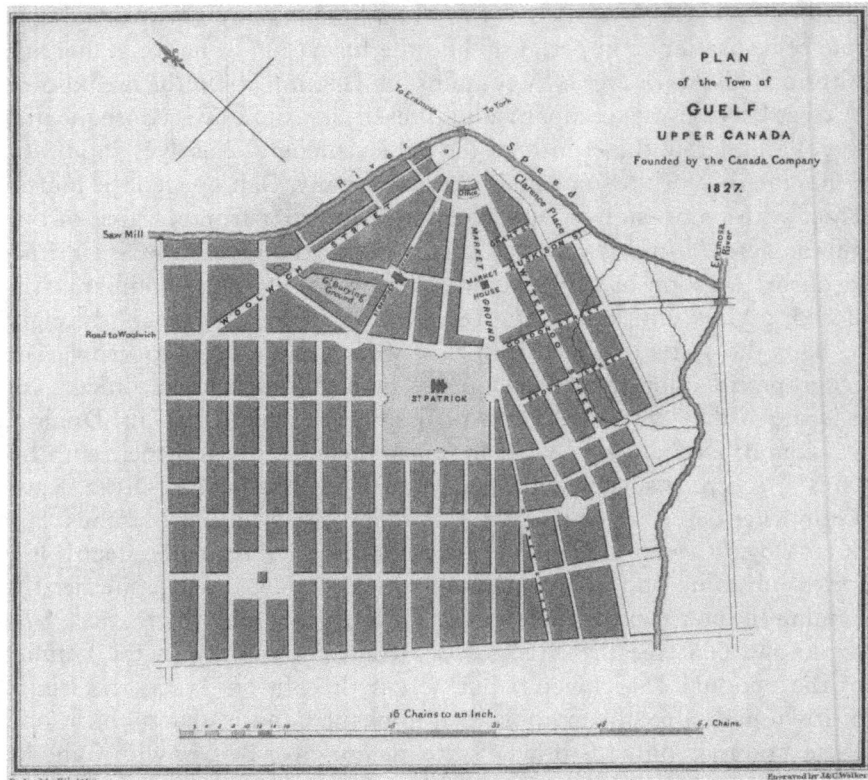

Figure 15 J. & C. Walker, *Plan of the Town of Guelf, Upper Canada* (1831). © McMaster University Library (Hamilton, Ontario).

City', which would seemingly connect these towns in their loyalty to the monarchy. However, Ian Gordon has noted that Galt's use of the phrase in *The Entail* was a simply a nod to the city becoming a royal burgh by charter in 1636.[87] It is therefore difficult to establish that Galt wanted to portray a shared sense of loyalty between Glasgow and Guelph. What we can be sure of is his connection between the two in *Bogle Corbet*, and the necessity of imperial 'alertness' – to return to Morton's phrase – that defined Glasgow's growth, whether or not loyal to the Hanoverians.

In terms of tracing identity, the problem arises in the separatist idea of Scottishness that permeates through colonial historiography, from the pre-Union attempts at colonisation to the post-Union diasporic development in the form of Caledonian Societies in almost every British colony.[88] All of these seek to conglomerate Scotland as a nation whose cultural motivations, literary heroes and collective identities are all on the same side, struggling together. This was symbolised in Robert Gibb's *Thin Red Line* (1881), a painting which offered the iconic image of the red-coated Sutherland Highlanders 93rd Regiment seeing off Russian cavalry in the Battle of Balaclava (1854). Joan Hichberger has noted how the image was used to popularise the role of Scots in the British army despite their 'numerical minority' in the late Victorian era.[89] The dominance of Victorian imagery has overshadowed the reality of the religious tensions in the seventeenth century and the Jacobite uprisings in the eighteenth century, therefore undermining the cultural identities that defined the Georgian era.

Before Galt's time the largest 'flow of emigration' to the 'underdeveloped and isolated provinces in British North America' was 'dominated by Highland Scots . . . led by the natural leaders of their local society'.[90] As of Galt's arrival, a great diversification of emigration ensued, wherein the 'Gaelic speaking Highland Scots [became] a much smaller percentage of the Scottish total', thus complicating the cultural make-up of Upper Canada in general.[91] These examples should remind us of the divisions of identity within Scotland which become deeper in the exploration and expansion of Britishness, and of the improbability of transporting a national collective identity across the Atlantic. Scottishness, it appears, was at one point harnessed and adopted, thus affecting the parochial novels of Galt within the context of cultural memory. As a result, certain myths become popularised, such as the story told by tour guides in Nova Scotia: that the wild heather in Point Pleasant Park 'found its way to Nova Scotia in the blankets of Highland troops . . . as they disembarked from their transports, the soldiers shook their bedding and the seeds that fell out found a new home across the Atlantic'.[92]

Murray Grigor's television film *Scotch Myths* (1981) illuminates the ways in which certain parts of Scotland's culture such as whisky drinking, Macpherson's *Ossian* fragments, and 'bringing in the bells' have come to represent the whole. In *The Invention of Scotland* (1991), Pittock put forth the idea that, far from a national identity falsely arising from Highland dress or, specifically, the rehearsed presentation of said dress during George IV's visit to Edinburgh in 1822, 'Scottish identity was, rather, the product of the continual reinterpretation of Scotland's relationship to the Stuart monarchy and to the Union throughout the eighteenth and nineteenth centuries.'[93] So, while we may be inclined to agree that, in theory, Tartan Day is a wholly American (or Canadian, if you consider its roots in 'Scottish Day', Nova Scotia) invention, we should also note that 'Highlandism was a Highland construction'.[94] To consider only the Victorian interpretation of Highland bravery (such as in Gibb's *The Thin Red Line*) is to significantly restrict the role of Highland culture in Scotland. With this logic we should realise that if we only recall Glasgow's industrial brilliance we risk neglecting its dual role as a city of Enlightenment and Empire, for better and for worse.

Following the retrieval of Galt in recent years we might begin to perceive him as a uniquely useful figure in retrieving the cultural memory of Georgian Glasgow. Because of his extensive references to the city and the various time-frames in which these references are set, we can use Galt's work to understand how certain places, people and events were being remembered at the close of the Georgian period. Combining these impressions with poems, paintings, etchings and statistical accounts from Galt's time amounts to a vast body of cultural memories. The process of using them in search of a city's prevailing image has recently been named 'cityscaping'.[95] But Galt's legacy straddles the Atlantic and is therefore stretched thin.

At a more local level Bruce Lenman has described Galt's literary depiction of Irvine, Galt's place of birth, as 'half-remembered, half-invented'.[96] But this need not be a bad thing. As we have touched on before, the process of remembering forces us to partially invent, to conjure reason in the construction of a narrative. Galt and his contemporaries, working as they were in the wake of the Scottish Enlightenment, were often unwittingly applying the rules of reason laid out in the eighteenth century. We have seen this in the tolerant, orderly plan for Guelph, and in Galt's many imagined town-planning schemes in his novels. At the heart of Galt's clearest, most repeated sketches of civic growth there exists a sort of utopia, a potential not at all unlike the twentieth-century literary craze that offered audacious visions of the future. One is also reminded of the seventeenth-century Darien Company, whose flag featured a blazing sun on the horizon: a symbol of the exotic and the unknown that connected exiles, emigrants and colonists from Scotland over centuries. In all of these cases we get a sense of great activity, of the Smithian 'hum of nations' that Dugald Moore described in his long poem about discovering Glasgow. The explosion of activity that would elevate the city to its height as the 'Second City of the Empire' was therefore initiated in the Georgian period which Galt and his contemporaries mapped out in their writing.

NOTES

1. T. M. Devine and Philip R. Rossner, 'Scots in the Atlantic Economy, 1600–1800', in John M. MacKenzie and T. M. Devine, eds, *Scotland*

and the British Empire (Oxford: Oxford University Press, 2011), 30–55 (37).
2. *Register of the Privy Council of Scotland 1681–1682*, 3:7 (Edinburgh: Morrison & Gibb, 1915), 664–5.
3. Gordon Jackson, 'Glasgow in transition, c.1660 to c.1740', in T. M. Devine and Gordon Jackson, eds, *Glasgow, Volume I: Beginnings to 1830* (Manchester: Manchester University Press, 1995), 63–105 (72).
4. George Pratt Insh, *Scottish Colonial Schemes 1620–1686* (Glasgow: Maclehose, Jackson & Co., 1922), 142.
5. Ibid.
6. This date is for the first English edition (see Bibliography for very full title), the first printing was in Latin: *Theologiae vere Christianae apologia* (Amsterdam: Typis excusa pro Jacob Claus, 1676).
7. Scott Sowerby's *Making Toleration* (2013) does much to elucidate the plight of Scottish Quakers and their treatment at the hands of the newly crowned James II and VII (1633–1701).
8. Insh, *Scottish Colonial Schemes*, 152.
9. Ibid., 188.
10. Ibid., 202.
11. Linda G. Fryer, 'Documents Relating to the Formation of the Carolina Company in Scotland, 1682', *The South Carolina Historical Magazine*, 99:2 (1998), 110–34 (120).
12. David Dobson, *Scottish Emigration to Colonial America, 1607–1785* (Athens, GA: University of Georgia Press, 1994), 64.
13. A. J. Mann, 'Gibson, Walter (b. c.1645, d. in or after 1717)', *Oxford Dictionary of National Biography*, <http://www.oxforddnb.com/view/article/67516> (last accessed 30 August 2020).
14. Lawrence S. Rowland et al., 'English, Scots, and Yemassee at Port Royal', *The History of Beaufort County, South Carolina: Volume 1, 1514–1861* (Columbia: University of South Carolina Press, 1996), 58–79 (72–4).
15. Dobson, *Scottish Emigration to Colonial America*, 65.
16. *The News and Courier*, Charleston, South Carolina, 158:172, 20 June 1960, 5. The artefact remains in the hands of the Charleston Library Society.
17. Michael Fry, *Scottish Empire* (Phantassie, East Lothian: Tuckwell Press, 2001), 25–6.
18. John Prebble, *The Darien Disaster* (London: Secker & Warburg, 1968), 315.
19. David Armitage, 'Paterson, William (1658–1719)', *Oxford Dictionary of National Biography*, <http://www.oxforddnb.com/view/article/21538> (last accessed 20 November 2019).
20. Ibid.
21. Julie Orr, *Scotland, Darien and the Atlantic World, 1698–1700* (Edinburgh: Edinburgh University Press, 2018).

22. The scope of the archival research was summed up in the review of Orr's monograph by Alasdair Raffe, 'Orr, *Scotland, Darien and the Atlantic World, 1698–1700*', *Scottish Historical Review*, 98:2 (October 2019), 318–19.
23. T. C. Smout, 'The Anglo-Scottish Union of 1707. I. The Economic Background', *The Economic History Review*, New Series, 16:3 (1964), 455–67 (459).
24. *Certain Propositions Relating to the Scots Plantation of Caledonia, and the National Address for Supporting thereof, briefly offered to Publick View, for removing of Mistakes and Prejudices* (Glasgow: 1700).
25. Ibid., 5.
26. Ibid., 30. For more on this pamphlet war, cf. Karin Bowie, 'Public Opinion, Popular Politics and the Union of 1707', *The Scottish Historical Review*, 82:214, Part 2 (2003), 226–60.
27. *Waverley; or, 'Tis Sixty Years Since*, vol. 3 (Edinburgh: John Ballantine & Co., 1814), 370.
28. Gifford, Dunnigan and McGillivray, eds, *Scottish Literature in English and Scots* (Edinburgh: Edinburgh University Press, 2002), 195.
29. Paul Barnaby, 'Timeline of the European Reception of Sir Walter Scott, 1802–2013', in Murray Pittock, ed., *The Reception of Sir Walter Scott in Europe* (London and New York: Bloomsbury, 2007), xxiv–lxxxii.
30. John Galt, *The Autobiography of John Galt*, vol. 2 (London: Cochrane and McCrone, 1833), 219.
31. Aleida Assmann, *Cultural Memory and Western Civilization* (Cambridge: Cambridge University Press, 2011), 323.
32. Paul Henderson Scott, 'Galt, John (1779–1839)', *Oxford Dictionary of National Biography*, <http://www.oxforddnb.com/view/article/10316> (last accessed 30 August 2020).
33. For more on this 'Glasgow School' see Craig Lamont, 'Finding Galt in Glasgow', in Gerard Carruthers and Colin Kidd, eds, *International Companion to John Galt* (Glasgow: Association for Scottish Literary Studies, 2017), 34–43 (37–41).
34. Bruce P. Lenman, *Integration and Enlightenment: Scotland 1746–1832* (Edinburgh: Edinburgh University Press, 1981), 134.
35. Anand C. Chitnis, 'The Scottish Enlightenment in the Age of Galt', in Christopher A. Whatley, ed., *John Galt (1779–1979)* (Edinburgh: The Ramsay Head Press, 1979), 31–50 (32–3).
36. John Galt, *Annals of the Parish; or, the chronicle of Dalmailing during the Ministry of the Rev. Micah Balwhidder, written by himself* (London and Edinburgh: T. N. Foulis, 1911 [1821]), 269–70.
37. John Galt, *The Entail; or, The Lairds of Grippy*, ed. Ian A. Gordon (Oxford: Oxford University Press, 1984 [1823]), 3.
38. Barbara A. Misztal, *Theories of Social Remembering* (Maidenhead: Open University Press, 2003), 17.

39. Ibid., 115.
40. Eliot Warburton, *Darien; or, The Merchant Prince. A Historical Romance*, vol. 1 (London: Colburn and Co., 1852), 31–3.
41. Ibid., 34.
42. John Galt, *The Literary Life, and Miscellanies, of John Galt*, vol. 2 (Edinburgh: William Blackwood, 1834), 39.
43. Hilary M. Carey, *God's Empire: Religion and Colonialism in the British World, c.1801–1908* (Cambridge: Cambridge University Press, 2011), 216.
44. *Report of Committee of General Assembly, on Colonial Churches, 28th May 1838, and deliverance of the assembly. With Appendix, containing correspondence with the Colonial Office, and Report of the North American Colonial Society of Glasgow for 1838* (Glasgow: G. Richardson, 1838), 4–5.
45. Carey, *God's Empire*, 219.
46. Maurice Halbwachs, *On Collective Memory*, ed. Lewis A. Coser (Chicago: University of Chicago Press, 1992 [1941]), 84.
47. Liam McIlvanney, 'The Glasgow Novel', in Gerard Carruthers and Liam McIlvanney, eds, *The Cambridge Companion to Scottish Literature* (Cambridge: Cambridge University Press, 2012), 217–32 (221).
48. Ibid., 221.
49. Ibid., 272.
50. John Galt, *The Ayrshire Legatees; or, The Pringle Family* (New York: W. B. Gilley, 1823), 14.
51. Miles Glendinning, Ranald MacInnes and Aonghus MacKechnie, *A History of Scottish Architecture: From the Renaissance to the Present Day* (Edinburgh: Edinburgh University Press, 1996 [2002]) 256–7.
52. Delivered 26 June 2012 at the University of Southampton and 10 May 2014 at the University of Aberdeen. Audio available online: <https://www.southampton.ac.uk/scnr/news/2012/06/26_faust_comes_to_town.page> (last accessed 30 August 2020).
53. Ian Duncan, *Scott's Shadow: The Novel in Romantic Edinburgh* (Princeton, NJ: Princeton University Press, 2007), 235.
54. Galt, *The Entail*, 11.
55. This is an oft-quoted piece of booster travel writing by Defoe, used to its full effect in nostalgic Victorian books on Glasgow's past, such as David Small, *By-gone Glasgow* (Glasgow: Morison Brothers, 1896), cf. section VI.
56. Ian Gordon, 'John Galt', *John Galt 1779–1979*, ed. Christopher A. Whatley (Edinburgh: The Ramsay Head Press, 1979), 19–30 (26–7).
57. Patricia J. Wilson, '*Ringan Gilhaize*: the product of an informing vision', *Scottish Literary Journal*, 8:1 (1981), 52–68 (52–3).
58. Hans Robert Jauss, 'Literary History as a Challenge to Literary Theory', *New Literary History*, 2:1 (1970), 7–37 (12).

59. Astrid Erll, *Memory in Culture*, trans. Sara B. Young (Basingstoke: Palgrave, 2011), 164
60. Wilson, '*Ringan Gilhaize:* the product of an informing vision', 61.
61. Ibid.
62. Patricia J. Wilson, '*Ringan Gilhaize:* A neglected masterpiece?', in Christopher A. Whatley, ed., *John Galt (1779–1979)* (Edinburgh: The Ramsay Head Press, 1979), 120–50 (132).
63. As described in: Jennie W. Aberdein, *John Galt* (Oxford: Oxford University Press, 1936), 108.
64. Charles E. Shain, 'John Galt's America', *American Quarterly*, 8:3 (1956), 254–63 (254).
65. Trumpener, *Bardic Nationalism: The Romantic Novel and the British Empire* (Princeton, NJ: Princeton University Press, 1997), 279.
66. John Galt, 'Memoir of Galt', *The Annals of the Parish and The Ayrshire Legatees* (Edinburgh: Blackwood and Sons, 1850), pp. lxxxix–xc.
67. John Galt, *Bogle Corbet; or, The Emigrants*, vol. 1 (London: Henry Colburn and Richard Bentley, 1831), iii.
68. Elizabeth Waterston, '*Bogle Corbet* and the Annals of New World Parishes', in Elizabeth Waterston, ed., *John Galt: Reappraisals* (Guelph: University of Guelph, 1985), 57–62 (61).
69. Trumpener, *Bardic Nationalism*, 278.
70. Kenneth McNeil, 'Time, Emigration, and the Circum-Atlantic World: John Galt's *Bogle Corbet*', in Regina Hewitt, ed., *John Galt: Observations and Conjectures on Literature, History, and Society* (Lewisburg, PA: Bucknell University Press, 2012), 299–322 (300).
71. Trumpener, *Bardic Nationalism*, 178.
72. Murray Pittock, *The Road to Independence? Scotland Since the Sixties* (London: Reaktion Books, 2008), 119–20.
73. Wulf Kansteiner, 'Finding Meaning in Memory: A Methodological Critique of Collective Memory Studies', *History and Theory*, 41:2 (2002), 179–97 (180).
74. John Galt, *The Steam-Boat* (Edinburgh: William Blackwood, 1822), 174.
75. This painting was placed at the beginning of the 2014 Glasgow Life Exhibition – *How Glasgow Flourished* – beside the Glassford family portrait. For more on this exhibition see Conclusion.
76. Galt, *Bogle Corbet*, vol. 1, 28.
77. Ibid., 69 [it is possible that Galt, having acknowledged Hamilton's *Cyril Thornton*, borrowed his 'canopy of smoke' line, pp. 88–9].
78. Gilbert A. Stelter, 'John Galt: The writer as Town Booster and Builder', in Elizabeth Waterston, ed., *John Galt: Reappraisals* (Guelph: University of Guelph, 1985), 17–43 (21–2).
79. Galt, *Bogle Corbet*, vol. 3, 38; cf. Lamont, 'Finding Galt in Glasgow,' 34–43.
80. Kenneth McNeil, 'Time, Emigration, and the Circum-Atlantic World: John

Galt's *Bogle Corbet*', in Regina Hewitt, ed., *John Galt: Observations and Conjectures on Literature, History, and Society* (Lewisburg, PA: Bucknell University Press, 2012), 299–322 (302).
81. Aberdein, *John Galt*, 172.
82. Paul Henderson Scott, 'Galt, John (1779–1839)', *Oxford Dictionary of National Biography*, <http://www.oxforddnb.com/view/article/10316> (last accessed 30 August 2020).
83. Robina and Kathleen Macfarlane Lizars, *In the Days of the Canada Company: The Story of the Settlement of the Huron Tract and a View of the Social Life of the Period, 1825–1850* (Toronto: William Briggs, 1896), 21.
84. Katie Trumpener, 'Annals of Ice: Formations of Empire, Place and History in John Galt and Alice Munro', in Michael Gardiner and Graeme Macdonald, eds, *Scottish Literature and Postcolonial Literature: Comparative Texts and Critical Perspectives* (Edinburgh: Edinburgh University Press, 2011), 43–56 (45).
85. Stelter, 'John Galt: The writer as Town Booster', 27.
86. Jeffrey Cass, 'John Galt, Happy Colonialist: *The Case of the Apostate; or, Atlantis Destroyed*', *Wordsworth Circle*, 41:3 (2010), 167–70 (170).
87. Galt, *The Entail*, 390.
88. John M. Mackenzie, 'Essay and Reflection: On Scotland and the Empire', *The International History Review*, 15:4 (1993), 714–39 (737).
89. J. W. M. Hichberger, *Images of the Army: The Military in British Art, 1815–1914* (Manchester: Manchester University Press, 1988), 106.
90. J. M. Bumsted, 'Scottish and Britishness in Canada, 1790–1914', in Marjory Harper and Michael E. Vance, eds, *Myth, Migration and the Making of Memory: Scotia and Nova Scotia c.1700–1990* (Halifax: Fernwood, 1999), 89–105 (98).
91. Ibid., 99.
92. Marjory Harper and Michael E. Vance, 'Introduction', in Marjory Harper and Michael E. Vance, eds, *Myth, Migration and the Making of Memory: Scotia and Nova Scotia c.1700–1990* (Halifax: Fernwood, 1999), 14.
93. Matthew P. Dziennik, 'Whig Tartan: Material Culture and its use in the Scottish Highlands, 1746–1815', *Past & Present*, 217 (2012), 117–47 (117).
94. Edward J. Cowan, 'Tartan Day in America', in Celeste Ray, ed., *Transatlantic Scots* (Tuscaloosa, AL: University of Alabama Press, 2005), 318–38 (321).
95. As per the title of the study: Therese Fuhrer, Felix Mundt, Jan Stenger, eds, *Cityscaping* (Berlin: De Gruyter, 2015).
96. Lenman, *Integration and Enlightenment*, 135.

PART IV

Commemorating Glasgow as the 'Second City'

With the echoes of Glasgow's Enlightenment and imperial histories still ringing, it is appropriate now to understand how these became deafened by the steady beat of industrial progress to which the city has been marching for centuries. This section takes us towards the end of Georgian era and beyond, focusing on the lamentations, commemorations and celebrations that ultimately locked in the image of Glasgow as we know it. When we find Georgian Glasgow at all the prevailing images are of a particular slant: rather than marking the many cultural achievements of the period they enshrine instead a sentimental and British National Romanticism. In the wake of the Enlightenment there was, it seems, an evolution. Glasgow became the 'Second City of the Empire', staking a claim in a new era of boldness, sometimes as 'the Workshop of the World'. While assuming these British and global epithets the city began to shed memories of its recent past, in a sense repositioning itself for new frontiers and conflicts. These were the foundations for the famous age of shipbuilding on the Clyde which remains Glasgow's most recognisable image.[1] But how did we get there?

The skies of the eighteenth century, once clear enough for stargazing at the College Observatory, were soon clouded with the progress of industry and towards the end of that century most of the leading lights of the Scottish Enlightenment had died out. James Watt lived until 1819 but few who can be said to match his colossal legacy lived beyond 1800. By the time William Hunter's collection arrived in Glasgow in 1807 in the form of the Hunterian Museum, it seemed strangely out of place on a campus somewhat living in the past.[2] Add into the equation John Anderson's tumultuous relationship with the College hierarchy and his decision to inaugurate a new College after his death and we can see a door closing in the history of the University. Advertisement pamphlets from the 1820s and 1830s show that the 'Andersonian University' was effectively competing with Glasgow University, offering classes on 'mechanical and chemical philosophy' and boasting new apparatus and books.[3] As this institution grew the University of Glasgow as a centre of the Scottish Enlightenment lost something of its former glory.

But the harnessing of eighteenth-century knowledge, and indeed the enhancement of it, ushered in a new age of 'Improvement'. It should be remembered that during the early decades of the nineteenth century there was a rise in social unrest and class consciousness. Political reform and continental wars dominated the newspapers. Slavery Acts were passed to bring about abolition but the trade continued regardless for another generation. This word 'generation' should give us pause. With the passing of one group of people who lived together (however we might divide them) to another group we essentially have a body of collective memories. Taking us back to the core strand of the book we have to ask ourselves what did Glasgow (i.e. its people) remember? What did it forget? As 'collective' or generational memory gives way to 'cultural' or transgenerational memory we can answer this by looking at what is left over. What did one group decide to remember *on behalf* of themselves, for when they were gone? In this section we will see what commemorative landmarks held ground throughout history and which areas of Georgian Glasgow were deemed less worthy. To begin we will look at how writers and travellers engendered a wave of movement and remembrance by consecrating people and things. Having opened up the New World during a century of imperial activity Scots became woven into the fabric of a strong (British) national identity. As a response to our increasing involvement in wars overseas many cities threw up statues and monuments to their war dead at an unprecedented rate. Poetry too was becoming more concerned with the heroic soldier and less with the stones and slabs of the city. As the Georgian period came to a close and the heavy industries began to change the face of the nation, Glasgow took centre-stage, refashioning itself as a powerhouse of the Empire. It became a hub of shipbuilding with such esteem that its legacy lasts today. It therefore begins to make sense that the histories we have traversed so far, with all their complications and implications, have been left in the dust of progress and improvement.

NOTES

1. Glaswegian comedian and writer Brian Limond (aka Limmy) often satirises the 'Men with a trade' characterisation of Glasgow.
2. This point was made in Chapter 3, in reference to Thomas Hamilton's novel *Cyril Thornton*.
3. University of Glasgow Library Special Collections: Sp Coll Bh12-y.25 (10).

6

Literary Tourists and Soldier Heroes

> From thy wild source to thy broad firth I passed,
>   The pilgrim of thy scene, romantic Clyde!
> Thy caves, and falls, as shrines beloved, I classed,
>   And, pilgrim-like, ne'er parted from thy side.
>
> Mary Macarthur, 'The Clyde' (1842)[1]

It is fair to say that Glasgow as a city has been surpassed by many others in terms of literary fame. When Edinburgh became the inaugural UNESCO City of Literature in 2004 its famous literary associations were enshrined with events and activity the likes of which Glasgow has rarely seen. It is also telling that in Kilpatrick's book on the *Literary Landmarks of Glasgow* (1898) there is an unfounded claim that Robert Burns touted his poetry in Glasgow before the famous Kilmarnock edition was published in 1786. Fame by association remained the norm for many years. Burns was often mentioned as being 'frequently in Glasgow' by apologetic writers concerned with the city's lack of literary prowess in Burns's era. But this kind of interpretation, still in play as recently as Oakley's *The Second City* (1946), pushed minor Glaswegian writers to the footnotes of literary history and taught an entire generation to look elsewhere for their poetry and novels.[2]

As a result of this the central figure in Glasgow's George Square is the Edinburgh celebrity Sir Walter Scott, towering high above Burns, the Alloway-born national poet, and Thomas Campbell, one of the few Glasgow-born poets whose fame extends beyond the city boundaries.[3] Unlike Campbell, the fame of Scott and Burns (whose memorials can be found across Scotland and beyond) is kept alive with their respective sites of memory or, to use Nora's popular term, *lieux de mémoire*. In particular, Burns's birthplace in Alloway, and the nearby Birthplace Museum draw masses of tourists. There is even a replica of the poet's birthplace in Atlanta, Georgia. The cottage, constructed by the Burns Club in 1911, is generally not open to the public and practically serves as a shrine to the memory of Burns. One can, however, visit Walter Scott's country estate Abbotsford, described on the official website as 'an enduring monument to the tastes, talents and personal tragedies of its creator'.[4] Scott's taste for historical nostalgia is renowned: he has even been credited with introducing a 'religion of names and of monuments' in Britain.[5] But Glasgow has no match for Edinburgh's Scott. In William Howitt's description of Campbell's house in *Homes and Haunts of the Most Eminent British Poets* (1877) he has little to say about the building. He can only lament the sad fact that it was 'swept away by the progress of modern improvement'.[6]

Ever since Nicola Watson's seminal book *The Literary Tourist* (2006) scholars have been using new case studies to understand the condition of cultural memory through the celebrations of writers. Watson posited that the 'portability and multiplicity of the published book seems to have induced since the late eighteenth century a desire to authenticate the reading experience in a more "personal" way'.[7] From the eighteenth century also sprung the popular and fashionable mode of visiting writers' graves, known as 'necro-tourism', which itself takes centre stage in Paul Westover's *Necromanticism* (2012).[8] In Scotland and England these phenomena accelerated in the nineteenth century, but as Harald Hendrix shows us with his study of Petrarch's birthplace in Arezzo, the consecration of literary celebrities is much older. Hendrix notes that Petrarch was both proud and embarrassed that the house in which he was born in 1304 ('but where he had never lived, not even as a child') was put 'under a special kind of protection' by local authorities to preserve its layout and aesthetic.[9] Indeed, we often fail to consider the relationship between the subject being remembered and the place in which we remember them. A more fitting example for the Georgian period is the multiform commemoration in the Lake District of the chief Romantic poet William Wordsworth and his sister Dorothy Wordsworth. Saeko Yoshikawa's *William Wordsworth and the Invention of Tourism* (2014) unpicks the various *lieux de mémoire* in the area, looking at the poet's houses and gardens in which the famous daffodils are grown.

With no comparative birthplace or famous residences in Glasgow, poets focus instead on the city spires and buildings. In his 'Elegy Written in Mull' (1795) Thomas Campbell writes:

Hail, happy Clutha! glad shall I survey
Thy gilded turrets from the distant way.[10]

For a Romantic-era poet Campbell is quite unique in his fixation here on the city itself. He expands on this idea, saying: 'I was better pleased to look on the kirk steeples and whinstone causeways of Glasgow than on all the eagles and wild deer of the Highlands.'[11] In this instance he associates the *Clutha* (Gaelic, i.e. Clyde) not with the sublime or with its picturesque course, but with its vantage point of the cityscape. There is a tradition of this association in verse, with glimpses of the city appearing to grow or move. The earliest examples in Scottish literature were written in Latin. The first, by John Johnston, was used as part of William Camden's unprecedented topographical and descriptive survey *Britannia* – first published in 1586 and going through several expansions and revisions throughout the seventeenth century. Johnston's Latin stanza on the Clyde appears as early as 1607, with the English translation appearing in 1695:

> Not haughty Prelates e'er adorn'd thee so,
> Nor stately Mitres cause of all thy woe,
> As Cluyd's muses grace thy blest abodes,
> And lift thy head among the deathless gods.
> Cluyd, great flood! for plenteous fish renown'd,
> And gentle streams that cheer the fruitful ground.
> But happy *Glascow*, *Cluyd*'s chiefest pride,
> Glory of that and all the world beside,
> Spreads round the richest of her noble tide.[12]

Another Latin dedication to Glasgow was written by the Aberdonian poet Arthur Johnston (no relation to John, above), published in 1642.[13] The English translation by John Barclay, also of Aberdeen, reads:

> Glasgow, to thee thy neighbouring towns give place.
> Bove them thou lifts thine head with comely grace;
> Scarce in the spacious earth can any see
> A city that's more beautifull than thee.
> [. . .]
> More pure than amber is the river Clyde,
> Whose gentle streams do by thy borders glyd;
> And here a thousand sail receive commands
> To traffick for thee unto forraign lands.[14]

It is intriguing that the first booster poem about Glasgow hailed from Aberdeen, and that the Clyde's value as a cultural and financial symbol was preserved in Latin during the first half of the seventeenth century. Barclay's rendering of Johnston's lines, specifically this notion that the Clyde is 'more pure than amber' (*electro purior*) is a very helpful metaphor in this discussion of memory. While the perseverance of the Clyde in Glasgow's imagery casts the old river as something of an eternal witness, this poetic process of reinscribing the Clyde and the cityscape as key images has probably diminished the importance of the Molendinar Burn in the origin story of Glasgow.

Following Johnston and Barclay we have James Arbuckle's anti-Jacobite poem *Glotta* (1721), John Wilson's celebratory poem 'Clyde' (1764), and Dugald Moore's 'Stanzas to the Clyde' (1833). John Mayne's *Glasgow* (1783) instead focused on the people, the streets and the buildings of the city. In a revised edition (1803), more people and places were added, and the focus was shifted outward to the surrounding natural scenes on the banks of the Clyde. This helped feed a new tradition wherein Glasgow's built environment was less attractive to visitors than the pastoral idylls beyond the city walls. None were more desirable than the falls of the Clyde known as Cora Linn. Between 1801 and 1845 William Turner sketched several paintings and drawings of the scene. In 1814 Wordsworth himself wrote about the 'little, trembling flowers' in his poem on Cora Linn.[15] Campbell, who was normally averse to romanticising his homeland, eventually returned to the scene in 1837 to commemorate 'a sweet Autumn Day / As ever shone on Clyde'.[16] That these sites have been the subject of artists time and time again helps us understand Glasgow's status for the would-be tourist. Where would they go? What would they want to tell people they had seen? Without a notable birthplace or shrine around which literary pilgrims might cluster, Glasgow had less traction than cities like Florence, Paris or London.

All of this leads us back to the Georgian period to examine how the city was imagined and reimagined by natives and travellers. The Edinburgh bookseller and poet Allan Ramsay paid homage to the majesty of Glasgow's river in 'Clyde's Welcome to his Prince' (1721), referring to the 'rival Thames'.[17] There are other examples in which Ramsay localises his neo-classical strain, effectively enshrining the memory of a place in verse. 'To the Ph— an Ode' (1721), itself an imitation of Horace, begged the reader to: Look up to *Pentland*'s towring Taps / Buried beneath great Wreaths of Snaw'.[18] This laid the groundwork for his masterpiece *The Gentle Shepherd* (1725) wherein the region of the Pentlands, and specifically Penicuik, replaced the traditionally anonymous idylls of pastoral verse. For the first time Scottish Romanticism had a meaningful and recognisable name and, more importantly, a locale which tourists could find and engage with.[19] It was Ramsay's friend James Arbuckle, student at the old College of Glasgow, who produced the poem *Glotta*, mentioned above. The name is the Latinised form of the Gaelic 'Clutha' for Clyde. His anti-Jacobite lines contrast nicely with Ramsay's take on the Clyde:

> Till all Disgusts, and secret Murmurs gone,
> The Realm in Int'rest as in Name be One:
> Impartial Riches flow in ev'ry Stream,
> And *Thames* and *Glotta* mutual Friendship claim.[20]

No longer rivals, these rivers are here unified in Arbuckle's unambiguous attempt to emblemise Glasgow as a staunchly pro-Hanoverian city. When the poem was reprinted in London in 1810 the effect of these political overtones was diminished by an entirely new phenomenon. In this new version an appended list of views were printed to correspond with 'Marshall's Extensive Panorama of the matchless Beauties of the Clyde, from the falls to the Irish sea, upon a new and interesting plan, as if travelling along the banks'.[21] The views included in this theatrical spectacle include 'distant' and 'extensive' views of Glasgow.[22] What is more, the poem itself is footnoted, often to match up a specific line with a view to be found in this panorama.[23] This subverted reading of *Glotta* from a political barb to a pleasant piece of faux-tourism can be considered alongside the secularisation of memory that we find in the physical world with writers' houses and graves. In this case, where Glasgow is the subject, the communicative effect of print culture is replaced by the novelty of the panorama, a fate that could hardly have been predicted by Glasgow's early-eighteenth-century printers.

Visual culture has an immediate locational effect which is naturally more memorable than words alone, hence the build-up of repeated images of ships on the Clyde cementing Glasgow's permanent legacy of shipbuilding. As regards the panorama's effect on poetry, there occurred a visual disruption. As Erkki Huhtamo (2002) explains, 'a moving panorama of the Clyde in Prince's Street [Edinburgh] as early as 1809'[24] allowed the spectator to be 'teleported' without leaving their 'familiar surroundings'.[25] At the same time, the political allusions throughout *Glotta* have been overshadowed by a new focus on place in an unusual corralling of the senses. In the case of John Mayne's poem *Glasgow* (1783), mentioned above, the new edition (1803) offers a new, expanded topography. Mayne has reviewed his portrait of the city and added content according to Glasgow's growth, development and fame. The original seventeen-stanza poem in the Standard Habbie style praised the College, the merchants, the Clyde, Glasgow Green and the city's writers. The revised edition saw a huge expansion of forty-three new stanzas in which Mayne name-checks the new buildings and institutions, as well as the great and good of Glasgow and beyond including Adam Smith and Robert Burns. That he lends a new emphasis to the commercial enterprises in Glasgow reveals Glasgow's shifting identity as a useful and industrious metropolis rather than a 'knacky' and flourishing town.[26]

But what else was there to see? With the heyday of the Enlightenment in the past what did Glasgow have to offer? The same famous buildings seem to have been in vogue for the majority of the nineteenth century, or for as long as they remained standing. We can see this in the stained glass work of the Edinburgh-born artist Stephen Adam. One particular piece made in the late nineteenth century portrays Glasgow's Trongate 'as it was' in 1800, a nice example of cultural memory (Adam was born in 1848).[27] In Elvira Anna Phipps's *Memorials of Clutha: or, Pencillings on the Clyde* (1842) she asks: 'Will the reader object to accompany me on my perambulations to Glasgow – that seat of commerce and of wealth?'[28] Chief among her recollections are the College, the Necropolis and the monument to John Knox. This monument, discussed already in Chapter 3, is often a focal point for would-be tourists. In Charles Mackenzie's *Interesting and Remarkable Places* (1849) the author gathers together an array of sites including Alexander Pope's Temple at Hagley, the birthplace of John Locke and Scott's Abbotsford. A medley of global hotspots including Constantinople and the Milan Cathedral make for a curious compendium of taste. Glasgow is represented solely by John Knox's monument (and a speculative engraving showing Knox's possible residence in the city).[29] And so it seems that Georgian – and indeed early Victorian – tourism in Glasgow is driven by its prestigious architecture and a religious reformer who probably only passed through town.[30]

The irony in this lack of commemoration of literary Glasgow is that the foundation story of Glasgow is remembered by its citizens in rhyme:

> Here's the bird that never flew;
> Here's the tree that never grew;
> Here's the bell that never rang;
> Here's the fish that never swam.

For centuries this has been considered a popular rhyme repeated by children.[31] It is a mnemonic device linked to the four elements of Glasgow's coat of arms, based on the miracles of the city's patron Saint Mungo. The legend is that Mungo's prayers brought a robin (the bird) back to life in his hands and caused some frozen olive branches (the tree) to catch fire. The fish 'that never swam' emblemises the miracle of rediscovering a lost ring. No matter which version of this story – normally involving an adulterous queen – is told, the consistent detail tends to be that the queen pled with Mungo to find the ring, that her life depended on it, and he responded by sending one of his monks to catch a fish and bring it from the river. In its mouth was the ring, and her life was saved. The bell 'that never rang' relates either to a bell that was given to Mungo by the Pope, or a fifteenth-century bell which John Stewart, the first provost of Glasgow left to the city as an emblem of the city's founder. The legends are now woven into a mantra that is well known by most Glaswegians, and the imagery associated is found everywhere in the city from bus shelters to dustbins, from parking meters to ironmongery containing the four main elements (you can see the four main elements on lamp posts at either side of the Livingstone statue in Figure 10). In terms of memory, this rhyme and these images remain the 'official' marker for civic identity as inscribed by the city itself. It takes us back to the 'site' of the foundation story we encountered in Part I. As we noted then, the discussion of memory concerning St Mungo's Cathedral and the nearby Necropolis is not quite the same as public commemorations on streets and in squares. Yes, tourists and citizens can wander into the cathedral and they can walk around the Necropolis as freely as they can any square, but new conditions are factored in. Quiet, respectful remembrance (if not religious) is almost expected in places like these. The remembering is therefore imbued with different unspoken rules.

In Florence, for instance, there was a medley of religious, social and cultural commemoration taking place all at once in certain churches. Anne O'Connor shows us this with various examples of Dante's importance in forming the cultural memory of the city in the nineteenth century (2008). 'From Santa Croce,' she says, 'to monuments around the city and prominent burial sites, the dead took their place among the city and contemporary landscape of the Tuscan capital.'[32] In so doing the landscape is given a new sense of purpose and, perhaps, esteem. Glasgow's Necropolis, following the Père Lachaise in Paris, can be seen as a similar act of civic enshrinement. In the preface to George Blair's *Biographic and Descriptive Sketches of Glasgow Necropolis* (1857) we get this sentiment in a sort of 'necro-touristic' mode. He says:

> The elegant and costly monuments with which it is now so richly embellished were never intended to be hid from view. They resemble a city that is literally 'set on a hill' – a silent but significant city of the dead – to draw the attention of the living to the memory and virtues of the departed.[33]

To justify his book, Blair backs this up by claiming: 'to render a visit to this very beautiful Cemetery really instructive and interesting, an adequate interpreter was required.'[34] What follows is a guide to the noble dead in the Necropolis with historical sketches interspersed with appropriate verse from Beattie, Cowper and Coleridge. Unsurprisingly, a chapter on the Knox monument contains great detail of its history, likeness and reception. Even its direction (facing the 'once Romish Cathedral' which his followers almost destroyed) is explained. As we have noted above, Knox's colossal presence in Glasgow speaks not only to a sense of religious identity in Glasgow – as, indeed, does the nearby William of Orange statue – but also to an absence. Without a home-grown 'hero' to which travellers flock in their thousands, the cultural memory of Glasgow ultimately clung to its engrained identity. The statue to Thomas Campbell in George Square was unveiled in 1867, ten years after Blair lamented the lack of a monument to Campbell in his book.[35] But Campbell never had the pull of a Wordsworth, a Scott, or a Dante.

It is probably for this reason that the Necropolis was conceived in the model of its Parisian predecessor. To install a site of memory can be seen as an overt attempt to define the city. Ironically, some of the poets who are buried there are not remembered at all. Take Dugald Moore for instance. Born in Glasgow and successful as a poet during his short life (1805–41), Moore's sonnet on Glasgow's Cathedral (1831) pays respect to the ancient edifice:

> . . . Ruin has been
> Busy upon the world; yet thou art green.
> Ten thousand sunsets now have tinged thy cheek,
> And yet thou look'st proudly in his eye
> As on that morn, when first his crimson streak
> Mellow'd thy infant turets from on high.[36]

In a similar vein, poet Mary Macarthur's *Necropolis: An Elegy* (1842) reveals the poetic preference for Glasgow's places over its people. Her elegies on Robert Burns and her close friends feature among verses on the Clyde and the different features of the Necropolis. Her titular poem ends:

> And now, my mission ended, I depart,
> The sky will soon be tinged with twilight's dyes,
> And, with a tranquil pleasure in my heart,
> I cross once more the bridge, the Bridge of Sighs.[37]

This was never the intended name for the main bridge connecting the Necropolis with the grounds of the cathedral, but, in taking its name from the Ponte dei Sospiri in Venice we see another connection between a Glasgow site of memory and a European counterpart. The semantics might be similar (the Venetian bridge connects a palace to a prison, not a cathedral to a graveyard) but the naming of this site reveals once again Glasgow's dependence on association and historical reference. However, it is also in Macarthur's book of poems that we find the turning point for this chapter, and the emergence of a culture of Soldier Hero worship.

Pieces such as 'The Recruit', 'The Old Soldier', and 'Nelson's Preparations for Battle' take us closer towards Glasgow's British nationalist sentiments. In the wake of Walter Scott's *Waverley* sensation, Dugald Moore's poems tried to encapsulate the Covenanter and Jacobite wars as well as more recent affairs including some verses on the death and legacy of Napoleon. Macarthur, working in this same medley of sentimentalism and servitude, dedicates 'The Hero and his Sword' to one of Glasgow's most commemorated sons, Sir John Moore of Corunna. As we have noted previously, Sir John Moore (1761–1809) was the son of the Glasgow Enlightenment figure Dr John Moore. Born in the Trongate, young John (or, as he was known in his family – Jack) went on to attend the Glasgow Grammar School but moved with his family to London at the age of ten. Following a short-lived and uneventful political career, Moore finally entered active service in 1788. Stationed originally in Chatham, England, Moore's military career took him to Gibraltar, Corsica, St Lucia, Ireland, Minorca, Egypt, the Mediterranean, Sweden and the Iberian Peninsula. He occasionally returned to the family home in Clifford Street, London, but was better pleased on the front than being stationed at home.[38] Though he never once returned to Scotland since setting off as a boy, his heroism and valour in the theatre of war led to the enshrinement of Moore as the quintessential Glasgow hero.

Moore's death in Corunna became one of the most symbolic instances of the ultimate sacrifice made by British soldiers in service to their country, prompting a tradition of celebration and commemoration at a national level. It was during an evacuation of his troops – left bewildered by a lack of Spanish support – from an 'overwhelming French force' that Moore ordered a counter-attack and was struck by a cannon shot. It was clear that the wounds were fatal and he was carried from the battlefield to the soldiers' quarters. In his final moments he said, 'I hope the people of England will be satisfied. I hope my country will do me justice.' He was buried nearby the next morning, his body shrouded in a military cloak.[39] A temporary memorial was installed and was soon converted from a wooden to a marble structure complete with a Latin inscription. Meanwhile the fame of Moore's memory was accelerated by contemporary artists and writers. The moment at which he received the wound, and his burial, were frequently sketched or painted in the decades following his death. T. Sutherland's *Death of Sir John Moore* (1815) and George Jones's *The Burial of Sir John Moore after Corunna* (c.1834) are two of the best examples, with the latter bearing some compositional resemblance to Benjamin West's *The Death of General Wolfe* (1770). The conjectural details of these scenes are necessary to capture the *image* of the event and to install cultural memory. For instance we know that Moore's burial service took place on the morning of 17 January 1809, yet some scenes, including Jones's, depict the soldiers burying Moore *on the spot* around midnight. Though it makes for a more compelling and memorable symbol of bravery and youth, it shows the power of images in transmitting and creating memories, sometimes at the expense of truth.

Indeed, where creativity is concerned there is always the issue of accuracy giving way to symbolism. Let us return to Macarthur's poem 'The Hero and His Sword'. Published in 1842 the poem is accompanied by a short paragraph taken from Southey's *History of the Peninsular War* (1823) from which the title is apparently taken:

> In raising him up, his sword, hanging on the wounded side, touched his arm [...] Captain Hardinge began to unbuckle it, but the General [i.e. Moore] said in his usual tone and manner, and in a distinct voice,— 'It is as well as it is; I should rather it should go out of the field with me.'[40]

Note the battlefield detail (the hanging sword) and the strength of Moore's voice despite having received a fatal wound. That he acknowledges death and wants to take his sword with him adds volumes to his heroism, so much so that Macarthur imaginatively extends his dying speech to two full stanzas, beginning: 'Nay, take not my sword from my wounded side,'

> Though 'tis drenched with its owner's gore;
> Its blade hath been often with life-blood dyed,
> But ne'er left on the field before.

> It hath served me well in perils past,
> Although now it hath failed to save;
> Of our battles we both have fought the last,—
> It shall lie with me in the grave![41]

Before taking on the perspective of the mourning citizen:

> He said, and the words drew many a tear
> From the hardy warrior band
> Who bore that chief and his sword to the rear,—
> They were sons of his native land.
> [...]
> Oh, might he but bear to his birth-place sleep,
> By his own majestic Clyde,
> Where they and their children could vigils keep,
> His place of sepulture beside![42]

More precisely we can pinpoint a Glasgow-centric mourner here. Macarthur, playing off the valorised image of the dying soldier, reinstates the romantic symbol of the River Clyde from poetic tradition and imagines the people of Glasgow remembering Moore *collectively*. She often draws on the home-versus-foreign soil dichotomy when discussing his 'early, though glorious doom', emphasising his sword and belongings as 'relics [...] in a stranger's tomb'.[43] And the footnote to Charles Wolfe's more famous song on the 'Burial of Sir John Moore' reveals an attempt on Macarthur's part to elevate Glasgow in the story of British imperialism. Wolfe's song, dated around 1814, has the soldiers digging their graves with their bayonets 'by the struggling moonbeam's misty light / and the lanthorn dimly burning'.[44] That they 'left him alone with his glory' has become a common phrase now associated with Moore, and undoubtedly helps construct the notion of the Soldier Hero for a British audience.

Graham Dawson was one of the first to interrogate this idea in his seminal work *Soldier Heroes* (1994), revealing the formative processes that linked the public's understanding of war to the duty of memory. Dawson shows how Sir Henry Havelock was exalted through a growing celebration of Empire and how the site of his death in Lucknow, like Moore's in Corunna, inscribed an 'imaginative landscape of adventure' in people's minds.[45] These images of bravery on foreign soil are followed up and commemorated by rituals in public life at home. Using Benedict Anderson's theory of the imagined community Dawson draws a line between the collective consumption of war-related news in the British press and the emergence of 'national recognition and commemoration'.[46] This process leads to what Paula Murphy calls the 'deification' of exalted heroes on public streets. In her book *Nineteenth-Century Irish Sculpture* (2010) Murphy shows how British Soldier Heroes such as Nelson and Wellington were enshrined with towering monuments in Dublin. Together with royal statues – *William of Orange*, 1701 and *George II*, 1758 – this new set of monuments affected the cultural memory of Dublin, boosting its reputation in the early nineteenth century as the Second City of the Empire. This 'title' would soon be contested by Glasgow, Liverpool, and later Birmingham. As with Dublin, the conglomeration of royal equestrian monuments and Soldier Heroes in Glasgow cast the city as a loyal and imperial centre. Indeed, the Protestant Ascendency brought about an age of commemoration placing Dublin on a similar plane to cities like Glasgow and Edinburgh, keen to inscribe their place in the British Empire.[47]

In terms of memory we might also consider how war inevitably shapes the pseudo-official identity of a nation. In his article on war discourse Ross Wilson (2015) examines how certain phrases first used in wartime news reporting – 'over the top', 'no man's land', 'in the trenches' – have been and are being recycled in popular culture and politics, thus keeping the memory of that specific war alive.[48] Wilson also shows how the canonisation of Siegfried Sassoon and Wilfred Owen as *the* poets of the trenches made it easy for their work to be 'mobilised' by political parties and the state during commemorative events.[49] But this osmosis of the Soldier Hero in the modern era has a completely different social and intellectual base. We have to remember that the move away from the glory toward the 'pity' of war – to quote Owen – came hand in hand with the decline of the British Empire, whereas the statesmen of the Georgian and Victorian periods promoted and relied upon the continuation of the Empire.

As we have seen, the ideas and images associated with war are often preserved in poetry. Simon Bainbridge shows us this in *British Poetry and the Revolutionary and Napoleonic Wars* (2003). For instance, the author draws our attention to Mark Twain's writings and his take on the unprecedented success of Walter Scott's historical fiction which produced, in some instances, a collapsing together of generational and cultural memory wherein 'the genuine and wholesome civilization of the nineteenth century is curiously confused and commingled with the Walter Scott Middle-Age sham civilization'.[50] This was not the last time that Scott was blamed for romanticised nationalism.[51] Indeed, the historical range of his work is a curious point of departure for anyone writing about memory. As Caroline McCracken-Flesher puts it, Scott had the ability to create a romantic distance or haze in his work that made memory all the more pertinent. Whether writing about 'events "sixty years since" (the 1745 rebellion) or only yesterday (Waterloo), his perspective was historicist.'[52] In 'The Field of Waterloo' (1815) Scott offers a 552-line poem where the natural beauty of the scene has returned to prevent an outright desolation of memory. The 'peasant's scythe' is juxtaposed with the 'bayonet', and fallen 'heroes' are likened to 'ripened grain [. . .] piled high as autumn shocks'. Described once as 'Bloody' and once as 'Immortal', Waterloo becomes a place of great bravery and great beauty, a *lieu de mémoire* of 'Britain's memory' and 'immortal claims!'[53] Like many poets in her day Macarthur was working in the tradition of Romanticism outlined by the likes of Scott as an integral factor in national taste and style. Her direct praise of Moore as a subject of remembrance seems to be influenced by the likes of Felicia Hemans who, incidentally, commemorates Moore herself in 'To my Younger Brother, on his return from Spain, after the fatal retreat under Sir John Moore, and the Battle of Corunna' (1812). Whether the site (i.e. the battlefield) or the person (i.e. Moore) are central to the poet's gaze, we see an overarching narrative of British pride and remembrance. Poetry like this links personal loss (such as Hemans's brother) to a renowned or notable loss (like Moore), which eventually sets the tone for remembrance as a dutiful act of collective mourning.

But to understand Glasgow's role in this more fully we must return to the city's principal civic square, in which Moore's statue was the first. It was described as 'the Pantheon of Glasgow' in Thomas Somerville's book on George Square (1891). Indeed we may find it difficult to imagine its origins as 'a marsh, surrounded by meadowlands and kitchen gardens' during Charles Edward Stuart's brief and unwelcome visit to Glasgow in 1745.[54] It was not until 1781 when the square was laid out simply 'to mark its boundary' following the ongoing development and sale of merchants' mansions in the area. The 'unabated' western development of Glasgow from that year through the nineteenth century saw new streets being named after royalty, politicians, bankers, provosts, lairds, and imperial efforts at sea and on the battlefield (including Corunna Street in Glasgow's West End).[55] Moore's statue in George Square is special not only because it was the first, but because of the speed in which the public subscription was filled for John Flaxman to begin work (see Figure 16). According to Cleland the people of Glasgow ('not confined to any class of the community') put up £4,000 within a few days of the news of Moore's death. We might also consider the symbolism of the final work: larger than life, cast in his cloak, and holding his famous sword. In a remarkable statement of victory the whole was 'made of brass cannon, taken from the enemy'.[56] In a lecture in Edinburgh in 1850, the artist Patric Park compared Flaxman's statue of Moore to the ancient statue of Phocion in the Vatican. The poise, cloak, and gripping left hand of both are indeed very similar.[57] That this image of antiquity has been transferred onto a British Soldier Hero makes it a more powerful example,

Figure 16 Sir John Moore statue, George Square, Glasgow. Photo: the author.

harking back to the invention of commemorative statues while revealing the fragility of memory and place. We also find monuments to Moore in the dramatic setting of St Paul's Cathedral, London, cast in his last moments being laid down gently by a group of mythic figures (1815), and on a stele in Kent (1909), near the site of one of his home bases.

In George Square, Moore's statue stood alone for just over ten years until James Watt's statue was placed nearby in 1830. In an 1825 issue of *The Northern Looking Glass* Moore's statue is seen in a less than ceremonial light. In the foreground young boys are throwing ropes around the statue and pelting it with mud, in the background women are washing their clothes and flipping sheets. All the while a pig rests wistfully on a heap. Caricatured though it is, this scene tells us something about the novelty of portrait statues in the city. Until then the only portrait statues in Glasgow were those depicting George and Thomas Hutcheson (both *c.*1649–57) and William of Orange (1734).[58] One year after Horatio Nelson's death in the Battle of Trafalgar (1805) a large obelisk monument was erected in Glasgow Green. This initiated a quick-response civic duty to commemorate Soldier Heroes in the city, but its design (by David Hamilton) speaks more to the classical period than the nineteenth century.[59] During a thunderstorm in August 1810 the obelisk was struck by lightning and sustained heavy damage. In the newspapers it was reported that a guard had to be put in place 'to keep at a distance the thoughtless or too daring spectators', while a poem by Mr J. Graham likened the resilience of the monument ('which Heaven's own fire hath trac'd') to Nelson himself:

> As nature's sculpture, trench'd by forky leven!
> As characters engrav'd by bolts from Heaven!
> Inscrib'd by fate. Leave then the unrivall'd plan;
> The monument and emblem of the man.[60]

The moment of the lightning strike was 'captured' in a painting by the Glasgow artist John Knox, ushering in a rather dramatic age of military monumentality in the city (see Figure 17). It should also be noted that Glasgow's monument to Nelson was the first on the British Isles, followed by a large column in Dublin (1808–9) in Sackville Street, and bronze statues in Birmingham (1809) and Liverpool (1813) which were the first publicly subscribed monuments in those cities. The Nelson tower in Edinburgh (1816) is over ten metres shorter than the Glasgow

Figure 17 John Knox, *The Nelson Monument Struck by Lightning* (c.1810). © The Hunterian, University of Glasgow.

obelisk, but its position at the highest point of Calton Hill gives it the highest vantage point of all (171 metres above sea level). The London column, which Paula Murphy notes for its striking similarity to the one in Dublin, was finished last (1843).[61] This brief cross-referencing of the response time of these cities in their commemoration of Nelson, the first Soldier Hero of the nineteenth century, reveals a sudden and growing popularity in public sculpture and a diversity of style and intent.

It also shows the fragility of these powerful structures when it comes to memory, especially in the comparison of Glasgow and Dublin. A bolt of lightning might have damaged the Glasgow obelisk, but the Dublin column no longer stands. The 1916 Easter Rising was commenced from the General Post Office, in full view of the Nelson column. Ten years later Sackville Street was renamed O'Connell Street in honour of the Irish Emancipator Daniel O'Connell.[62] And as the fiftieth anniversary of the Rising approached, explosives were used to destroy the column and reduce the once-proud symbol of the British Empire to half its size, *sans* Nelson. The potential for cultural memory to play a major part in emerging political and social powers is emphasised in examples like this. And yet in other similar sites we can see how memory is as powerful as it is unstable. The Marian Column erected in Prague's Old Town Square in 1650 was destroyed by a rioting crowd in 1918. As Cynthia Paces explains, the column 'originally commemorated the Habsburg defeat of Sweden and the subsequent Swedish retreat from Prague at the end of the Thirty Years' War'. At the beginning of the twentieth century in the midst of new social strife and nationalism the baroque column took on new meanings, with 'most nineteenth-century Czechs' seeing it instead as a commemoration of 'the Habsburg's victory over Bohemian Protestant nobles at the Battle of White Mountain'.[63] In this 'triumphalist' light the column came under attack and was destroyed.[64] After the formation of the Marian Column Restoration Society (1990), decades of debate with atheists, Protestants and other groups ensued. Eventually, on 4 June 2020, a replica perfectly matching the original Baroque column was reinstalled. As we will see below, the social context of these public monuments often reveal much about the cultural memory of a city.

Though not the first Soldier Hero symbol in Glasgow (Nelson), the Moore monument was the city's first nineteenth-century portrait statue. But as George Square filled up with more portraits (work on the last, of William Ewart Gladstone, commenced in 1899 and finished in 1902) Moore's star never faltered. In the 1840s Scottish and English newspapers make reference to the Sir John Moore Tavern facing George Square.[65] Since at least 1844 there was a 'U.O.O.F Lodge' named the

'Loyal Sir John Moore's' in Glasgow.[66] A merchant's ship named *The Sir John Moore* set sail from Glasgow to Bombay in 1860, and in the *Glasgow Herald* seven years later we find for sale a 'RELIC FROM SIR JOHN MOORE, OF GLASGOW: HIS CAMP BEDSTEAD, which he used until his last moments at Corunna'.[67] In this last example especially we find the closest Glasgow comparison with the likes of Burns, Scott, and other Romantic writers whose names became part of relic-hunting and memory-making in the modern period. In the National Army Museum, London, some of Moore's items are stored and exhibited, including a General Officer's sword, a telescope and a watch ('taken from the body of General Sir John Moore after his death'). The ephemeral markers such as the ship and the camp bed help us understand how Moore's memory was maintained in the short term, but when we cross the line from collective to cultural memory we have no choice but to interrogate what the permanent markers, such as monuments, mean now.

Moore's statue in George Square, once alone and therefore significant in its own way, is now surrounded by eleven others. This 'set' does not constitute a single meaning, it is not an exclusive showcase of Glasgow's famous sons: half of the statues commemorate people born outside Glasgow. With the exception of Burns (Alloway) and Scott (Edinburgh) the site helps Glasgow position itself as an integral part of the British state. Royalty (Victoria and Albert) and politicians (Peel and Gladstone) share a platform with Glaswegian men of science (Watt, Graham), of trade (Oswald), of letters (Campbell), and of war (Moore, Baron Clyde). In 1888 Queen Victoria opened the colossal City Chambers building which dominates the east side of the square, and in 1924 the lion-flanked Cenotaph was unveiled to commemorate the fallen of the First World War. It now serves as the principal focal point in Glasgow during Remembrance services, which, unlike the other statues, serves as an 'active site of memory' in the sense that ceremonies maintain its purpose. For Jay Winter, sites like the Cenotaph are so widespread in France and Britain – 'in every city, in every town, in every village' – that public remembrance is easily achieved.[68] In the moments before it was unveiled the Cenotaph was draped in a Union flag, and the same flag tends to feature in and around the site during Remembrance services. The connections between symbols of British national pride (in a Scottish context) is an intriguing point of departure here because the standard flag of the City Chambers today is the Saltire. At certain moments the flag changes to commemorate an event. For instance, the Union flag was in place during the sixtieth anniversary of the Queen's coronation (2013) and, controversially, the flag of Palestine was raised as a gesture of support during the ongoing conflict in Gaza (2014). Radically different in their reception, these recent tropes of symbolism take us toward Michael Billig's theories outlined in *Banal Nationalism* (1995), in which he stresses the difference between 'routine flags' and 'those that seem to call attention to themselves and their symbolic message'.[69] For example, Christopher Whatley's study of Burns monuments in a Unionist context points out the Masonic and pro-British overtones during an otherwise Scottish foundation-stone-laying event in Kilmarnock in 1878, and the Union flag covering the Dundee Burns monument before its unveiling in 1880.[70] While few would question the suitability of the Union flag during commemoration services for war dead, the Saltire/Union flag dichotomy on civic buildings and other monuments across Scotland continues to spark (often furious) debate.

Yet, in many ways sites like George Square are arguably 'flattened out'. No longer in any real flux, our view of the square is 'complete' with the City Chambers and the thirteen monuments (twelve portraits and the Cenotaph). In this stasis we gain an idea of what Glasgow means, what it is *for*. But we also lose a great amount of detail with this flatter view. Staying with the Soldier Hero for the moment, we might see Moore and Baron Clyde as two halves of the imperial story. Moore was killed in the same war in which Clyde first served in uniform. Suitably, they stand side by side on the southern edge of the square. But we are only seeing the top layer of their cultural memory. Beneath this layer – out of view, in the archives, in bookshops – we find the morbid gristle of imperialism.

In *The Life of Lieutenant-General Sir John Moore* (1833) by Moore's brother and *The Diary of Sir John Moore* (1904) one can read about his contact with the 1796 slave insurrection in St Lucia. Through Moore's letters the editors portray a distressed-but-diligent commander quelling the barbaric threat of armed 'negroes', or 'Brigands'. In one instance Moore admits he 'cried like a child' when he learned that his mother was sick with worry about his wellbeing. In the same letter he describes his movements and attacks on the Brigands' supplies: 'I wish to embark every black I take, or who surrenders. Their hatred to us and attachment to the Republic, which they think had given them liberty, is great.'[71] At almost every turn of the St Lucia period, readers are reminded of two things: that the black corps have the advantage of being acclimatised to the conditions of the island, and that the Brigands were essentially unpredictable in their rampage. 'I have been forced to adopt other violent measures,' Moore admits, 'which at first I had flattered myself would not have been necessary; but true republicanism seems, at least in this country, to be an excuse for every species of treachery, want of faith, and even of common honesty.'[72] In passages like this Moore assumes the credentials of the ideal Briton (i.e. 'faith', 'honesty') and writes not as an individual but as a conduit of the Empire to justify his actions. That Moore reinstated slavery and continued to suppress the black population on the island is justified in these books by the threat of the French and the emotional admissions found in his letters. Michael Morris describes this as 'a remarkable example of imperial tensions between human sympathy eventually overrun by devotion to military duty'.[73] This side of Moore is not visible today, like so much of the Glasgow connection with slavery and Empire.

By comparison, Dawson takes an interesting approach in his work on Havelock by quantifying the periods of the soldier's life which receive the most attention in the edited *Memoirs*, essentially counting how his Heroic qualities were promoted.[74] After Moore's skirmishes with the Brigands in St Lucia we might consider Baron Clyde's leading role in the suppression of the Indian Rebellion in 1857. The fortified villa Sikandar Bagh, in Lucknow, was the setting of a furious battle in which over 2,000 'mutineers' were slaughtered by the 93rd Highlanders and 4th Punjab Infantry. Clyde's tactical awareness and bravery are portrayed in vivid detail in Archibald Forbes's biography (1895), but so too is his apparent dismay at the unrelenting bloodshed, giving us yet again an exemplary all-round Soldier Hero.[75] This need for biographers to balance the scales of their subject's morality is part of the conditioning process which affects cultural memory. That Moore and Clyde were 'men of war' is an important part of their legacy and should feature as a leading qualifier in our discussions of the Empire and its commemoration in Glasgow. Nonetheless, in penetrating the layers of memory (portraits, statues, street names, objects, biographies) concerning such men we can encounter the systematic racial oppression and imperial tyranny of the Empire.

In 2017 Mélina Valdelievre started a petition to remove the 'racist, colonial statue' of British soldier Frederick Sleigh (1st Earl) Roberts (1832–1914). Her reasoning – that Roberts 'burned farms and created concentration camps for Boers to force them to submit'[76] – is based on sound historical accounts, but is tellingly absent from his biography in the *Oxford Dictionary of National Biography*.[77] These aspects of Roberts's life are also missing, perhaps more understandably, from Ray McKenzie's brief biography of the soldier in his book on Glasgow sculpture. Instead, a fascinating exchange of memory is outlined by McKenzie, wherein around 4,000 volunteers distributed 250,000 souvenirs of Roberts on 26 December 1914, each for a small fee that would help cover the cost of the monument.[78] That Valdelievre's petition to remove the statue closed with only 108 supporters tells us something about the stasis of cultural memory. Not only are people arguably disengaged with who Roberts is or was, but those who care tend to rely on the positive, heroic elements that flank the pedestal of the statue itself.

We should concede that our ability to shine a light on the atrocities committed in the name of Britain is an advantage allowed to us by our distance from the subject, and that with the progression of social theory and technology we have further critical advantages over those living during the eighteenth and nineteenth centuries. In the guide books and light histories printed during the height of Empire we can analyse language to glimpse a collective frame of mind. In J. A. Hammerton's *Sketches from Glasgow* (1893) the author takes us on a walk around George Square. Pausing at the statues of Moore and Clyde, Hammerton says, 'War has naturally been the subject of our thoughts what time we have been worshipping at the shrines of these two heroes of the battlefield.'[79] This essentially confirms the Soldier Hero status of these men while elucidating something of the seemingly collective thought, or memory, which defined them. As Whatley notes in his review of Dundee's public memorials, Glasgow's relatively strong tradition of hero worship was typical of the movement sweeping Europe in the nineteenth century.[80] Near the Moore and Clyde statues in George Square we have the Cenotaph: the focal point of the exaltation of the Soldier Hero in Glasgow. The monument was occasionally guarded by Unionists during the spate of protests in June 2020, but we will return to those in the Conclusion. Wreaths of poppies are also laid by the Highland Light Infantry Memorial for the Boer War (1906) and the Cameronians Memorial (1924) in Kelvingrove Park.[81] The sombre rituals surrounding these modern monuments separate them to an extent from other nineteenth- and twentieth-century memorials around which no rituals take place. The Australian artist Will Longstaff captures the essence of this in his paintings *Menin Gate at Midnight* (1927) and *Immortal Shrine* – also known as *Eternal Silence* (1928) – in which the ghosts of soldiers are seen marching in and around these monuments as if conjured by collective remembering.

Yet for all this memory-making Glasgow has an extremely unique and iconic statue in which purpose is completely overawed by humour and chance. In J. E. Cookson's essay (2004) on the Edinburgh and Glasgow Duke of Wellington Statues as symbols of Tory-led Unionist Nationalism in the mid nineteenth century we are reminded that Wellington never visited Scotland. It is also shown that the subscription list for Carlo Marochetti's equestrian statue (1844) was not as popular as previous public statues in Glasgow.[82] Again we see how a British hero with little (or, in this case, zero) association with Scotland was constructed as a popular figure through the reporting of English events, toasts, and festivals in Wellington's name in the Scottish press. And while Scotland's 'antipathy' to Toryism and to Wellington 'surpassed' England's, the presence of the statue in front of the Royal Exchange (previously the home of the slave-owning merchant William Cunningham, now the Gallery of Modern Art) says something about the power of the state in dictating our landscapes of memory. But, as seen on many advertisements and souvenir mugs, the Wellington statue in Glasgow is better known for its traffic cone hat than its political stance. Beginning at some point in the 1980s, the famous cone on Wellington's head has been woven into the civic identity of Glasgow. This ironic triumph of plastic over bronze reminds us how unpredictably cultural memory takes shape. As we noted above, the fragility of monuments is not their material, but the context which they are powerless to control. Who could have predicted, for example, that the bronze *Wall Street Bull* (1989), a symbol of American resilience, would be recast as a symbol of the oppressive patriarchal business world by the presence of the *Fearless Girl* sculpture (2017), standing in the bull's path?[83]

The point is that all things change to some degree. Even the objects designed to be permanent are typically uprooted, destroyed, or, if left alone, are altered by the shifting environment around them. Think of Shelley's 'Ozymandias' (1818).[84] In Glasgow's case another monument was literally created out of circumstance, eventually becoming one of the chief symbols of the city's heritage. The Finnieston Crane, erected in 1931, stands at 175 feet and once had a capacity of 175 tons. The decline of Glasgow's manufacturing in the mid twentieth century cut short the legacy of this engineering marvel, and, although it has not been used for heavy-duty lifting since the 1980s, it has become the focal point of art installations and Glasgow's tourist sector. So prominent in the Glasgow skyline, it is nothing short of a monument to the era of shipbuilding, featuring as such in the opening ceremony of the 2014 Commonwealth Games in Glasgow. And so we recognise that the cultural memory of Glasgow was carved out not only in the form of its monuments, but in the popularisation of the city through phraseology, unofficial titles, and, most of all, as will be explored in Chapter 7, the International Exhibitions which sought to promote Glasgow to the world.

NOTES

1. Mary Macarthur (as 'Mrs. James Macarthur'), *Necropolis: An Elegy, and other poems* (Glasgow, David Bryce, 1842), 71.
2. C. A. Oakley, *The Second City* (London and Glasgow: Blackie and Son, Limited, 1946), 55.
3. Besides the Mossman statue in George Square, there is a bronze plaque to mark the place where his house once stood in the High Street, facing the site of the Old College. Outside Scotland Campbell has a statue at Poet's Corner in Westminster Abbey.
4. See <https://www.scottsabbotsford.com/history> (last accessed 30 August 2020).
5. Beth S. Wright, quoting Charles Nodier (1823), in '"Seeing with the Painter's Eye": Sir Walter Scott's Challenge to Nineteenth-Century Art', in Murray Pittock, ed., *The Reception of Sir Walter Scott in Europe* (London and New York: Bloomsbury, 2007), 293–312 (303).
6. William Howitt, *Homes and Haunts of the Most Eminent British Poets* (London: George Routledge & Sons, 1877), 488.
7. Nicola J. Watson, *The Literary Tourist: Readers and Place in Romantic & Victorian Britain* (Basingstoke and New York: Palgrave Macmillan, 2006), 13.
8. Ibid., 33.
9. Harald Hendrix, 'The Early Modern Invention of Literary Tourism: Petrarch's Houses in France and Italy', in Harald Hendrix, ed., *Writers' Houses and the Making of Memory* (New York: Routledge, 2008), 15–30 (15–16).
10. J. Logie Robertson, *The Complete Poetical Works of Thomas Campbell* (London: John Frowde, 1907), 369–70.
11. Quoted in John L. Hardie, 'Thomas Campbell and Glasgow', *Old Glasgow Club Transactions, Volume VII, Session 1933–1934* (Glasgow: Aird and Coghill Ltd, 1934), 18–28 (22).
12. My thanks to Dr Kelsey Jackson Williams, who brought this particular verse to my attention. For reference, the earlier appearance of this verse in Latin is in *Britannia* (London, 1607), 696; the English translation here from the 1695 edition, p. 918.
13. Arthur Johnston, *Poemata Omnia* (Middleburg, 1642), 433–4.
14. George Eyre-Todd, ed., *The Glasgow Poets: Their Lives and Poems* (Paisley: Alexander Gardner, 1906 [1903]), 2.
15. *The Poetical Works of William Wordsworth. A New Edition. In Six Volumes. Vol. III.* (London: Edward Moxon, 1837), 160.
16. *The Eclectic Review MDCCCXLII: January–June, New Series, Vol. XI* (London: Thomas Ward & Co., 1842), 715.
17. Allan Ramsay, *Poems* (Edinburgh: Thomas Ruddiman, 1721), 364.
18. Ibid., 346.

19. This concept of 'the Pentland *locus amoenus*' was introduced in conjunction with Ramsay's chief play, *The Gentle Shepherd* (1725) by Murray Pittock in his book *Scottish and Irish Romanticism* (Oxford: Oxford University Press, 2008), 53.
20. James Arbuckle, *Glotta: A Poem* (Glasgow: William Duncan, 1721), 21.
21. James Arbuckle, *Glotta; or, The Clyde: A Poem* (London: Henry Reynell, 1810), 3.
22. Ibid., 4.
23. Ibid., 7.
24. Erkki Huhtamo, 'Global Glimpses for Local Realities: The Moving Panorama, a Forgotten Mass Medium of the 19th Century' (2002), 10 n. 26, <http://gebseng.com/media_archeology/reading_materials/Erkki_Huhtamo-Moving_Panorama.pdf> (last accessed 20 November 2019).
25. Ibid., 2.
26. The first edition of 1783 is reproduced in Richard B. Sher's chapter 'Images of Glasgow in Late Eighteenth-Century Popular Poetry', in Andrew Hook and Richard B. Sher, eds, *The Glasgow Enlightenment* (Phantassie, East Lothian: Tuckwell Press, 1995), 190–213; the 1803 version was published in London: <http://xtf.lib.virginia.edu/xtf/view?docId=chadwyck_ep/uvaGenText/tei/chep_2.1234.xml> (last accessed 30 August 2020).
27. On display during the 2018 Charles Rennie Mackintosh exhibition at the Kelvingrove Art Gallery and Museum, Glasgow Museums: PP.2018.31.
28. Elvira Anna Phipps, *Memorials of Clutha; or, Pencillings of the Clyde* (London: Smith, Elder and Co., 1842), 35.
29. Charles Mackenzie, *Interesting and Remarkable Places; with Historical & Topographical Descriptions* (London: John Reynolds, 1849) 29–30.
30. Knox never lived in Glasgow, and Mackenzie's companion text to the engraving does admit that placing the alleged residence had 'been subject of much dispute.' The only evidence that Knox had been in Glasgow is derived from his signing off a letter to Archibald Campbell, 5th Earl of Argyll, 'in haste from Glasgow, 7 May 1563.' cf. W. C. Dickson, ed., *John Knox's History of the Reformation in Scotland*, vol. 2 (London: Nelson, 1949), 76. My thanks to Jane Dawson, Professor Emerita of Reformation History at the University of Edinburgh for helping me with this question.
31. John M'Ure, *The History of Glasgow: A New Edition* (Glasgow: Hutchison and Brookman, 1830), 119.
32. Anne O'Connor, *Florence: City and Memory in the Nineteenth Century* (Florence: Città di Vita, 2008), 7.
33. George Blair, *Biographic and Descriptive Sketches of Glasgow Necropolis* (Glasgow: Maurice Ogle & Son, 1857), vii–viii.
34. Ibid., viii.
35. Ibid., 9.
36. Dugald Moore, *The Bridal Night; The First Poet; and other Poems* (Glasgow: Blackie, Fullarton & Co., 1831), 247.

37. Mary Macarthur, *Necropolis: An Elegy, and other poems* (Glasgow: David Bryce, 1842), 14.
38. John Sweetman, 'Moore, Sir John (1761–1809)', *Oxford Dictionary of National Biography*, <https://doi.org/10.1093/ref:odnb/19132> (last accessed 30 August 2020).
39. Ibid.
40. Macarthur, *Necropolis*, 81.
41. Ibid.
42. Ibid., 82.
43. Ibid.
44. Jon Stallworthy, ed., *The New Oxford Book of War Poetry* (Oxford: Oxford University Press, 2014), 86.
45. Graham Dawson, *Soldier Heroes: British Adventure, Empire and the Imagining of Masculinities* (London and New York: Routledge, 1994), 104.
46. Ibid., 114–15.
47. Paula Murphy, *Nineteenth-Century Irish Sculpture: Native Genius Reaffirmed* (New Haven and London: Yale University Press, 2010), 13.
48. Ross J. Wilson, 'Still fighting in the trenches: "War Discourse" and the memory of the First World War in Britain', *Memory Studies*, 8:4 (2015), 454–69 (457).
49. Ibid., 464.
50. Simon Bainbridge, *British Poetry and the Revolutionary and Napoleonic Wars: Visions of Conflict* (Oxford: Oxford University Press, 2003), 226.
51. Scott (and Burns) were famously lambasted as 'sham bards of a sham nation' in his poem 'Scotland 1941', cf. P. Butter, ed., *Edwin Muir: The Complete Poems* (Aberdeen: Association for Scottish Literary Studies, 1991), 100.
52. Caroline McCracken-Flesher, 'Future Scotts: The Aliens have Landed', The Bottle Imp, 16, <https://www.thebottleimp.org.uk/2014/11/future-scotts-the-aliens-have-landed/> (last accessed 30 August 2020).
53. Walter Scott, *The Field of Waterloo; a poem: second edition* (Edinburgh: Archibald Constable, 1815).
54. Thomas Somerville, *George Square, Glasgow; and the lives of those whom its statues commemorate* (Glasgow: John N. MacKinlay, 1891), 9.
55. Ibid., 12–13.
56. James Cleland, *Enumeration of the Inhabitants of the City of Glasgow and County of Lanark. Second Edition* (Glasgow: John Smith and Son, 1832), 267.
57. *Caledonian Mercury* (Edinburgh, 24 October 1850), 1. This comparison is no mistake. Flaxman had seen the statue of Phocion before he began working on Moore's monument. His sketch of it was reproduced in *The Saturday Magazine*, No. 583 (London: July, 1841), 1.

58. This excludes the bust of Zachary Boyd, fixed in the court of the old College campus of the University of Glasgow.
59. Edinburgh's commemorative response time is similar to Glasgow's in the sense that royalty and politicians are commemorated much sooner than artists, writers, etc. Cf. Craig Lamont, 'Allan Ramsay and Edinburgh: Commemoration in the City of Forgetting', *Scottish Literary Review*, 10:1 (2018), 117–37.
60. *The Weekly Entertainer: or, Agreeable and Instructive Repository*, 24 September 1810 (Sherborne: R. Goadby), 776.
61. Murphy, *Nineteenth-Century Irish Sculpture*, 18.
62. W. N. Osborough, *Law and the Emergence of Modern Dublin: A Litigation Topography for a Capital City* (Dublin: Irish Academic Press in association with the Irish Legal History Society, 1996), 46.
63. Cynthia Paces, 'The Fall and Rise of Prague's Marian Column', *Radical History Review*, 79 (2001), 141–55 (141).
64. Alfred Thomas, *Prague Palimpsest: Writing, Memory, and the City* (Chicago: University of Chicago Press, 2010), 4.
65. Such as in *The Morning Post*, London, 21 February 1844, 7. In Argyle Street, Glasgow now stands the Sir John Moore (Wetherspoons) bar.
66. This might mean United Order of Odd Fellows: *Accounts and Papers [of the House of Commons]: Forty-Four Volumes, Trade, &c. continues, (Friendly Societies and Trade Unions)* Vol. LXIX. (1876), 510 (number 205).
67. The Sir John Moore ship, from Glasgow to Bombay, advertised in the *Glasgow Herald*, 27 August 1860; the camp bed in the same newspaper on 26 July 1867.
68. Jay Winter, 'Sites of Memory', in Susannah Radstone and Bill Schwarz, eds, *Memory: Histories, Theories, Debates* (New York: Fordham University Press, 2010), 312–24 (319).
69. Michael Billig, *Banal Nationalism* (London: Sage, 2013 [1995]), 41.
70. Christopher A. Whatley, 'Contested Commemorations: Robert Burns, Urban Scotland and Scottish Nationality in the Nineteenth Century', in Gerard Carruthers and Colin Kidd, eds, *Literature and Union: Scottish Texts, British Contexts* (Oxford: Oxford University Press, 2018), 221–43 (238).
71. James Carrick Moore, *The Life of Lieutenant-General Sir John Moore, K. B.*, vol. I. (London: John Murray, 1833), 143–6.
72. Ibid., 154.
73. Michael Morris, 'Multi-directional Memory, Many-Headed Hydras and Glasgow', in Katie Donington, Ryan Hanley, Jessica Moody, eds, *Britain's History and Memory of Transatlantic Slavery: Local Nuances of a 'National Sin'*, (Liverpool: Liverpool University Press, 2016), 195–215 (213).
74. Dawson, *Soldier Heroes*, 131–2.

75. Archibald Forbes, *Colin Campbell Lord Clyde* (London: Macmillan and Co., 1895), 129.
76. See <https://www.change.org/p/glasgow-city-council-remove-the-racist-colonial-statue-of-frederick-roberts-in-the-kelvingrove-park> (last accessed 30 August 2020).
77. For Roberts's involvement in these atrocities, cf. James S. Olson and Robert Shadle, eds, *Historical Dictionary of the British Empire A–J* (Westport, CT: Greenwood Press, 1996), 46; Adrian Gilbert, *The Encyclopedia of Warfare: From Earliest Time to the Present Day* (London: Fitzroy Dearborn, 2000), 205. For the *Oxford Dictionary of National Biography* on Roberts see Brian Robson, 'Roberts, Frederick Sleigh, first Earl Roberts (1832–1914)', <https://doi.org/10.1093/ref:odnb/35768> (last accessed 20 November 2019).
78. Ray McKenzie et al., *Public Sculpture of Glasgow: Public Sculpture of Britain, Vol. 5* (Liverpool: Liverpool University Press, 2002), 232.
79. J. A. Hammerton, *Sketches from Glasgow* (Glasgow and Edinburgh: John Menzies & Co., 1893), 101.
80. Christopher A. Whatley, 'Contesting Memory and Public Places: Albert Square and Dundee's Pantheon of Heroes', in Christopher A. Whatley, Bob Harris, and Louise Miskell, eds, *Victorian Dundee: Image and Realities*, second edition (Dundee: Dundee University Press, 2011 [2000]), 173–96 (174).
81. The Boer War memorial was vandalised in February 2019. Both of the Soldier's feet were hammered off and the face was badly damaged. The memorial was restored in the summer of the same year. It is unclear whether the vandals were making a point with this statue or if the damage was mindless.
82. J. E. Cookson, 'The Edinburgh and Glasgow Duke of Wellington Statues: Early Nineteenth-Century Unionist Nationalism as a Tory Project', *The Scottish Historical Review* 83:205, Part 1 (2004), 23–40 (27).
83. The removal of the *Fearless Girl* prompted new discussion on the issues it raised, as reported in *The Guardian*, 28 November 2018, <https://www.theguardian.com/us-news/2018/nov/28/new-york-fearless-girl-charging-bull-wall-street> (last accessed 30 August 2020).
84. Percy Bysshe Shelley, 'Ozymandias', *The Examiner* (London: 11 January 1818), 24.

7

The Great Exhibitions: 1888–1938

We have seen how self-reflective literature portrayed the city as a proud and growing metropolis and how the consecration of war heroes in verse was made permanent in monuments. Following this first phase of post-Enlightenment commemorative practice we witness the growth of designated phrases, markers and verbal associations that strive to uphold Glasgow's status. Our review of civic poetry revealed a tradition of boosterism via the literal growth of the city in its architecture and the always inspiring River Clyde. These landmark images became vehicles for poets to write about Glasgow's worth to trade, commerce and empire. But when exactly did Glasgow become known as the 'Second City of the Empire'? Few histories of the city are written without some mention of this phrase, so iconic in the golden age of industry and shipbuilding. John MacKenzie's chapter on Glasgow as an 'imperial municipality' in *Imperial Cities* (1999) is an excellent study of the city's development and self-staging in the nineteenth and twentieth centuries. MacKenzie makes the point that 'the Glasgow elite' were 'in the business of negotiating a municipal identity' by 'relentlessly pursuing the shibboleth of "Second City of the Empire" and other extravagant claims'.[1] As we will see, they achieved this by staging the city in the context of the World's Fairs (or Exhibitions) between 1888 and 1938. But the ascription of the 'Second City' had been in use for the majority of the nineteenth century.

Tom Devine has traced an early instance of the phrase to a Police Minute Book in 1825.[2] There are, however, earlier examples. Glasgow was described as 'the second city in the empire' in an account of a town meeting held in Edinburgh in December 1820.[3] In a report bemoaning foreign loans in *The Morning Chronicle* (London: 18 September 1822), Glasgow is described yet again as 'the second city in the empire', with the population of Paisley included, and the point is made that other cities such as Leeds, Manchester and Birmingham are disadvantaged by not having ample representation in the House of Commons. From this, the phrase was taken up, adapted, and more or less accepted as Glasgow's unofficial title. In an advertisement for a new bank printed in the *Caledonian Mercury* on 19 October 1843 the city is described as 'the second City in Great Britain for population and commercial enterprise'. When Victoria visited Glasgow in 1849 eager citizens lined the streets and the Tolbooth steeple boasted a large Union flag. This was the first royal visit to the city since the seventeenth century, a time when the same steeple was decorated with the heads of traitors and religious dissenters. Anticipating her visit, the *Glasgow Herald* ran some booster pieces on Glasgow, adopting a topographical approach to describe scenes the Queen might enjoy. These included 'our venerable University and Cathedral; our spacious and picturesque streets, continually crowded with an industrious and loyal population' and 'The Falls of Clyde—which usually attract a large share of the notice of tourists'. And Glasgow, the reader is reminded, is 'the second city in her dominions'.

The totems of industry and sovereignty at the heart of the Victorian era came to define Glasgow holistically, thus affecting our memory of Georgian Glasgow. Both Ann Rigney (2005) and Murray Pittock (2013) have cited Michel Foucault's principle of 'scarcity' (*loi de rareté*) as regards the construction of cultural memory. As Rigney puts it, utterances of a particular subject 'acquire a value that is relative to [its] usefulness in given situations and, *faute de mieux*, to the lack of immediate alternatives'.[4] In applying this to the historical character of Glasgow, we can point to the plenitude of Victorian aspects and the scarcity of Georgian ones. Going further, it can be argued that, rather than being the *strongest* image of Glasgow in the public – as perhaps it deserves to be – the nineteenth-century metropolis has become the *defining* image. This may be the result of the unprecedented increase in population: from 77,000 in 1801 to a staggering 762,000 in 1901. As Glasgow's population and industrial landscape expanded, the defence of its unofficial title was fortified. And as MacKenzie shows, Glasgow held on to the title until the 1920s or 1930s, 'even when decline and contraction had clearly robbed the city of such a status'.[5]

Let us remember that while this title was becoming part of Glasgow's civic vocabulary and memory the colossal statue of Knox was erected, facing the cathedral, before the famous Necropolis came into being. Indeed, Glasgow's religious identity had been its proudest civic marker for centuries and was only gradually giving way to the British imperial character that brought about the Soldier Hero. Quite often the two would converge. During the furore caused by Glasgow's emancipation societies for the rights of slaves, the city's religious identity came to be strongly foregrounded. Before images of Livingstone reading the Bible to Africans reached home, these societies were using churches and quoting scripture to further their cause, calling the national sins of slavery into question.[6] This seems to convey an increase in tolerance and inclusivity in Glasgow, but sectarian tensions still pervaded public life. Take the example of an Orange procession in the city on 12 July 1822, when a number of Catholics confronted an Orangeman before his fellow marchers drew swords to ward them off.[7] Broadsides and pamphlets in the 1820s also advertised meetings held in opposition to the new freedoms being allowed to Catholics by the government, and in one particularly loaded diatribe we can glimpse a throng of civic identifiers:

> Let it not be said, that the second city in the Empire, with a population of upwards of 200,000 was amongst the last, to step forward in defence of its religion [...] be not unmindful of protecting that path which your forefathers made and paved with their blood for you.[8]

In this example the wars of the Covenanters take priority over the Napoleonic wars which would come to define Glasgow's proud British stance. But the term 'Second City' is still deployed in a powerful union of imperial and religious identity to which many Glaswegians fully subscribed.

The next phase of Glasgow's nineteenth-century development allowed the expansion of the Second City and the added moniker 'Workshop of the World'. Indeed, we might think of the phrase as a link connecting the city's own commercial empire with its industrial hinterland. As R. H. Campbell says, 'Glasgow's reputation as an industrial city was not obtained by breaking from its commercial past but by building on it.'[9] If this was a study of Victorian Glasgow we might take a closer look at the trajectory charted in Campbell's study (1995) of Glasgow's lighter industries and the move towards ironworking or Christopher Whatley's *The Industrial Revolution in Scotland* (1997), in which he suggests that Glasgow's eighteenth-century merchants played a chief role in Scotland's industrialisation. The point is made that at the turn of the nineteenth century 60 per cent of Scotland's shipping fleet was based in Glasgow ports.[10] A formidable number, and an opportunity to remind ourselves how the slave economy in which Glasgow's merchant class were involved impacted the city's financial standing for generations to come. But in this chapter on commemoration we are more concerned with the ways in which the cultural memory of Glasgow's industrial and commercial 'edge' (as Whatley calls it) was first found.[11] So, we return to the Exhibitions, the showcase events where Glasgow built on its Second City status.

These World's Fairs were inaugurated in London in 1851: the Great Exhibition of the Works of Industry of All Nations held in the Crystal Palace is often seen as the first truly international stage of great societal progress. With this in mind we might say that Glasgow's debut on the international stage in 1888 was the first grand portrayal of the character of the city. There had been industrial exhibitions in the city from 1847 to 1886, 'devoted to setting the industries and manufacturers of the city in their wider global and imperial context while also displaying the products of other cultures, thereby improving and educating the working classes'.[12] But these smaller affairs were not intended as self-portraits of Glasgow. Instead, London's 1851 Exhibition was the model Glasgow could follow, showcasing itself once again as London's understudy, as the Second City. The show was set in Glasgow's West End, far from the older, overcrowded centre. Its full title was the International Exhibition of Science, Art and Industry. We should be wary of reading too much into the order of these categories: the prospectus strayed from the advertised title in that Industry was first and Art last.[13] More important is the map of the Exhibition, and the obvious preference of industrial over artistic achievement. The main, temporary exhibition building was designed 'in the Moorish style' by James Sellars and James Barr, with a '150-foot-high dome at its centre, surrounded by four square towers, each topped with a minaret'.[14] As a result, the site was often referred to in the press as 'Baghdad by Kelvin'.[15] As an important architectural structure its importance can only be considered via its time and in the minds of attendants and visitors, unlike the extant Municipal Chambers which were opened by Queen Victoria in the same year: a much more permanent expression of Glasgow's 'status as a great industrial power'.[16]

One of the most curious features was the reconstructed Bishop's Castle. It was noted as a major tourist attraction in *Pen and Ink Notes at the Glasgow Exhibition* (1888): 'the imitation of antiquity has been very successfully carried out in the construction of the Bishop's Castle, and wood and paint and canvas have been so put together as quite to cheat the eye into a belief that it is a genuine old building'.[17] This follows Edinburgh's 'large-scale reconstruction of a typical 17th century street complete with legendary buildings that had long since been demolished' in 1886.[18] Among these buildings was Cardinal Beaton's House, which also featured on a postcard. It would seem that the religious troubles still resonant in the Georgian era were, by the late nineteenth century, distant enough to allow such a fantastical gaze into the past. Walker's introduction to the mock Bishop's Castle structure is telling of this new attitude to old Glasgow as he considers the architect's 'good deed' in 'restoring' the 'ancient building which clung round historic associations'.[19]

It is ironic, then, that such language is used in the Exhibition to combine the idea of the city's lost buildings with the valour found in a temporary copy of an ancient structure, reinvented and relocated (the mock castle stood near the University, roughly on the spot 'where the statue of Lord Kelvin now stands').[20] The Victorian era's ability to define itself through growth and industrial progress also brought about the reappropriation and trivialisation of medieval history. Many of the objects on display in the reconstructed castle included an oak cradle used by James VI, an oak work box and an embroidered velvet bed-hanging depicting thistles which belonged to Mary, Queen of Scots, and a two-handed sword from Bannockburn. While these were on show, there was also a lighter way of remembering the Stuart era at J. Lyons' Bishop's Palace Temperance Restaurant, where waitresses were dressed as the Scottish queen.[21] As such, the experience of the relics in the mock castle take on a sort of carnival light, for, while the interior was designed to enhance the visitors' experience, the placement of their worth may be negated in going for a meal thereafter, and being served by many a living version of said ancient and tragic queen.

In effect, there was a sort of compression of history being enacted throughout the Exhibition. This adds to the idea of a miniature empire. That different nations can be conglomerated is in keeping with the bringing together of different eras in time – a disorienting and isolating effect of displaying a large range of historical objects in the hope to define any one cultural aspect which, in this event, was ancient Scotland as a Kingdom contrasted with modern Scotland in the British Empire. Writing after the 1851 London Exhibition, William Whewell stated: 'By annihilating the space which separates different nations, we produce a spectacle in which is annihilated the time which separates one stage of a nation's progress from another.'[22] Not only did Glasgow's 'spectacle' introduce the Empire to the visitors, but it imbricated it into and initiated the 'spectacle' of Victorian civic pride which lasts to this day. The inaugural ode of the Exhibition reveals this pride. Written by poet and novelist Robert Buchanan and set to music by Dr A. C. Mackenzie, 'The New Covenant' was performed as part of the opening ceremony. It goes:

> Dark, sea-born city, with thy throne
>   Set on the surge-vex'd shore,

> The trumpet of the storm was blown
>   To break thy rest of yore . . .[23]

Glasgow as 'dark, sea-born city' is unusually anonymous. The name Glasgow, and any local characteristics of the city, are absent in the ode. Flying in the face of the topographical tradition of Glasgow verse this was perhaps a subtle attempt to elevate Glasgow beyond its origins and recent past into a glorious stronghold of the British Empire.

Glasgow's second International Exhibition was held in the same location in 1901, drawing 11.5 million visitors. Compared to the 5.8 million passing through the previous halls, we can safely say that the city's greatness had been successfully showcased.[24] The main new attraction was Kelvingrove Art Gallery and Museum. The legacy of that building today makes the 1901 Exhibition unlike the others for its ability to remember specific cultural ideas of the city. In terms of layout, the main building of 1888 which contained the art section was long gone (as was the reinvented Bishop's Castle). This time, the area was divided between three main buildings: the aforementioned Kelvingrove building, the 200,000-square-foot Industrial Hall, and the 160,000-square-foot Machinery Hall (the latter two being connected by the 1,000-foot-long Grand Avenue).[25] In surrounding the newly built Art Gallery with these vast, temporary halls dedicated to industry and technology the organisers were making a statement. Glasgow was being promoted as a powerhouse. In Thomas Richards' *The Commodity Culture of Victorian England* (1990) emphasis is placed on 'the elevation of a form of technology into a form of culture', wherein 'machines [are] put on the stage, and after a time the machines *became* the stage'.[26] This was definitely true in Glasgow, whose literary scene was, as we know, lagging behind the rest of Scotland in terms of prestige and marketability. On the other hand its bold new industrial frontier was leading the way. Roland Quinault's 'The Cult of the Centenary' (1998) shows how commemorative events were designed to 'revive' or 'create' in the public imagination certain 'perceptions of past events and people' in connection with collective memory.[27] For example, it is stated that:

> Neo-classicism was soon blended with other eclectic historical elements, including romantic medievalism, which led to the staging of costume pageants and period-style dinners. Such entertainments were designed to attract large numbers of ordinary people and reflected the Victorian taste for spectacle.[28]

If we look briefly at the example of Edinburgh it seems that 'romantic medievalism' had been on the rise since the middle of the nineteenth century. Mock heraldic shields and ornate stonework became commonplace on Edinburgh buildings in the wake of a lecture by John Ruskin in 1858, and in 1891 the Scottish National Portrait Gallery put on a *Heraldic Exhibition* to explore the visual culture of medieval times.[29] We have seen how the Edinburgh (1886) and Glasgow (1888) Exhibitions encouraged an interactive, even playful approach the past. It was less to do with commemoration than with wonder, with awe. In Glasgow's 1901 Exhibition however there was another anniversary to be marked. As the first British host city of the twentieth century it also served 'to commemorate the fiftieth anniversary of London's Great Exhibition of 1851'.[30] Therefore, the Exhibitions had taken on a new prominence in the construction of civic pride. Where it was once great men and women who were idolised and commemorated, it was now the events themselves which were being remembered. And what modern memories they were.

As touched on above, the spectacle of the machine *on* and *as* the stage ushered in new collective experiences and, in the case of these World's Fairs, dressing them up as symbols of progression. All this before the unprecedented and dehumanising experience of World War I. As Daniel Pick puts it: 'the industrial revolution was perceived as central to the question of war' by the 1860s, 'even if for a further period chivalric and Napoleonic war codes and images still persisted alongside'.[31] These 'codes and images' were cultural memories of an increasingly antiquated mode of combat. That they were gradually eroded by mechanised war shows us the capacity for the industrial revolution to alter collective ideas of history. The pageantry of these International Exhibitions was made hyper-real by the convergence of old and new, that is, the physically new being conducted in an old-fashioned manner. Spencer R. Weart describes this in relation to the 1893 Chicago International Exposition – nicknamed the 'White City' – containing 'broad avenues and sparkling fountains, incandescent at night under the new electric lamps with steel dynamos gleaming alongside alabaster sculptures of virgins, a picture of the future harmony between technology and art'.[32] And while these commemorations were in honour of the 400th anniversary of Christopher Columbus's arrival in the New World, the Chicago and other American affairs were also based on the models of London and Glasgow, with their purpose-built temporary halls which, no matter the commemorative purpose, ended up showcasing the best and brightest of technological and industrial invention.

The very idea of defining Glasgow within temporary halls was part of a city-wide attempt to 'explain' Glasgow to tourists. *Glasgow in*

1901 was 'written to satisfy the curiosity of visitors to the International Exhibition ... as to the qualities of Glasgow and her citizens'.³³ The author, James Hamilton Muir, was the combined pseudonym of James Bone, A. H. Charteris, and Muirhead Bone (the latter supplying the illustrations of Glasgow unique to this year).³⁴ The book is divided into three parts, offering distinctive frames through which the city may be experienced. They are: 'Glasgow of the Imagination', offering topographical writing, features of industry which make the city famous, and the city's placement as 'The Heart of Scotland'; 'Glasgow of Fact – the Place', offering a history from early Glasgow to the Union, extensive remarks on the River Clyde and the shipbuilding industries, and a look at the city's modern architecture as compared to remaining ancient edifices; and finally 'Glasgow of Fiction – the Man and his Haunts', which considers 'The City Man ... His Howffs ... The Working Man ... Quayside Folk', and some words on the Exhibition itself.³⁵ It is telling that the frontispiece to this publication is a photogravure entitled 'Clyde Shipbuilders', further perpetuating the idea that shipbuilding alone forged Glasgow's place in the world. There is a deliberate romanticising of working-class daily life – anticipating George Blake's iconic novel *The Shipbuilders* – in the section entitled 'Our Milieu':

> The *milieu* of a town means very much more than the tale of sun or rain on its stone. It is not the fame of her towers or the beauty of her sunsets that attracts the traveller to Glasgow, and she does not take her stand on these ... Perhaps our friend came nearest it when, looking in at the open door of a workshop, he was almost blinded by the smoke and iron dust, and deafened by the roar ... the gasps of the exhaust pipes pushing their way through blackened roofs, toiling Glasgow drawing hard her breath.³⁶

These ideas compete with the equally proud testament to the newly built Art Gallery and Museum: 'No British municipality has erected so important a palace of art, and one could wish that this one deserved better the praises of the discerning.'³⁷ These definitions of Glasgow as a working city and a cultured city are still very much in play; readable in the rhetoric of almost all local cultural sites.

In 1901, the *Official Guide* declared that its collection of nineteenth-century oil paintings would 'give the Glasgow Exhibition a unique place in the artistic annals of the country'.³⁸ From the eighteenth-century Foulis Academy, to Archibald McLellan's galleries in Sauchiehall Street, to Kelvingrove Art Gallery and, eventually, Charles Rennie Mackintosh's Glasgow School of Art, the city's history of engagement with the visual and fine arts is long and complex. It is full of contradiction and selective remembering, harking back to the concepts of memory at the beginning of this book. For instance: the same Glasgow Boys who were commissioned to paint the murals in the City Chambers had a poor showing at the 1901 Exhibition.[39] It is also said that 'only three' of their paintings were purchased for Glasgow City Art Gallery 'before any of them died'.[40] Mackintosh had a similarly limited input to the 1901 event, having designs rejected by the organisers based largely on the notion that his 'work was generally regarded in his home city as uncomfortably odd'.[41] Now, the underappreciation of artists at home during their most active years is not a Glaswegian phenomenon: Johannes Vermeer and Paul Cézanne lived to enjoy only a fraction of the critical success we afford them now. The enshrinement of the Glasgow Boys and Mackintosh as the quintessential Glasgow artists does, however, reveal something about the city's shifting identity.

We might ask: how does Mackintosh not only survive these initial setbacks, but come to embody Glasgow's answer to the arts overall? Perhaps the answer lies in the rhetoric used in a 1996 Mackintosh exhibition held in the McLellan Galleries. Murray Grigor's review denotes the absence of Alexander 'Greek' Thomson in the exhibition narrative, despite the fact that Mackintosh used neo-Greek motifs in the design which won him the Alexander Thomson travelling scholarship in 1890.[42] More interestingly in the context of this chapter: it seems that Mackintosh's legacy was folded into the popular, industrial character of Glasgow. As Grigor puts it, 'the compendious [exhibition] catalogue explores ... how Glasgow merchants engendered radical architecture', and 'how the essential craft traditions of the city allowed half the world's shipping to be fitted out with such *fin de siècle* panache'.[43] Indeed, Mackintosh's style, with its international influence, seemed custom-made for a progressive Glasgow: streamlined, minimalistic, strong on the outside and refined on the inside.[44] Add for good measure that Mackintosh worked as a junior member of staff for the Fairfield Shipbuilding and Engineering Co. around 1888 and the manipulation of Glasgow's art history as a tangent of its celebrated industrial character is made much easier.[45] On this same issue we might consider Maryhill Burgh Halls as an appropriate *lieu de mémoire*. More specifically, the twenty stained-glass panels by Stephen Adam (1878) showcased typical Glasgow role models (The Teacher, The Soldier) among the city's industrial workforce (wheelwrights, sawyers, railwaymen, papermakers, linen bleachers, joiners, iron moulders, glassblowers, gas workers, engineers, chemical workers, canal boatmen, calico printers, bricklayers, boat-builders, blacksmiths, zinc spelters and dye-press workers). To a large extent Glasgow still promotes this version of its character above all else. In the 1911 Exhibition this character was adapted and taken forward in the new context of *Scotland*'s national story.

The 'Scottish Exhibition' as it was called, also held in Kelvingrove Park, raised the question of national identity immediately. The stated purpose of the Exhibition was 'to create a greater public interest in Scottish History and Literature . . . to celebrate distinguished Scotsmen', and to 'represent a realistic picture of Scottish Burghal Life in bygone times'.[46] The most recognisable difference between this Exhibition and the foregoing Victorian pair – aside from the Scottish name – was the layout. The emphasis was shifted from the site of the new art galleries completely, and with no clearly defined main building, the park was littered with different smaller buildings including the Palace of Art, the Palace of History, the Palace of Industries and the Aviation Building. Elfie Rembold's consideration of the 1911 Exhibition notes the new, Edwardian preference for 'cultural achievements' over 'technological performances' in representing a nation.[47] In the introduction to *Glasgow, Volume II* (1996), W. Hamish Fraser suggests that 'the Scottish emphasis . . . may itself have unconsciously signified a narrowing of horizons'.[48] For Bruce Lenman, it was the emphasis of 'folk' values and traditions that led the charge for the main purpose of the Exhibition: to fund a new Chair in Scottish history and literature at Glasgow[49] similar to that which had existed in Edinburgh for ten years.[50] It is said that 'members of the Historical Committee of the exhibition could or would not present Scottish history in either a positive or negative way'[51] and that 'the advocates of a history chair were divided between those who located Scotland within the context of the Union and the Empire, those who directed their attention toward Europe, and finally those who confined their view solely to Scotland'.[52] It is therefore more reasonable to suggest that the Scottish branding of the Exhibition marks not a narrowing of cultural horizons, but rather an unresolved issue of identity made clear in the light of such conflicted curatorial visions. As has been suggested above, Glasgow's 'delayed interest in Scottish history' was a result of the city's 'swift and revolutionary' industrial rise, during which it was 'distanced from ancient and role-bound formal aesthetic traditions'.[53]

According to Rembold, the national press branded the Exhibition 'troubled' and 'checkered' despite the fact that it was planned to the point of exhaustion, including several subcategories of history and literature which were said to cover the period between James III and Sir Walter Scott.[54] Besides the expected venerable relics ('It was with pride we gazed at the Wallace letter . . . the Brooch of Lorn . . . [the] sword . . .

of Bannockburn'), the catalogue also reveals that the 1911 Exhibition did exhibit some of the figures of Glasgow's literary enlightenment.[55] These included portraits of Tobias Smollett, Thomas Campbell and Dugald Moore alongside portraits of Burns and Scott, reproductions of letters including one from the Glasgow physician and author John Moore to Burns advising him 'to deal more sparingly for the future in the Provincial Dialect', and a varied display of books printed in the city, with three copies of *The Protestation of The Generall Assemblie of the Church of Scotland* (1638) alongside several examples by the Foulis brothers.[56]

Perhaps the real issue in 1911 was that for the first time Glasgow displayed its connection with historical literary roots to an emerging modern audience with a limited collective memory. In other words, the British Empire was a more secure notion than specifically Scottish history. This is not to deny that generations of readers familiar with the novels of Scott and his contemporaries would have enjoyed the historic objects on display, but rather that Glasgow had already rejected this world in the previous Exhibitions in favour of a modern British one. It is understandable that the historical elements could have been slightly disorienting for those who expected a similar layout to the 1901 Exhibition; but little could have prepared visitors for the developed faux-Scottish designs that took place. As with the panorama companion to *Glotta*, above, the immersive quality of the 1911 Exhibition would have been an unprecedented novelty. The removal (or replacement) of context has featured in all the Glasgow Exhibitions. John Lavery's painting *Potter at Work*, (1888) depicts a Bengali potter working on a piece of his display during the Exhibition. It offers a glimpse into the interactive element of the event as well as revealing the carefully planned authenticity, as though being transported, to an Indian marketplace.

In 1911 there were new additions which maintained this tradition, none more notable than the Highland Clachan. John MacKenzie suggests that such 'reconstructions ... set out to reconcile Lowland and Gaelic culture, while suggesting their joint role in the creation of the Scottish spirit that had produced modern technology and industry'.[57] On the Exhibition map, however, one can spot two ironically adjacent sections: West Africans and Laplanders. Perilla Kinchin and Juliet Kinchin use the *Souvenir of a Visit to the West African Colonies* as an example of the common ethnographic attitudes of the visitors. Therefore, 'exhibiting' Scottish 'natives' takes the parochialism of the event beyond a simple exploitation of 'the world's weakness for tartan and the romance of Scotland'.[58] Any doubts about the distinction between historical re-enactment and plain exploitation should be quelled by the fact that these 1911 exhibits, being in the 'amusement section', charged a separate admission fee.[59]

Behind the Clachan's saleability was cultural compression. Just as the relocation of the Bishop's Castle from the east to the west of the city was revelatory of its new purpose, so too was the imagined relocation of the Highlands to the Lowlands. Such a convergence of two distinct aspects of Scotland can be seen as a symbol of the uncertain, overwhelming nature of the Exhibition itself. The roots of *An Clachan* in Glasgow can be traced to the Highland Association's Bazaar in St Andrew's Halls in 1907, which featured 'a typical representation of a "Clachan" or village of the Western Highlands and Islands ... panoramic views of Highland scenery painted by Colin Mackintosh', and even 'a reproduction of Prince Charlie's Cave'.[60] In 1911, spanning three acres and in the context of Kelvingrove Park, it resembled a 'dream village' – to borrow Bob Crampsey's words – complete with Gaelic-speaking employees and customised tartan.[61]

The souvenirs and objects of these Exhibitions which recorded the experience are also important in the pursuit of authenticity. For instance, a photograph taken in the Clachan was edited and mass-produced as a postcard. This change (the buildings in the background are gone) represents a false memory, an act of invented authenticity: not only has a Highland village been transported to Kelvingrove Park, but its placement in Kelvingrove Park has been erased. This double removal makes the site an interesting focal point of the Exhibition, not least for questions it raises over historical significance. In terms of identity, and the pomp which surrounds it when it reappears in 1938, one is reminded of Sir Walter Scott's organisation of George IV's state visit to Scotland in 1822. In Raphael Samuel's *Patriotism: The Making and Unmaking of British National Identity* (1989), Christopher Harvie opines the following:

> It was the political apotheosis of Scott's combination of unionism and cultural nationalism, the symbolic confirmation of the Hanoverian line, the transference of remaining Jacobite and nationalist sentiments to wider British imperial loyalties ... reminding the political metropolis and élite that Scots loyalty, though full-hearted, was not wholly unconditional.[62]

It would seem difficult to dispute that the tartanry of the Scottish Exhibition of 1911 serves as the continuation of this placement of Scotland in Britain. Empire was a powerful notion elsewhere in the western world, as Anthony Gristwood shows through the example of

Seville (1999). The 1929 Iberoamerican Fair was a pivotal showcase of imperial Spain's mythology, history, and lingering power. Just as Glasgow did and would do again in 1938, the Fair in Seville 'tapped a vein of nostalgia for past splendours embodied in the monuments and relics of an imperial and maritime past' while at the same time showcasing the new industries and regeneration of the city.[63] There are further similarities to Glasgow's Exhibitions here in terms of indigenous and foreign communities as 'amusement zones'. In the case of Seville there were pavilions dedicated to the Gulf of Guinea, Mexico, Peru and Colombia. As we will see below, the efforts to recreate authentic environments were spectacular, commercial and objectifying.

The 1938 Empire Exhibition (Scotland) was the only major Exhibition in Glasgow to be held anywhere other than Kelvingrove, this time in Bellahouston Park. The site itself was once home to Bellahouston House, formerly Dumbreck House, with a history dating back to the Rowan family in the seventeenth century. It attracted 12.6 million visitors, making it the most popular Exhibition in Glasgow's history.[64] Beside the change of location, there is a distinct tone which separates this event from those held in the West End which, ironically, adds weight to the conflicting issues surrounding national identity. For one, there is a sense of urgency in the representations of growth, unlike the grand Exhibitions of 1888 and 1901, wherein Glasgow seemed confident in its longevity as Second City in the Empire. The layout of the Exhibition grounds with the huge spaces dedicated to the Palace of Engineering and the Palaces of Industries (note the plurals) shows the same favouritism for Glasgow's heavy industry that was present in 1888 and 1901. As Kinchin and Kinchin point out, World War I aided Glasgow's industrial workforces but that impact soon dissipated, and 'Scotland as a whole' was 'lagging behind in industrial recovery'. The confidence emblematised in the Industrial Halls in previous affairs was much less apparent in 1938, with the need to advertise what made Glasgow so strong in the first place taking centre-stage.[65] Findling's *Historical Dictionary of World's Fairs* makes this clear: 'The idea for an Empire Exhibition in Glasgow was conceived in 1931 at the height of the depression in conscious effort to promote employment and to advertise the industries of Scotland.'[66] It is here at the point of the word 'advertise' that we can begin to think about Glasgow as a commercial concept.

The style of 1938 was certainly more modern, pertaining to new ideas representative of Great Britain far more than the frozen-in-time, all-encompassing compressions of space that featured previously. Perhaps the biggest shift in style can be interpreted in Mark Crinson's analysis of the design choices made by Thomas Smith Tait. Crinson says that 'Tait was anxious to emphasize the fact that the buildings were steel framed and prefabricated and could be easily erected and dismantled'.[67] This turn to Modernism was fairly new. As Findling puts it: 'Whereas previous British exhibitions had adopted pastiche, eclectic, or antique styles, Glasgow was unashamedly modern.'[68] The symbol of this newfound modernity was the Tower of Empire. According to Goldsmith, the Tower was to be a permanent feature, but as World War II began it was 'seen as a possible navigation aid for enemy aircraft' and was taken down.[69] The Tower certainly would have reiterated and memorialised the Victorian self-confidence the city once enjoyed, but in reading this inter-war Exhibition it is difficult to ignore the sense of urgency in promoting employment and regrowth which were missing in 1888 and 1901. In the *Official Guide*, the Tower becomes something like a beacon of Utopia:

> The finished effort, dominating the Exhibition ... is symbolic of all that is enterprising, and is the crowning achievement of the imagination which envisaged the Empire city of Bellahouston rising from the wooded slopes and spacious lawns of a beautiful public park.

The idea of an 'Empire city' is resonant of the city as a 'miniature Empire' discussed above. Also, the 'rising' steel and concrete is a powerful colonial image, further inscribing the cultural memories of Empire. Ultimately, the Exhibition Tower conforms to what Eric Hobsbawm calls 'the legitimacy of prosperity'. Indeed, his discussion of the role of the Eiffel Tower in the transformation of 'the heritage of the [French] revolution into a combined expression of state pomp and power and the citizens' pleasure' can be applied to the modernisation of Glasgow out of the Scottish past and into the realm of the New World.[70] After all, the *Official Guide*'s description of the Empire Tower likens 'the skyscrapers of Manhattan' to 'the constancy of man's aspiration towards the heavens'.[71]

For all this, the use of Burns, Scott, Carlyle, Livingstone and Watt (the 'great Scottish achievers') on the wall of the North Pavilion and the reappearance of the Clachan within the official 'Empire' context complicates the lingering issues of national identity.[72] In Colin McArthur's account of the Exhibition, he states: 'The Clachan and the Tower of Empire are the polar points of the dialectic which threatens to render individual Scots schizoid ... illustrating the generality of the ideological struggle between cores and peripheries.'[73] He goes on: 'Great national moments of self-presentation ... were the occasions when the ongoing dialectic of modern/urban against rural/ancient emerged in its most public and delirious form.'[74] John MacKenzie adds weight to McArthur's use of the Tower and the Clachan as opposite cultural symbols, stating that the Clachan was an 'idyllic vision of a rural past' awkwardly 'displayed within a dramatically modern architectural context'. His accompanying illustration shows the Tower 'rising above the funfair', informing us that, seen from everywhere in the park, the Tower rose above the supposedly authentic Highland Village.[75] As though the parenthesis surrounding '(Scotland)' was not enough, Tait's Tower above the Clachan is suggestive of the imperial narrative of the Exhibition. While Glasgow's buildings were removed from photographs of the Highland Village in 1911, the Tower became central to the marketing campaign in 1938, instilling this new modern style in the minds of tourists and locals. Its appearance on the front page of the *Glasgow Herald* on 28 April 1938 illustrates this well.

The recycling of these new structures as symbols is crucial to our understanding of Glasgow's trajectory. Laurence Gouriévidis' comments (2010) on the Clachan further develop the role of memory in such native exhibits. '*An Clachan*,' he states, 'was certainly devised around the collective imaginaries enveloping the Highlands and Islands as it was meant to "raise many memories in the minds of returned exiles and ... give to others some impression of the real old Scotland, the Land of the Gaels, the Scotland that is fast passing before the relentless onrush of modernity".'[76] Indeed, it is this kind of analysis which renders the consideration of the actual content of the Clachan subsidiary to comments of cultural identity. There is perhaps no account of the 1938 Exhibition more striking in this dichotomy of old versus new than King George VI and Queen Elizabeth's visit to the top of Tait's Tower and then to the Clachan, 'where Mary Morrison from Barra sang them a lament while working at her spinning wheel'.[77] This level of spectacle is an unusual occurrence of encased cultural memory, dislocated from its source and therefore somehow out of time. The performative element, drawn out by the presence of royalty, speaks to an even stranger continuation of folk culture. In these examples the argument of preservation versus exploitation is inevitable. Not only imperial but racist tones are perceived the more we examine the roots of colonial heritage. This becomes clear if we return for a moment to the 1929 Iberoamerican Fair in Seville, during which Spanish royals in the Guinean pavilion were treated to the spectacle of local fauna, gorillas, and 'two nude Pamúes [indigenous tribespeople].'[78] Like Mary Morrison from Barra, these 'natives' performed for their royal visitors as part of an exchange designed to nullify tensions between old and new. When these Exhibitions pack up and move on, the sensational images linger, and become woven into the prominent branding images which become the surviving memory of the host place (and nation).

For Thomas Richards, the 'image of Victoria became a common text and a prevailing context for the nation' in English Exhibitions after the Jubilee of 1887, thus merging 'advertising and spectacle'.[79] Since then, Exhibitions have been viewed synonymously with branding and propaganda. For instance, John MacKenzie says that 1938 can 'be placed in the classic exhibition tradition, combining fun with information, economic propaganda with ethnic display'.[80] For Kenneth Luckhurst, 'the exhibition can be a most powerful instrument for propaganda', saying that it was unlikely for a visitor to Glasgow's Exhibition to leave without 'some new and lasting impression of the significance of the British Empire as a whole'.[81] To achieve this 'lasting impression', the site would have to be memorable. Mark Crinson points to the use of colour which unified all the buildings in the Exhibition, and the continuation of these colours 'in the street furniture: in the kiosks, information stands, signposts, lamps and litter bins'.[82]

This design-led unification process is perhaps one of the strongest examples of modernisation in Glasgow's history of Exhibitions. Here we had the lion rampant designed into any and all objects connected to the Exhibition, itself a reaction, perhaps, to the English 'Wembley' lion that had been used in guides and postage stamps in the 1924/25 Empire Exhibition. For Irene Maver 'using old symbols in a new context ... potently combined imperial and Scottish aspirations'.[83] In 1901, most of the souvenirs from the Exhibition featured the image of the Main Building, as can be seen in its presence on brooches, medals and handkerchiefs. Some souvenir lockets (see Figure 18) commemorated the Exhibition site alongside other noteworthy Glasgow buildings including the Cathedral, the Exchange (now the GoMA), and the City Chambers. In 1938, the distinctly Scottish Empire lion was used across printed materials such as guides, programmes, pamphlets and official souvenirs such as silverware, key-rings, handkerchiefs and postcards. Being an instantly recognisable motif, the lion perpetrated the position of Scotland in the Empire far more effectively than the superimposed palatial Main Building of 1901.

The repetition of one image throughout the 1938 Exhibition was a powerful associative technique which unified Glasgow in Scotland, and Scotland in Britain. It epitomises the blurred lines of Scottish Nationalism, as Murray Pittock puts it, after the merging of the National Party of

The Great Exhibitions: 185

Figure 18 Miniature enamelled book locket from the 1901 Glasgow Exhibition (200 mm × 160 mm), showing the front (main), and two sample 'pages' inside. Photo: the author.

Scotland with the Scottish Party to become the Scottish National Party in 1934. The competing agendas (independence versus home rule within the British Empire) within this new party, as well as the increasing diversity of Scottish literature in the 1920s and 1930s form the cultural context to this Exhibition.[84] In other words, using the lion rampant as a logo certainly gives Glasgow a nationalist stamp, but images like this can outlast (and even skew) the cultural memory of a certain place and time. Billed as 'Scotland's Greatest Exhibit', some of the other images found on the 1938 pamphlets combined tartan, ancient churches, battles, the Tower of Empire and the Empire lion, offer a sort of progression of Scotland's journey from its roots to its British modernity. Just like the banquet halls of the Victorian City Chambers, Glasgow's Georgian history is completely absent in this trajectory.

And so Glasgow's character had come full circle in these bold exhibitions from an anonymous 'dark' city to an equally anonymous modern one, built nonetheless on the recent memories of imperial and industrial strength. As put by Martin Bellamy (2006), 'shipbuilding had become tamed in the public imagination' following the abundance of novels, plays and films that portrayed the industry, but was ultimately rooted in that Victorian sense of pride that crystallised between 1888 and 1901.[85] As Kinchin and Kinchin remind us, however, the Festival of Britain in 1951 effectively usurped the modernist architecture introduced by Tait in Glasgow. Also in that year the first post-war census revealed that Birmingham, not Glasgow, had become the Second City of the Empire.[86]

NOTES

1. John M. MacKenzie, '"The Second City of the Empire": Glasgow – imperial municipality', in Felix Driver and David Gilbert, eds, *Imperial Cities: Landscape, Display and Identity* (Manchester: Manchester University Press, 1999), 215–37 (232).
2. T. M. Devine, 'The Urban Crisis', in T. M. Devine and Gordon Jackson, eds, *Glasgow, Volume I: Beginnings to 1830* (Manchester: Manchester University Press, 1995), 415 n. 2.
3. *Caledonian Mercury*, 23 December 1820.
4. Ann Rigney, 'Plenitude, scarcity and the circulation of cultural memory', *Journal of European Studies*, 35:1 (2006), 11–28 (16); Murray Pittock, *Material Culture and Sedition, 1688–1760: Treacherous Objects, Secret Places* (Basingstoke: Palgrave Macmillan, 2013), 60–1.
5. MacKenzie, '"The Second City of the Empire"', 215.
6. For more on the Abolitionist histories see C. Duncan Rice's *The Scots Abolitionists, 1833–1861* (Baton Rouge: Louisiana State University Press,1981) and Iain Whyte's *Scotland and the Abolition of Black Slavery* (Edinburgh: Edinburgh University Press, 2006).
7. Broadside news report, Glasgow University Special Collections, Bh12-y.3 (8).
8. University of Glasgow Library Special Collections, Broadside Collection, Bh14-x.5, 11.
9. R. H. Campbell, 'The Making of the Industrial City', in T. M. Devine and Gordon Jackson, eds, *Glasgow, Volume I: Beginnings to 1830* (Manchester: Manchester University Press, 1995), 184–213 (209).
10. Christopher A. Whatley, *The Industrial Revolution in Scotland* (Cambridge: Cambridge University Press, 1997), 60.
11. Ibid.
12. MacKenzie, '"The Second City of the Empire"', 226.
13. University of Glasgow Library Special Collections, Call Number: Mu23-x.20. Related ephemera from the Exhibition; prospectus begins on page 164.

14. John E. Findling ed., *Historical Dictionary of World's Fairs and Expositions, 1851–1988* (New York: Greenwood Press, 1990), 103.
15. Alastair Lindsay Goldsmith, *The Glasgow International Exhibitions, 1888–1938*, (MLitt thesis: University of Strathclyde, 1985), 54.
16. Perilla Kinchin and Juliet Kinchin, *Glasgow's Great Exhibitions: 1888, 1901, 1911, 1938, 1988* (Oxon: White Cockade, 1988), 18.
17. Robert Walker and T. Raffles Davison, *Pen and Ink Notes at the Glasgow Exhibition* (London: J. S. Virtue & Co., 1888) 103.
18. David McLean, 'Lost Edinburgh: Edinburgh International Exhibition 1886', *The Scotsman*, 15 April 2013, <http://www.scotsman.com/whats-on/arts-and-entertainment/lost-edinburgh-edinburgh-international-exhibition-1886-1579533> (last accessed 30 August 2020).
19. Walker and Davison, *Pen and Ink Notes*, 102.
20. Henry C. Cornish, 'First Glasgow International Exhibition, 1888', *Old Glasgow Club Transactions, Volume V, Session 1923–1928* (Glasgow: Aird and Coghill Ltd, 1928), 42–9 (46).
21. Kinchin and Kinchin, *Glasgow's Great Exhibitions*, 46.
22. William Whewell, 'On the General Bearing of the Great Exhibition', *Lectures on the Results of the Great Exhibition of 1851* (London: David Bogue, 1852), 3–25 (11).
23. This official ode was printed in *The Electrical Engineer*, 27 April 1888 (London: Biggs and Co.), 395.
24. Kinchin and Kinchin, *Glasgow's Great Exhibitions*, 15.
25. Findling, *Historical Dictionary of World's Fairs and Expositions*, 172.
26. Thomas Richards, The Commodity Culture of Victorian England: Advertising and Spectacle, 1851–1914 (Stanford, CA: Stanford University Press, 1990), 57.
27. Roland Quinault, 'The Cult of the Centenary, c.1784–1914' in *Historical Research*, 71:176 (1998), 303–23 (303).
28. Ibid., 321.
29. Lamont, 'Allan Ramsay and Edinburgh', 131.
30. Findling, *Historical Dictionary of World's Fairs and Expositions*, 172.
31. Daniel Pick, *War Marchine: The Rationalisation of Slaughter in the Modern Age* (New Haven and London: Yale University Press, 1993), 177.
32. Spencer R. Weart, *Nuclear Fear: A History of Images* (Cambridge, MA: Harvard University Press, 1988), 7.
33. Simon Berry and Hamish Whyte, eds, *Glasgow Observed* (Edinburgh: John Donald, 1987), 179.
34. Ibid., 178.
35. Derived from table of contents of James Hamilton Muir, *Glasgow in 1901* (Glasgow and Edinburgh: William Hodge & Company, 1901).
36. James Hamilton Muir, *Glasgow in 1901* (Glasgow and Edinburgh: William Hodge & Company, 1901), 20.
37. Ibid., 148.

38. *Glasgow International Exhibition 1901: Official Guide* (Glasgow: C. P. Watson, 1901), 101.
39. Kinchin and Kinchin, *Glasgow's Great Exhibitions*, 65.
40. Roger Billcliffe, 'A Brush with Europe: visual art in Glasgow 1890–1990' in *RSA Journal* 139:5417 (1991), 330–42 (341).
41. Kinchin and Kinchin, *Glasgow's Great Exhibitions*, 59.
42. Murray Grigor, 'Not in architectural order', *RSA Journal*, 144:5473 (1996), 39.
43. Ibid.
44. Scottish architect James Miller (1860–1947), who designed many of the buildings for the 1901 Glasgow Exhibition, carried his eclectic style into the interior of the Cunard liner RMS *Lusitania*: an amalgamation of Georgian, Queen Anne, and Louis XVI styles.
45. David Stark, *Charles Rennie Mackintosh and Co: 1854 to 2004* (Catrine, Ayrshire: Stenlake, 2004), 139.
46. Quoted in Kinchin and Kinchin, *Glasgow's Great Exhibitions*, 96–7.
47. Elfie Rembold, 'Negotiating Scottish Identity: The Glasgow History Exhibition 1911', *National Identities*, 1:3 (1999), 265–85 (266).
48. W. Hamish Fraser, 'Introduction: "Let Glasgow Flourish"', *Glasgow, Volume II: 1830–1912*, W. Hamish Fraser and Irene Maver, eds, (Manchester: Manchester University Press, 1996), 1–7 (6).
49. Bruce P. Lenman, 'The Teaching of Scottish History in the Scottish Universities', *The Scottish Historical Review*, 52:154 (1973), 165–90 (177).
50. Rembold, 'Negotiating Scottish Identity', 271.
51. Ibid., 267.
52. Ibid., 272.
53. James Schmiechen: quoted in Rembold, 'Negotiating Scottish Identity', 271.
54. Rembold, 'Negotiating Scottish Identity', 267.
55. James Baillie, 'The Scottish Exhibition of National History, Art, and Industry, Glasgow, 1911', *Old Glasgow Club Transactions, Volume 7, Session 1934–1935* (Glasgow: Aird and Coghill Ltd, 1935), 7–15 (11).
56. *Scottish Exhibition of National History, Art and Industry: Palace of History, Catalogue of exhibits, vol. 1* (Glasgow: Dalross, 1911), 184.
57. John M. MacKenzie, 'Empire and National Identities: the Case of Scotland', *Transactions of the Royal Historical Society*, 8 (1998), 215–31 (227).
58. Kinchin and Kinchin, *Glasgow's Great Exhibitions*, 97.
59. Ibid., 121.
60. *Souvenir and handbook of Feill a' Chomuinn Ghaidhealaich* (The Highland Association Bazaar) 1907 (Glasgow: J. M. Munro, 1907), 71.
61. Bob Crampsey, *The Empire Exhibition of 1938: The Last Durbar* (Edinburgh: Mainstream, 1988), 49.

62. Christopher Harvie, 'Scott and the Image of Scotland,' in Raphael Samuel, ed., *Patriotism: The Making and Unmaking of British National Identity, Volume II: Minorities and Outsiders* (London and New York: Routledge, 1989), 173–92 (184).
63. Anthony Gristwood, 'Commemorating empire in twentieth-century Seville', in Felix Driver and David Gilbert, eds, *Imperial Cities: Landscape, Display and Identity* (Manchester: Manchester University Press, 1999), 155–73 (156).
64. Kinchin and Kinchin, *Glasgow's Great Exhibitions*, 15.
65. Ibid., 127–8.
66. Findling, *Historical Dictionary of World's Fairs and Expositions*, 291.
67. Mark Crinson, *Modern Architecture and the End of Empire* (Aldershot: Ashgate, 2003), 96.
68. Findling, *Historical Dictionary of World's Fairs and Expositions*, 291.
69. Goldsmith, *The Glasgow International Exhibitions*, 96.
70. Eric Hobsbawm, 'Mass-Producing Traditions: Europe, 1870–1914', in Eric Hobsbawm and Terence Ranger, eds, *The Invention of Tradition* (Cambridge: Cambridge University Press – Canto, 1996 [1983]), 263–307 (271).
71. *Empire Exhibition Scotland – 1938, Official Guide* (Glasgow: McCorquodale & Co. Ltd, 1938), 76.
72. Kinchin and Kinchin, *Glasgow's Great Exhibitions*, 153.
73. Colin McArthur, 'The dialectic of national identity: The Glasgow Empire Exhibition of 1938', in Tony Bennett, Colin Mercer and Janet Woollacott, eds, *Popular Culture and Social Relations* (Milton Keynes and Philadelphia: Open University Press, 1986), 117–34 (131–2).
74. Ibid., 132.
75. MacKenzie, '"The Second City of the Empire"', 229–230.
76. Laurence Gouriévidis, *The Dynamics of Heritage: History, Memory and the Highland Clearances* (Farnham: Ashgate, 2010), 123, quoting from p. 121 of Empire Exhibition Scotland – 1938, Official Guide.
77. Kinchin and Kinchin, *Glasgow's Great Exhibitions*, 138.
78. Gristwood, 'Commemorating empire in twentieth-century Seville', 163.
79. Richards, *The Commodity Culture of Victorian England*, 105.
80. John M. MacKenzie, *Propaganda and Empire: The Manipulation of British Public Opinion, 1880–1960* (Manchester: Manchester University Press, 1984), 113.
81. Kenneth W. Luckhurst, *The Story of Exhibitions* (London: The Studio Publications, 1951), 11.
82. Crinson, *Modern Architecture and the End of Empire*, 96.
83. Irene Maver, *Glasgow* (Edinburgh: Edinburgh University Press, 2000), 256.
84. Murray Pittock, *The Road to Independence? Scotland Since the Sixties* (London: Reaktion Books, 2008), 55.

85. Martin Bellamy, 'Shipbuilding and cultural identity on Clydeside', *Journal for Maritime Research*, 8:1 (2006), 1–33 (19).
86. Kinchin and Kinchin, *Glasgow's Great Exhibitions*, 168–70.

Conclusion

After relinquishing the title 'Second City' to Birmingham, Glasgow was left to reinvent itself. But before we proceed we must keep in mind that such epithets, honorary in nature, can become arbitrary. What good is having the title if four or five other cities still claim it? More useful for us, then, is the understanding of the *persistence* of these titles even after the metaphorical baton of civic triumph has moved hundreds of miles in another direction. Brian Groom's piece 'Splendidly pointless second city debate' in the *Financial Times* sums up the ongoing debate well: many of the former powerhouses of the industrial age still make the claim while capital cities Edinburgh, Belfast, and Cardiff feel the title should be theirs.[1] That there is 'no official mechanism' to decide which of these is *the* Second City asks us to look back across the history of the UK and witness the rise and fall of its many proud metropolises. In Scotland, cultural memories are exchanged between the Highlands and the Lowlands to such a disproportionate extent history and geography are often blurred. Our legends of Wallace and Bruce figure in the battles of the first half of the second millennium while in the second half a decadent swathe of dances and (more) battles surround, first, Mary, Queen of Scots and, later, the Jacobites. In none of these stories do we find Glasgow in a starring role. And so with an unerring loyalty to the antagonists of Scotland's popular histories Glasgow expanded rapidly to forge a new, modern image of itself in the nineteenth and early twentieth centuries.

Whether or not we remember it as the Second City of Britain does not prevent Glasgow's self-preservation vis-à-vis the nostalgia of its industrial greatness. The wisdom of Burns's famous lines should encourage us to consider not what *we* think Glasgow is, but what our neighbours think: 'O wad some Pow'r the giftie gie us / *To see oursels as others see us!*'² To this day the surviving image of Glasgow is more or less what the city constructed during its Great Exhibitions. Take, for instance, one of the objects on display in the Glasgow City Chambers. A commemorative glass trophy for the World Irish Dance Championships held in 2018 features the Finnieston Crane, a Mackintosh pendant and 'GLASGOW 2018' in the classic Mackintosh-style typography (ITC Willow). The base of the trophy is in the shape of a ship, and the logo for the Championships reincorporates a ship and the crane. This combination of industry and modern art is Glasgow's favourite self-portrait despite the unravelling of its social and economic fabric. As this book has shown time and again: memory can be more powerful than fact.

Indeed, with any study of a single city we are required, perhaps, to acknowledge the impossibility of accumulating every fact, figure and statistic. We depend on shifting cultural trends and major events to gauge public perception. In his book on Prague (2010) Alfred Thomas makes the point that the city was popularised as being unscathed by European wars as 'an unbroken historical continuum or as a site of the imagination *tout court*'.³ That the epithet 'mother of cities' survives in popular culture and guide books helps perpetuate the historically resilient character of Prague. To a lesser extent we might say the same about Edinburgh, where most major histories of Scotland can somehow find root. But, crucially, every city achieves its identity through what Thomas describes as an 'interplay between remembering and forgetting'. The destruction of the Jewish ghetto in Prague in the late 1890s 'as part of an extensive slum clearance and sanitation program' is the example of choice, and a powerful one too where modern European history is concerned.⁴ In Glasgow we have the documentary evidence of the slum clearances in the old heart of the city: photographs captured by Thomas Annan depicting the overcrowded tenement flats on High Street. These slow-exposure images are often haunting, with the ghostly outlines of people refusing to sit still reminding us that the buildings in which they live are as fleeting and as temporary as we are. In Paris, Eugène Atget captured similar images of the old city during Georges-Eugène Haussmann's legacy of rebuilding which came to epitomise creative destruction elsewhere.⁵ This 'Haussmannisation' can be examined in the context of many places, and may well be seen as a precursor to Robert Bruce's unsuccessful plan to rebuild Glasgow that we touched on in the introduction. In these cases, it seems, cities are able to identify and promote themselves as 'survivors' of history through a handful of powerful images, regardless of the evidence of their actual demise.

As regards Glasgow's popular history we can make the case that some of the more prevalent images have begun to fade. Many of these relate to antisocial issues or infamous poor health, though these too have been questioned and reconsidered. For an overview of what these are one might begin with Carol Craig's *The Tears that Made the Clyde* (2010) in which Glasgow's image as a 'macho city' is interrogated together with other social stereotypes. Tracing a line through the popular novels – none more prevalent than *No Mean City* (1935) – and shipyard songs of the early twentieth century, Craig's summary of Glasgow's 'claim to fame' includes 'punch-ups, alcohol-fuelled social disorder, domestic violence and gangs'.[6] That these images hover determinedly in the twenty-first century reinforces the idea that cultural memory can be more powerful than we want it to be. Four years before Craig's book a report by the Glasgow Centre for Population Health was published. The lengthy study by Hanlon, Walsh and Whyte (aptly named *Let Glasgow Flourish*) includes 'an analysis of what is getting better in Glasgow' with a view to 'challenge a number of stereotypes'.[7] Inequalities in health and wellbeing are still flagged, but their desire to 'illuminate' improvements indicates the notion that perceptions of the city's social problems are not always as they seem.

So how does Glasgow transform itself in the public imagination, or, put another way: how does it curate its own cultural memory? In Clark and Wright's study of Urban Regeneration in Glasgow (2018) the city's recurring self-promotion is explained thus:

> By [the 1990s] Glasgow had firmly established a strategy of event-based regeneration, a boosterist policy approach that the city initiated in the late 1980s with the 1988 Glasgow Garden Festival, which was held on a reclaimed former shipping quay. The event helped create a new image of Glasgow, which was later consolidated by successful bids to become the 1990 European City of Culture and the 1999 City of Architecture. Glasgow was emerging from its post-industrial slump, with the city council actively marketing Glasgow as a cultural and shopping venue in Scotland, the UK and Europe. Much has been made of the city's industrial and working-class heritage, which has been deployed in regeneration to attract tourists, conferences or simply more affluent residents. [. . .] Glasgow was no longer a 'mean city'.[8]

There are several threads in this excellent summation of Glasgow's tradition of 'event-based regeneration' that we might pick up. The symbolism of a reclaimed shipping quay signifies the importance of place in people's minds, proving, perhaps, that we sometimes buy into an image of the past to accept the future. But it is this idea that a 'new image' of Glasgow was forged within the last thirty years that is most compelling.

Within the framework of collective – or generational – memory we can see for ourselves the ways in which nostalgia for working-class life plays out in gift shops and popular histories. Tenement life and Glasgow's wit (banter) are among the common selling points laid out in various forms for tourists and proud citizens looking to reinforce their identity. All of this memory making brings us to the first question this book asked. *Where is Georgian Glasgow?* What we might do to consolidate the relatively invisible Georgian period of Glasgow's history is examine the attempts made in recent years to bring it into focus.

2014 AND BEYOND: NEW PERSPECTIVES ON GEORGIAN GLASGOW

The same 'event-based regeneration' policy explained by Clark and Wright was most recently used to boost the pertinent images of Glasgow during 2014. From 23 July to 3 August the city hosted the XX Commonwealth Games, an event which brought about an attempted overhaul of the city's deprived East End. The Athletes' Village became a new residential area and the Commonwealth Arena and Sir Chris Hoy Velodrome became the Emirates Arena, completely transforming the area. Until then, Celtic Park sat in the midst of an otherwise run-down community with little connection to the city and its events. Of course, another major event was dominating the headlines in 2014. Scotland's Independence Referendum took place on 18 September and, with an unprecedented 85 per cent of the electorate showing up to vote, 55 per cent of them decided that Scotland should remain in the UK. The margin of votes was around 400,000. Notably, Glasgow (53.49 per cent) and Dundee (57.35 per cent) were the only two locales in which Independence was more favourable.[9] But it was in Glasgow where the unsavoury side of what had been a passionate few years of debate spilled over. In response to the 'No' outcome a group of Unionists lit flares, taunted and charged at the defeated supporters of Independence who had dominated George Square before and during the vote.[10] Similar battles took place throughout June 2020, during the resurgence of the Black Lives Matter movement. Although peaceful protests against racism were held in Glasgow Green, more trouble spilled over in George Square, with members of the National Defence League and other loyalist groups staging counter-protests, defending statues and singing 'Rule Britannia'.[11] These flashpoints remind us that perceptions of history, often skewed by an impaired or biased cultural memory, can strengthen the identity of different groups. The symbolic importance of royal and imperial statues became clear to see during these conflicts.

These Commonwealth Games which the city had used to exalt its new image in 2014 and celebrate its old ones have their roots in more telling nomenclature. Beginning in Hamilton, Canada, in 1930 as the British Empire Games, they became the British Empire and Commonwealth Games in Vancouver in 1954, the British Commonwealth Games in Edinburgh in 1970, and finally the Commonwealth Games in Edmonton, Canada in 1978.[12] The loss of the words 'Empire' and 'British' from the official advertising and merchandise says something about the context, and awareness, of British colonial history. The semantics become crucial when we look at particular cases, such as the 1966 Games in Jamaica, in which the word 'Empire', and all that it entails, was used on commemorative stamps and other signage. Today an entire generation of athletes and spectators are largely unaware of the imperial roots of these games and it is no wonder that certain histories, such as slavery, have been neglected. During those clashes in George Square we might suggest that the spectre of Glasgow's imperial history was not vanquished after all. Perhaps it revealed that national identity in Scotland is an evolution, not just of symbols, colours and flags on buildings and in football stadia, but of ideas and beliefs spanning centuries. That the battleground of choice for these ideas was the city's chief square, laid out in the Georgian period, following a global sporting event which – whether explicitly or not – placed Glasgow in an imperial context, is more than a little symbolic.

In the midst of these contests, Georgian Glasgow was being put on display in the Kelvingrove Art Gallery and Museum. From 18 April to 17 August, and thus coinciding with the Commonwealth Games, Glasgow Life ran the major exhibition *How Glasgow Flourished: 1714–1837*. As a collaborative doctoral student, I was directly involved with the planning and curation of this exhibition.[13] The access I gained to the careful preparation and the processes involved by the staff offered a unique insight into the importance of reviving lost narratives while appealing to people's expectations of Glasgow. A precarious balancing act. The most serious issue in dealing with Georgian Glasgow in the city museums is simply that it has been unrepresented for too long. As the original interpretation plan puts it: 'The collections of this period held by Glasgow Museums are among the finest of any civic museum service in Great Britain. Alas, they have never been displayed in a major exhibition about the city's history.'[14] The purpose of *How Glasgow Flourished* was to change this: to bring these objects to the public. But, as discussed throughout this book, the term Georgian seems uncomfortable and almost insecure beside the familiar character of Victorian Glasgow. Other than the histories of the Tobacco Lords in the People's Palace and the Foulis Academy Exhibition held in the Mitchell Library in 2001, the civic contextualisation of Glasgow and its eighteenth-century history has been more or less ignored since the literary relics of Smollett, Moore and others were put on show as part of the Scottish Exhibition in 1911. Therefore, we may argue that the 2014 exhibition was long overdue.

As we know, the majority of Glasgow's Georgian architecture is lost. While buildings such as Kelvingrove Art Gallery and Museum were being built, the surfeit of socialist and working-class culture that responded to the pomp of the late Victorian period brought about a sense of separation from the origins of Glasgow's wealth through tobacco, sugar and cotton. In a way this is not unlike the marginalisation of history in English culture which, as Paul Readman puts it, was 'swept from the high place it had won for itself' by 'the rapid pace of change in the late nineteenth and early twentieth centuries'.[15] But what histories remain? Which of them have survived the passage of time and the many technological revolutions since the International Exhibitions outlined above? The Merchant City remains a popular bar and restaurant district of Glasgow, but its name bears little resemblance to the cultural memory of Glasgow as it is today, and as it has been for the past century. In fact, the Merchant City area *should* be the exact location in which Georgian Glasgow is evoked. The concentration of the few remaining Georgian buildings such as the Trades Hall on Glassford Street and the churches in the Saltmarket area, not to mention the Trongate and the High Street on which the original University of Glasgow was built, should offer locals and tourists in Glasgow an impression of this era. Instead, it represents a cordoned off, increasingly unpopular subcategory of the Georgian era: the merchants themselves. This celebration of the select few wealthy men has overshadowed their ties to slavery and, yes, their connections with figures of Glasgow's Enlightenment including Adam Smith and the Foulis brothers. This localised imbalance has complicated the public's perception of Glasgow's already-skewed historical character.

In *Selling Places* (1998) Stephen Ward declares: 'It was Glasgow, traditionally perceived as hard, dirty and violent, a seemingly unstormable stronghold of the left, which took Britain into this new era of place marketing in 1983–84.'[16] The slogan which brought Glasgow into the spotlight was the famous 'Glasgow's Miles Better', with a smiling Mr Happy in place of the 'o' in Glasgow. For Ward, the success of the slogan was built partially on the 'I ♥ New York' campaign, opening

Glasgow to a global audience.[17] The spatial compression of the city's meaning in the Great Exhibitions is echoed in such campaigns. As Ward says, 'these campaigns have commodified places and denied or trivialized their subtle meanings.'[18] It is possible that these 'subtle meanings' are only discoverable by living in or visiting a place for a long period of time. In other words, day visitors and general passers-by would take little from the Georgian period other than the names of a couple of merchants. Raphael Samuel's analysis of the Merchant City as a site of memory allows us to consider the city's sudden focus on the city centre in a new light:

> Glasgow's 'Merchant City' is an apparently successful example [of municipal idealism and civic pride], the restoration and refurbishment of a run-down district of sweatshops and warehouses into one that is simultaneously pre-industrial and post-modern, exorcising memories of the shipyards by resurrecting the commercial glories of the age of Adam Smith, while at the same time providing a showcase for modern fashion and a new business headquarters for information technology.[19]

Samuel's words above suggest that the contradictory nature of the reinvented Merchant City is concomitant with the presence of new and old in the Exhibitions, particularly 1911 and 1938. A recent symbol of this may be the 'illumination of the Gothic skyline of the Necropolis' during 1990: a literal combination of the older part of the city with new technologies without recreation or pomp.[20] Glasgow, it seems, has always merged visions of the past – however industrial the focus may have been – with visions of the future.

In Mark O'Neill's summary (2009) of Glasgow's cultural sites he acknowledges Glasgow as having 'the best preserved Victorian urban architecture in the UK'.[21] Going on, he makes that point that Glasgow's self-definition 'is not unitary or without conflict, and is to a degree, very consciously, commodified in response to global economic forces'. This is a measured response to the present state of Glasgow's remembrance of its past. The issue is not that the 'main directions and content' of museum displays 'are decided locally and reflect local realities and aspirations' but that the city has been intrinsically involved in dictating imperial values onto the public as a sort of erasure of its social problems, rendering everything that came before the Victorian period as a sort of tributary flowing into the all-powerful Clyde of the shipbuilding era. This returns us to the chronology of the murals in the City Chambers, and the tremendous gap only recently being filled by such events as the 2014 exhibition in Kelvingrove Museum.[22]

Upon closing on 17 August 2014 *How Glasgow Flourished* had counted 57,753 visitors, almost double the amount expected.[23] The exhibition dealt with several themes and narratives particular to Glasgow in the Georgian era, including the Tobacco Lords, the 'elite', social order, education, textiles, coal mining, steam power, radicalism and reform, printing and publications, slavery and family histories. The use of objects was therefore carefully considered and diverse, including paintings, etchings, drawings, models, sculptures, precious metals, banners, books, glass, pottery, various dress types, weapons, and an array of digital media from projections to interactive touchscreens showing the physical growth of the city in Georgian period.

Getting the tone right proved to be difficult in the planning stages, as the organisers found in their consultation days, seeking a suitable title that would attract a diverse audience with little knowledge of Georgian Glasgow to build on. As my PhD thesis (2015) showed, the early 'working titles' leaned towards the built environment of Glasgow and the city's renowned merchants.[24] That the term 'Georgian Glasgow' was so unpopular with the public during these consultations helps us understand just how dominant Victorian Glasgow has become, as we will discuss shortly. The Enlightenment, meanwhile, proved to be a more popular hook, but was essentially elided throughout the exhibition, at least in name, perhaps due to the presence of slavery. With Glasgow's role in slavery being discussed in the media there was, it seems, some apprehension about making claims of being an enlightened city on one hand while pointing out its guilt with the other.[25]

This is not to say that the figures of the Scottish Enlightenment local to Glasgow were not part of the exhibition. Indeed, many – if not most – of the people in this book comprised part of the narrative of *How Glasgow Flourished*, it was only the concept of the Enlightenment that was unfortunately absent. Walking round the exhibition space you would encounter a portrait of William Cullen, the renowned image of Glasgow University from the seventeenth century by John Slezer (d. 1717), both of Robert Paul's *Views of Glasgow from the South East* (1760s), his engravings *From the South on the East Side of St. Mungo's Church*, and *A View of St. Andrew's Church from the Battlements of the Old Town House*, as well as tourist books and histories of Glasgow, displaying the early-Victorian taste for local historical tourism which we touched on in Chapter 6.[26] Each book was opened to show other topographical views – suggesting the legacy of Paul's work in the Foulis Academy – and, in the case of the history book (1881), the image on display was David Allan's *Fine Art Exhibition in the Court of Old*

College (1761).[27] It should also be noted that this image, from an essentially forgotten aspect of Glasgow's history, was used as the primary image in Glasgow Life's marketing strategy for the exhibition. A poster was designed based on Allan's work, representing the starting point for a new feature of Glasgow's exhibited character, taking its cue from a lively social scene in the arts rather than a bustling, masculine scene of industry (see Figure 19). This departure from the norm is certainly a step in the right direction.

LOCALISING CULTURAL MEMORY AND THE PERSISTENCE OF VICTORIAN GLASGOW

In this concluding chapter the development of Glasgow's character has been the focus. It is therefore fitting to end by rounding off some ideas on cultural memory and the potential that existed for the 2014 exhibition, and that continues to exist for other museum spaces in Glasgow, to affect new interpretations of what is, at present, a persistently Victorian city. In relation to this book, the problematic role of slavery and the elision of the Scottish Enlightenment in *How Glasgow Flourished* are the clearest examples of the exhibition's unfulfilled potential. What is more, the complex interrelationship of slavery *and* Enlightenment seems to have prohibited either theme being properly explored, leaving the familiar narrative of industry with much more exhibition space than was perhaps necessary. Before any more is said on cultural memory, however, it should be stated that the 2014 exhibition successfully promoted Georgian Glasgow as a new, meaningful term for the public to use and interpret.

The permanent 'Glasgow Stories' section in Kelvingrove Art Gallery and Museum was renewed in March 2014, changing its angle from a focus on the city post-1990 to a chronological narrative of Glasgow in its various stages of development. The Victorian era is given the largest space, exploiting the prominence of industry and shipbuilding in the public imagination as outlined above. This is understandable. However, it is made all the more effective by the presence of Georgian Glasgow. This section includes a portrait of Lord Provost Arthur Connell (1772–4), a map of Glasgow from 1775, and yet another topographical view of the city from Foulis Academy pupil Robert Paul. The importance of the Georgian era is explained in an official press release, in which it is stated that the Glasgow Story 'moves on to Georgian Glasgow and the 18th Century, charting a period in which the city grew significantly in size, stature and international influence'.[28] Herein lies the beginning of

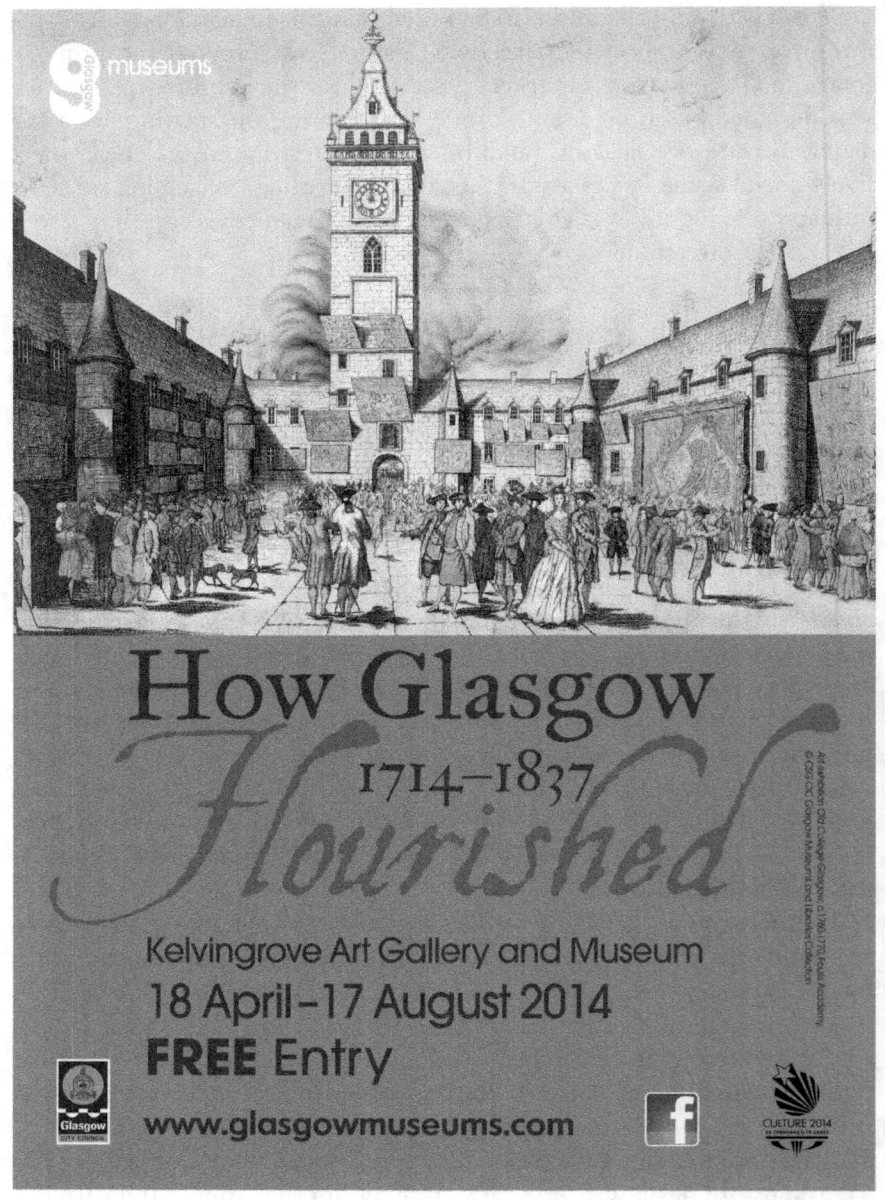

Figure 19 Marketing poster design for *How Glasgow Flourished: 1714–1837* (2014). © Culture and Sport Glasgow (Museums).

the officially renewed interest in Georgian Glasgow by its chief cultural body, Glasgow Life.

My involvement in this is rooted in my arguments for a considered use of the term 'Georgian', in spite of its initial lack of popularity as an exhibition title. Together with repeated images such as the Foulis Academy landscapes which I had been researching, the era may become recognisable over time. In Carol Foreman's text *Lost Glasgow* we find a chapter dedicated to the Georgian era. It is not titled as such: instead, 1707–1837 is titled 'From Merchant City to Victorian City' while 1837–1901 is clearly marked 'The Victorian City'.[29] This is symbolic of Glasgow's historical issue with the Georgian period. From the Union to the height of industrialisation, Glasgow has been under-represented, mislabelled and entirely overshadowed by Edinburgh in a national context. This book has tried to make the case for a longer and more involved showcase of Glasgow's history. The wealth of the collections at the core of Glasgow's museums has highlighted the need for more exhibitions, themed according to specific subjects which, rooted in the important work done in 2014, can fill the gap in cultural memory which has only recently been addressed. It may even be said that the forgotten people and ideas of the Georgian era can evolve and belong to Glasgow alongside the more familiar, reinforced character of the city.

The importance of cultural memory is implied by the interdisciplinary relationships that helped produce the 2014 exhibition and the issues of ownership, selectivity and distinctive strategies therein. Unlike the civic affairs of the late nineteenth and early twentieth centuries, the ceremony and pomp of Glasgow's character was not the concern. But, as I have argued, the cultural memory of this confident, Victorian *version* of Glasgow, including its industrial motifs, has never been adequately challenged. Therefore the issue of Georgian Glasgow's subservient place in Glasgow's projected character – whether in museums or city streets – has been dormant and invisible without any context. A statement such as this, in reference to periods of history in certain places, is reliant on theories of memory studies. In particular, the relationship between cultural and communicative memory in shaping collective memories (the shared experience of a particular exhibition and its effect on the perceived character of Glasgow) as well as the importance of location are at the heart of this final analysis.[30]

To sum up the use of cultural memory thus far, this book has dealt with printed material such as books and pamphlets in the proliferation of religious and classical ideas, the issue of the ownership of individuals from history and the ideas they represent, the issue of ownership and location as regards the remembrance of transatlantic slavery, and the dominance of Empire in the shaping of national identity. In each of these cases, comparative scholarship has been used to exemplify the role of printed literature, paintings, etchings, statues and artefacts in the preservation of cultural memory specific to Glasgow-based people, institutions, and buildings. In *How Glasgow Flourished*, a similar dialogue was in play. Of course, objects and scenes from the past suggest the bygone people and places of that period. This is the most common relationship between the curator and the audience. Its invisibility, however, suggests an equally important cultural memory which has *not* been evoked. This is what we might call 'archival' memory: that which Aleida Assmann has described, through the words of Jacques Derrida, as being a 'political power'.[31] In the case of Glasgow's cultural memory, the main archival store is the Glasgow Museums Resource Centre in Nitshill, mentioned above. Outside specially acquired loans and relocated objects from other Glasgow museums, all exhibitions rely on this store in order to label the provenance of each object and therefore facilitate its correct historical use. But, if 'control of the archive means control of memory',[32] as Assmann puts it, the potential for certain objects and associated narratives to be elided is increased.

Let us step outside the exhibition space for a moment and look at the location itself, for there is a curious occurrence of collective memory particular to Kelvingrove Art Gallery and Museum worth noting. Eviatar Zerubavel has said that across all age groups 'museums are one of the institutional forms in which communities shape their collective memory'.[33] This is, of course, applicable to all museums, and is therefore as suitable to Kelvingrove Art Gallery and Museum as it is to the People's Palace, despite their many historical and cultural differences. Zerubavel goes on to say 'it is important to consider not only what is represented, but also what is not represented', confirming the issues of elision raised above.[34] In his discussion on the representation of the Highland Clearances in museums (2000), Laurence Gouriévidis says that the opening of the National Museum of Scotland in Edinburgh on St Andrew's Day 1998 was a symbolic, commemorative act challenging 'head-on the notion that Scotland only began to flourish properly after [the Union with England in] 1707'.[35] Given that the Georgian era began in 1714, may we assume that *How Glasgow Flourished* was constructed with an imperial view of Scotland in mind? Based on the above, may we even say that a more British than Scottish context for Georgian Glasgow was evoked? As we know, Glasgow has long been viewed as the Second City of the Empire and an insular experience such as that which is offered in Kelvingrove Art Gallery and Museum has its own cultural conditions. To go further, we may even consider Kelvingrove as a *lieu* of memory which conjures images of Victorian Glasgow regardless of the content of its exhibitions.

Built at the end of the Victorian period, in time for the Glasgow International Exhibition in 1901, the impressive Kelvingrove building symbolised the Victorian wealth and splendour of the city. Flanking the names of famous artists from home and abroad on the exterior walls of the building are three-dimensional shipping motifs. It is no wonder, then, that a showcase of Georgian Glasgow should lean, literally, on Victorian Glasgow. Indeed, we have said so much about the forgetting and misrepresentation of Georgian Glasgow in the public imagination that the presence of Victorian Glasgow, even when it is not the focus, has so obviously, if silently, remained. In effect, *How Glasgow Flourished* operated with not one dialogue (the narrative constructed by the curators), but two. The second was the popular, ever-present Victorian prism in the form of the building itself through which Georgian Glasgow was observed. This is when we can once again consider the time-frames in question. Today, one can visit a permanent exhibition called *Glasgow and the World*, displaying paintings, souvenirs and models which were originally on display during the initial Glasgow Exhibitions. As such, this exhibition exemplifies how objects of collective memory (bought, sold and gazed upon in 1888 and 1901) can become objects of collective memory for visitors today, who view them all in a new context. The sense of refraction from the original experience is limitless here, like a hall of mirrors.

With Kelvingrove Art Gallery and Museum emblemising its own time, the Georgian world on show in 2014 was arguably weakened by the comparative splendour and survivability of this great Victorian building. While it was a case of transportation with the Hunterian Museum in Chapter 3, we might say that exhibiting Georgian Glasgow in the West End relies on a unique set of negotiable characteristics. Glancing at slavery and the Scottish Enlightenment in the first instance might have been deemed necessary to introduce an almost-forgotten era. This crisis of cultural memory is aided by another look at the existing scholarship. As Peter Meusburger et al. have said, the 'social process of remembering requires a bodily practice of commemoration, often in the form of ritualised performances. Buildings, squares, statues, and street names "facilitate commemorative performance by reproducing and producing social relations".'[36] It is useful here to recall the point made in Chapter 4 that semantics of memory such as 'amnesia' must be handled carefully:

the most obvious example being that, while Virginia Street and Jamaica Street can connect the passer-by to Glasgow's relationship with slavery, it does not always succeed, the reason being that the public do not share the same level of knowledge or cultural memory of this aspect of the city's history. In the same way, Glassford Street and the other Merchant City markers cannot stand as suitable markers of the Georgian era. To borrow Michael Billig's term, there is an insurmountable 'banality' that, like 'unwaved flags in civic spaces', lies dormant with little effect on cultural memory.[37]

Having said this, it can be argued that the Kelvingrove Art Gallery and Museum building in the West End of Glasgow – detached from the Merchant City, High Street, George Square, and other *lieux* of Georgian Glasgow – was instrumenting a sense of Victorian Glasgow throughout the duration of *How Glasgow Flourished*. This is why 'place-bound rituals' (such as museum-going) and 'cultural artefacts' (such as those on display during the exhibition) were effectively 'solidifying' predominant notions of the city 'in the conscious and the subconscious mind[s]' of the museum-goers. Anthony Smith has called this the "territorialization of memory".[38] In Glasgow, it is clear that the built environment and the public imagination are bound by the prevailing image of the Victorian era.

So, how do we go forward from here? By opening these Glasgow-centric issues to a wider, interdisciplinary scholarly audience I believe that new questions on the use of cultural memory have been asked. This Conclusion has shown that being in partnership with cultural institutions such as museum services allows these questions to be brought to the public. With this transcultural approach, questions of remembering and forgetting can be answered more fully. In this case, the perceivable absence of the Georgian era in Glasgow's cultural memory has invited a critique of the dominant character of the city. From here, particular themes such as literature, religion, slavery and the Enlightenment (with its own subsections of medicine, science and philosophy) can be contextualised in suitable places. While the Victorian cultural memories of Kelvingrove Art Gallery and Museum offered an introduction to the Georgian era through *How Glasgow Flourished*, harnessing the cultural memories of other institutions allows for the evolution of Georgian Glasgow.

The Hunterian, for instance, has the potential to exhibit the men and women of Glasgow's Enlightenment while the Mitchell Library can provide a fitting format for the men and women of Glasgow literature.

These institutions need not always be steeped in time or history specifically (especially since there is not enough Georgian architecture left in Glasgow to facilitate this history), but the relevance of the building is intrinsic to the success of the public experience. This was shown in 2014, during the course of the Commonwealth Games in Glasgow. As stated before, the Games were an opportunity for Glasgow to showcase its international appeal. At the same time, however, the lingering issues of Empire in Glasgow's cultural memory were addressed by Jude Barber and Louise Welsh in the form of the aptly named Empire Café. Held at the Briggait in Glasgow, the location itself – in the Merchant City, with the Merchant's Steeple looming overhead – was meant to aid the exploration of 'Scotland's relationship with the North Atlantic slave trade through coffee, sugar, tea, cotton, music, visual art, academic lectures, poetry, debate, workshops, historical walks, film and literature.'[39] These kinds of events are examples of what we might consider as multi-dimensional instances of collective remembering which – without ignoring the inevitable issues of ownership and selectivity that occurs in every public event – can offer an alternate experience to museums in publicising underdeveloped issues.

To put it this way: there are various ways to exhibit an impression of the past. As Gaynor Kavanagh has said: 'the images created by museums can buttress social identity, and consolidate social positions and class interests'. In Glasgow this seems undeniably true. She goes on to say that these images can also enable 'the opening of new ideas and the articulation of long silent questions. They can even provide the basis for an agenda for change.'[40] *How Glasgow Flourished*, I believe, has provided this agenda. Glasgow Life's final interpretation of 'Georgian Glasgow' in the exhibition may have drawn criticism but without it we would have less to say about the 'images' of Glasgow which can now be interpreted and remembered by upcoming generations of the public as well as academics and professionals from a wide range of fields. Institutional issues of ownership and misrepresentation become less prominent when more voices are heard. A public debate – '(Re)moving statues: should statues ever be removed for political reasons?' – hosted by Glasgow City Heritage Trust in St Andrew's in the Square on 27 March 2019 offered a suitable platform for both new voices and old. And as we listen in order to use these voices to enhance the presence of Glasgow's history, other educational and cultural institutions can, hopefully, draw from the case of Georgian Glasgow as a blueprint for analysing their own unique cultural memories.

And so we come full circle to the notion in Gray's *Lanark* that Glasgow is relatively unimaginative, that it evokes only a limited number of references. 'Imaginatively,' he writes, 'Glasgow exists as a music hall song and a few bad novels. That's all we've given to the world outside. It's all we've given to ourselves.'[41] We come back to this to challenge how relevant it is today, how it stacks up to the recent, often heated, debates on Glasgow's complicity in the slave trade and to the deep-cut political and religious divides that can be traced back through the centuries. Is it not the case that the more we uncover about Glasgow's past the more we might also imagine? Those 'bad novels' that Gray's characters mock often clamoured around the Georgian period, reviving the romance of the Jacobites, the greed of merchants and the adventures of emigrants. Although they are not named, Gray's predecessors are often derided for their sentimentality. Authors such as Catherine Carswell and Margaret Thomson Davis might be cast in a genre of postmodern romance but their evocation of the eighteenth century has preserved much of Georgian Glasgow, imaginatively, in print.

As Glasgow continues to change and keep pace with the technological advances of the twenty-first century we can barely imagine how it might look to the next generation, and the next, and so on. Buildings and monuments may fall. Streets might be renamed. But lost histories can be always found in the tapestry of cultural memory.

NOTES

1. Brian Groom, *Financial Times*, 23 February 2013 <https://www.ft.com/content/6f4d18a6-7f3f-11e2-89ed-00144feabdc0> (last accessed 20 November 2019).
2. Robert Burns, *Poems, Chiefly in the Scottish Dialect* (Kilmarnock: John Wilson, 1786), 194.
3. Alfred Thomas, *Prague Palimpsest: Writing, Memory, and the City* (Chicago: University of Chicago Press, 2010), 2.
4. Ibid., 3.
5. I am indebted to my wife Sarah-Louise for making this same comparison in her work as a student at the Glasgow School of Art.
6. Carol Craig, *The Tears that Made the Clyde: Well-being in Glasgow* (Glendaruel: Argyll Publishing, 2010), 131–2.
7. Phil Hanlon, David Walsh and Bruce Whyte, *Let Glasgow Flourish: A comprehensive report on health and its determinants in Glasgow and West Central Scotland* (Glasgow: Glasgow Centre for Population Health, 2006), 12, <https://www.gcph.co.uk/assets/0000/0377/LetGlasgowFlourish_full.pdf> (last accessed 20 November 2019).
8. Julie Clark and Valerie Wright, 'Urban Regeneration in Glasgow: Looking

to the Past to Build the Future? The Case of the "New Gorbals"', in Julie Clark and Nicholas Wise, eds, *Urban Renewal, Community and Participation* (Cham, Switzerland: Springer International, 2018), 45–70 (56).
9. BBC, 'Scotland Decides: Results' <https://www.bbc.co.uk/news/events/scotland-decides/results> (last accessed 30 August 2020).
10. BBC, 'Scottish referendum: More arrests pledged over George Square disorder' <https://www.bbc.co.uk/news/uk-scotland-glasgow-west-29294562> (last accessed 20 November 2019).
11. *The Scotsman*, 18 June 2020 <https://www.scotsman.com/news/crime/glasgow-violence-heres-what-happened-george-square-between-loyalist-defence-league-and-no-evictions-group-2888577> (last accessed 29 June 2020).
12. For a breakdown of all these Games see the official webpages <https://thecgf.com/games> (last accessed 20 November 2019).
13. In 2012 I was awarded an AHRC-funded Collaborative Doctoral Award, shared by the University of Glasgow and Glasgow Life ('Georgian Glasgow', PI: Murray Pittock).
14. As stated in Glasgow Life's Interpretation Plan (19 October 2011).
15. Paul Readman, 'The Place of the Past in English Culture c.1890–1914', *Past & Present*, 186 (2005), 147–99 (148).
16. Stephen V. Ward, *Selling Places: The marketing and promotion of towns and cities, 1850–2000* (London: Routledge – E. & F. N. Spon, 1998), 191.
17. Ibid., 192.
18. Ibid., 239.
19. Raphael Samuel, *Theatres of Memory, Volume 1: Past and Present in Contemporary Culture* (London and New York: Verso, 1994), 146.
20. Ibid., 180.
21. Mark O'Neill, 'Museums, Meaning and Money in Glasgow', *Journal of Irish Studies*, 2:2 (2009), 139–52 (140).
22. Ibid., 150.
23. Figures courtesy of Dr Anthony Lewis (18 August 2014).
24. Craig Lamont, *Georgian Glasgow: the city remembered through literature, objects, and cultural memory theory* (PhD thesis: University of Glasgow, 2015), 249.
25. Ibid.
26. They were: *Select Views of Glasgow and its Environs* (1829); *Glasgow Delineated* (1839); *Views and Notices of Glasgow of Former Times* (1848 [1843]); and George MacGregor's *History of Glasgow* (1881).
27. See Figure 2.
28. See <https://newsroom.peoplemakeglasgow.com/news/news-archive/march-2014/kelvingrove-glasgow-stories/> (last accessed 20 November 2019).

29. Carol Foreman, *Lost Glasgow: Glasgow's Lost Architectural Heritage* (Edinburgh: Birlinn, 2002), contents page.
30. Christina West, 'Memory—Recollection—Culture—Identity—Space: Social Context, Identity Formation, and Self-construction of the Calé (Gitanos) in Spain', in Peter Meusburger, Michael Heffernan and Edgar Wunder, eds, *Cultural Memories: The Geographical Point of View* (London: Springer, 2011), 101–19 (104).
31. Aleida Assmann, *Cultural Memory and Western Civilization* (Cambridge: Cambridge University Press, 2011), 328.
32. Ibid.
33. Mauro Spicci, 'Museums, Memory and the Shaping of Identity: a conversation with Professor Eviatar Zerubavel', *Altre Modernità*; 5 (2011), 115–18 (116).
34. Ibid., 117.
35. Quoted in Laurence Gouriévidis, 'Representing the Disrupted Past of Northern Scotland: The Highland Clearances in Museums', *History & Memory*, 12:2 (2000), 122–41 (124).
36. Peter Meusburger, Michael Heffernan and Edgar Wunder, 'Cultural Memories: An Introduction', in Peter Meusburger, Michael Heffernan and Edgar Wunder, eds, *Cultural Memories: The Geographical Point of View* (London: Springer, 2011), 2–14 (8).
37. Michael Billig, *Banal Nationalism* (London: Sage, 2013 [1995]), 49–50.
38. Quoted in Meusburger et al., 'Cultural Memories: An Introduction', (2011), 8.
39. See <http://www.empire-cafe.org/about> (last accessed 30 August 2020).
40. Gaynor Kavanagh, 'History in the Museum – and out of it', in Timothy Ambrose, ed., *Presenting Scotland's Story* (Edinburgh: Scottish Museums Council, 1989), 27–37 (36).
41. Alasdair Gray, *Lanark: A Life in Four Books* (Edinburgh: Canongate, 2007 [1981]), 243–4.

Bibliography

PRIMARY SOURCES

Manuscripts

Edinburgh University Library, Archives Services
　LA. III. 363. 1, ff. 1–47: 'Memorial of Robert Foulis & Company'.
Mitchell Library, Glasgow
　MS. 73: Unpublished collection of poems by William Campbell.
National Records of Scotland, Edinburgh
　GD393/91, f. 10: Letter from Alexander Harvie, Barbados, to Claud Alexander, merchant in Glasgow.

Printed works

A Society in Glasgow, *An Address to the Inhabitants of Glasgow, Paisley, and the Neighbourhood, Concerning the African Slave Trade, 1791, from The Slave Trade Debate: contemporary writings for and against* [reprint] (Oxford: Bodleian Library, 2007).
A vindication of Mr. Hutcheson from the calumnious aspersions of a late pamphlet, by several of his scholars (1738).
Accounts and Papers [of the House of Commons]: Forty-Four Volumes, Trade, &c. continues, (Friendly Societies and Trade Unions) Vol. LXIX (1876).
Autobiographical Accounts of Persons Under Spiritual Concern at Cambuslang (Glasgow) during the Revival of 1741–1743, Part One (Shropshire: Quinta Press, 2008), 342, <http://quintapress.macmate.me/PDF_Books/-Cambuslang_Testimonies_Vol_1.pdf> (last accessed 20 November 2019).
Arbuckle, James, *Glotta: A Poem* (Glasgow: William Duncan, 1721).
Barclay, Robert, *Theologiae vere Christianae apologia* (Amsterdam: Typis excusa pro Jacob Claus, 1676).

Black, Joseph, 'Experiments upon magnesia alba, quicklime, and some other alcaline substances', *Essays and Observations, Physical and Literary. Read before a Society in Edinburgh, and published by them. Volume II* (Edinburgh: G. Hamilton and J. Balfour, 1756), 157–225.

Blake, George, *The Shipbuilders* (London: Faber, 1935).

Boswell, James, *An Account of Corsica* (London: Edward and Charles Dilly, 1769).

[Boswell, James], *No Abolition of Slavery; or the Universal Empire of Love: a poem* (London: R. Faulder, 1791).

Bruce, Robert, *Folio of maps, plans and drawings accompanying the First Planning Report to the Highways and Planning Committee* (Glasgow: Corporation of the City of Glasgow, 1945).

Burns, Robert, *Poems, Chiefly in the Scottish Dialect* (Kilmarnock: John Wilson, 1786).

Butter, P., ed., *Edwin Muir: The Complete Poems* (Aberdeen: Association for Scottish Literary Studies, 1991).

Caledonian Mercury, 23 December 1820.

Caledonian Mercury, 24 October 1850.

Camden, William, *Britannia, sive florentissimorum regnorum angliae, scotiae, hiberniae, et insularum adiacentium ex intima antiquitate chorographica description* (London: Bishop and Norton, 1607).

[Camden, William,], *Britannia, Newly Translated into English: with large Additions and Improvements* (Oxford: Edmund Gibson, editor, of Queens College, 1695).

Catalogue of the Foulis Exhibition Held in the University of Glasgow April 1913 (Glasgow: James MacLehose and Sons, 1913).

Certain Propositions Relating to the Scots Plantation of Caledonia, and the National Address for Supporting thereof, briefly offered to Publick View, for removing of Mistakes and Prejudices (Glasgow: 1700).

Chambers, Robert, *The Gazetteer of Scotland* (Edinburgh: Balfour & Jack, 1836).

The Eclectic Review MDCCCXLII: January – June, New Series, Vol. XI (London: Thomas Ward & Co., 1842).

The Electrical Engineer, 27 April 1888.

Empire Exhibition Scotland – 1938, Official Guide (Glasgow: McCorquodale & Co., Ltd, 1938).

The Examiner (London), 11 January 1818.

Financial Times, 23 February 2013.

Gaitens, Edward, *Dance of the Apprentices* (Edinburgh: Canongate Classics, 2001 [1948]).

Galt, John, *Annals of the Parish; or, the chronicle of Dalmailing during the Ministry of the Rev. Micah Balwhidder, written by himself* (London and Edinburgh: T. N. Foulis, 1911 [1821]).

Galt, John, *The Steam-Boat* (Edinburgh: William Blackwood, 1822).

Galt, John, *The Ayrshire Legatees; or, The Pringle Family* (New York: W. B. Gilley, 1823).
Galt, John, *The Entail; or, The Lairds of Grippy*, ed. Ian A. Gordon (Oxford: Oxford University Press, 1984 [1823]).
Galt, John, *Bogle Corbet; or, The Emigrants*, 3 vols (London: Henry Colburn & Richard Bentley, 1831).
[Galt, John], *The Autobiography of John Galt*, vol. 2 (London: Cochrane and McCrone, 1833).
Galt, John, *The Literary Life, and Miscellanies, of John Galt*, vol. 2 (Edinburgh: William Blackwood, 1834).
[Galt, John], 'Memoir of Galt', *The Annals of the Parish and The Ayrshire Legatees* (Edinburgh: Blackwood and Sons, 1850), pp. lxxxix–xc.
The Guardian, 28 November 2018.
Gillies, John, *Historical Collections Relating to Remarkable Periods of The Success of The Gospel and Eminent Instruments Employed in Promoting It, Volume I* (Glasgow: Robert and Andrew Foulis, 1754).
Glasgow Herald, 27 August 1860.
Glasgow Herald, 26 July 1867.
Glasgow International Exhibition 1901: Official Guide (Glasgow: C. P. Watson, 1901).
Gray, Alasdair, *Lanark: A Life in Four Books* (Edinburgh: Canongate, 2007 [1981]).
Hamilton, Thomas, *The Youth and Manhood of Cyril Thornton*, ed. Maurice Lindsay (Aberdeen: The Association for Scottish Literary Studies, 1990 [1827]).
Hamilton (of Gilbertfield), William, *A new edition of the life and heroick actions of the renoun'd Sir William Wallace, general and governour of Scotland. Wherein the old obsolete words are rendered more intelligible; and adapted to the understanding of such who have not leisure to study the meaning, and import of such phrases without the help of a glossary* (Glasgow: William Duncan, 1722).
Hamilton (of Gilbertfield), William, *Blind Harry's Wallace* (Edinburgh: Luath Press, 1998 [1722]).
Hind, Archie, *The Dear Green Place & Fur Sadie* (Edinburgh: Polygon, 2008 [1966]).
[Home, Henry (Lord Kames)], *Sketches of the History of Man. In two volumes* (Edinburgh: William Creech, 1774).
Howitt, William, *Homes and Haunts of the Most Eminent British Poets* (London: George Routledge & Sons, 1877).
Hunter, William, *Anatomia uteri humani gravidi tabulis illustrata, auctore Gulielmo Hunter, serenissimae Reginae Charlottae medico extraordinario, in Academia Regali anatomiae professore, et Societatum Regiae et Antiquariae, socio* (Birmingham: John Baskerville, 1774).
Johnston, Arthur, *Poemata Omnia* (Middleburg, 1642).

Kyle, Elizabeth, *The Tontine Belle* (London: Peter Davies, 1951).
Lee, Arthur, *An essay in vindication of the continental colonies of America, from a censure of Mr Adam Smith, in his Theory of moral sentiments. By an American.* (London: T. Becket and P. A. De Hont, 1764).
M'Ure, John, *A View of the City of Glasgow; Or, an Account of its Origin, Rise and Progress, with a more particular Description thereof than has hitherto been known* (Glasgow: James Duncan, 1736)
M'Ure, John, *The History of Glasgow: A New Edition* (Glasgow: Hutchison and Brookman, 1830).
Macarthur, Mary, *Necropolis: An Elegy, and other poems* (Glasgow, David Bryce, 1842).
McArthur, Alexander and Long, H. Kingsley, *No Mean City: A Story of the Glasgow Slums* (London: Longmans, Green & Co., 1935).
The Meditations of the Emperor Marcus Aurelius Antoninus. Newly translated from the Greek: with notes, and an account of his life. (Glasgow: Robert Foulis, 1742).
Mayne, John, 'Glasgow', in George Eyre-Todd, ed., *The Glasgow Poets: Their Lives and Poems* (Paisley: Alexander Gardner, 1906 [1903]), 73–87.
Millar, John, *Observations Concerning the Distinction of Ranks in Society*, second edition (London: J. Murray, 1773).
Moore, Dugald, *The Bridal Night; The First Poet; and other Poems* (Glasgow: Blackie, Fullarton & Co., 1831).
Moore, Dugald, *The Bard of the North: A Series of Poetical Tales, Illustrative of Highland Scenery and Character* (Glasgow: David Robertson, 1833).
The Morning Chronicle (London), 18 September 1822.
The Morning Post (London), 21 February 1844.
The News and Courier (Charleston, South Carolina, 158:172), 20 June 1960.
Phipps, Elvira Anna, *Memorials of Clutha; or, Pencillings of the Clyde* (London: Smith, Elder and Co., 1842).
The Protestation of the Generall Assemblie of the Church of Scotland (Glasgow: George Anderson, 1638).
Ramsay, Allan, *Poems* (Edinburgh: Thomas Ruddiman, 1721).
Ramsay, Allan, *The Gentle Shepherd; A Scots Pastoral Comedy* (Edinburgh: Thomas Ruddiman, 1725).
Register of the Privy Council of Scotland 1681–1682, 3:7 (Edinburgh: Morrison & Gibb, 1915).
'Remove the racist, colonial statue of Frederick Roberts in the Kelvingrove Park, Glasgow.' change.org [Mélina Valdelievre] < https://www.change.org/-p/glasgow-city-council-remove-the-racist-colonial-statue-of-frederick-roberts-in-the-kelvingrove-park> (last accessed 20 November 2019)
Report of Committee of General Assembly, on Colonial Churches, 28th May 1838, and deliverance of the assembly. With Appendix, containing correspondence with the Colonial Office, and Report of the North American Colonial Society of Glasgow for 1838 (Glasgow: G. Richardson, 1838).

Robertson, J. Logie, ed., *The Complete Poetical Works of Thomas Campbell* (London: John Frowde, 1907).
Robertson, James, *Joseph Knight* (London: Fourth Estate, 2003).
The Saturday Magazine, No. 583 (London: July, 1841).
The Scotsman, 15 April 2013.
Scottish Exhibition of National History, Art and Industry: Palace of History, Catalogue of Exhibits, vol. 1 (Glasgow: Dalross, 1911).
[Scott, Walter], *Waverley; or, 'Tis Sixty Years Since*, vol. 3 (Edinburgh: John Ballantine & Co., 1814).
Scott, Walter, *The Field of Waterloo; a poem: second edition* (Edinburgh: Archibald Constable, 1815).
Smellie, William, *A Treatise on the Theory and Practice of Midwifery*, 3 vols (London: D. Wilson, 1752–64).
Smith, Adam, *The Theory of Moral Sentiments*, second edition (London: A. Millar, 1761).
Smith, Adam, *Glasgow Edition of the Works and Correspondence, Vol. 5, Lectures on Jurisprudence* (Oxford: Oxford University Press, 1976 [1762]).
Smith, Adam, *The Wealth of Nations, Books I–III* (London: Penguin, 1986 [1776]).
Smollett, Tobias, *An essay on the external use of water. In a letter to Dr. **** with Particular Remarks upon the present Method of using the Mineral Waters at Bath in Somersetshire, and a Plan for rendering them more safe, agreeable, and efficacious.* (London: M. Cooper, 1752).
Smollett, Tobias, *Travels Through France and Italy* (London: The Folio Society, 1979 [1766]).
Smollett, Tobias, *The Expedition of Humphry Clinker* (London: Penguin, 1985 [1771]).
Smollett, Tobias, *Ode to Independence. By the Late T. Smollett, M. D., with notes and observations* (Glasgow: Robert and Andrew Foulis, 1773).
Smollett, Tobias, *The Miscellaneous Works of Tobias Smollett, M.D. with a Life of the Author in Twelve Volumes, Volume 4* (London: Otridge and Rackham et al., 1824).
Southey, Robert, *History of the Peninsular War*, 3 vols (London: J. Murray, 1823).
Souvenir and handbook of Feill a' Chomuinn Ghaidhealaich (The Highland Association Bazaar) 1907 (Glasgow: J. M. Munro, 1907).
Stuart, Charles Edward, *Letter to the Town Council of Glasgow, 13 September 1745* (facsimile), University of Glasgow Library, Special Collections Eph. A/106.
Subscription Call for Foulis Library, 1866, University of Glasgow Library Special Collections, Call Number: Mu2-x.9/13c.
Thom, William, *The Defects of an University Education, and its unsuitableness to a commercial people: with the expediency and necessity of erecting at*

Glasgow, an academy, for the instruction of youth. In a letter to J.M. Esq. from a society interested in the success of this public spirited proposal (London: E. Dilly, 1762).

The Trans-Atlantic Slave Trade Database <http://www.slavevoyages.org> (last accessed 20 November 2019).

Walker, Robert and Davison, T. Raffles, *Pen and Ink Notes at the Glasgow Exhibition* (London: J. S. Virtue & Co., 1888).

Warburton, Eliot, *Darien; or, The Merchant Prince. A Historical Romance*, vol. 1 (London: Colburn and Co., 1852).

The Weekly Entertainer: or, Agreeable and Instructive Repository, 24 September 1810 (Sherborne: R. Goadby).

Wordsworth, William, *The Poetical Works of William Wordsworth. A New Edition. In Six Volumes, Vol. III.* (London: Edward Moxon, 1837).

SECONDARY SOURCES

Unpublished theses

Goldsmith, Alastair Lindsay, *The Glasgow International Exhibitions, 1888–1938*, (MLitt thesis: University of Strathclyde, 1985).

McLean, Ralph R., *Rhetoric and literary criticism in the early Scottish Enlightenment* (PhD thesis: University of Glasgow, 2009).

Mullen, Stephen, *The 'Glasgow West India interest': integration, collaboration and exploitation in the British Atlantic World, 1776–1846* (PhD thesis: University of Glasgow, 2015).

Published works

Aberdein, Jennie W., *John Galt* (Oxford: Oxford University Press, 1936).

Abrams, Lynn, *Oral History Theory* (London: Routledge, 2010).

Armitage, David, 'Paterson, William (1658–1719)', *Oxford Dictionary of National Biography*, <http://www.oxforddnb.com/view/article/21538> (last accessed 20 November 2019).

Assmann, Aleida, *Cultural Memory and Western Civilization* (Cambridge: Cambridge University Press, 2011).

Assmann, Jan, 'Collective Memory and Cultural Identity', *New German Critique*, 65 (1995), 125–33.

Assmann, Jan, *Religion and Cultural Memory: Ten Studies* (Stanford, CA: Stanford University Press, 2006).

Assmann, Jan, 'Communicative and Cultural Memory', in Astrid Erll and Ansgar Nünning, eds, *Media and Cultural Memory: An International and Interdisciplinary Handbook* (Berlin: Walter de Gruyter GmbH & Co., 2008), 109–18.

Baillie, James, 'The Scottish Exhibition of National History, Art, and Industry,

Glasgow, 1911', *Old Glasgow Club Transactions, Volume 7, Session 1934–1935* (Glasgow: Aird and Coghill Ltd, 1935), 7–15.

Bainbridge, Simon, *British Poetry and the Revolutionary and Napoleonic Wars: Visions of Conflict* (Oxford: Oxford University Press, 2003).

Barfoot, Mike, 'Philosophy and method in Cullen's medical teaching', in A. Doig et al., eds, *William Cullen and the Eighteenth Century Medical World* (Edinburgh: Edinburgh University Press, 1993), 110–32.

Barfoot, Mike, *An Account of the Life, Lectures, and Writings of William Cullen*, vol. 1 (Bristol: Thoemmes, 1997).

Barnaby, Paul, 'Timeline of the European Reception of Sir Walter Scott, 1802–2013', in Murray Pittock, ed., *The Reception of Sir Walter Scott in Europe* (London and New York: Bloomsbury, 2007), xxiv–lxxxii.

Barthes, Ronald, *Camera Lucida: Reflections on Photography* (New York: Hill & Wang, 1980).

Bellamy, Martin, 'Shipbuilding and cultural identity on Clydeside', *Journal for Maritime Research*, 8:1 (2006), 1–33.

Berry, Christopher, J., *The Idea of Commercial Society in the Scottish Enlightenment* (Edinburgh: Edinburgh University Press, 2013).

Berry, Simon and Whyte, Hamish, eds, *Glasgow Observed* (Edinburgh: John Donald, 1987).

Benjamin, Walter, 'The Work of Art in the Age of Mechanical Reproduction, in Hannah Arendt, ed., *Illuminations* (New York: Schocken Books, 1969).

Bickham, Troy O., *Savages Within the Empire: Representations of American Indians in Eighteenth-Century Britain* (Oxford: Clarendon Press, 2005).

Billcliffe, Roger, 'A brush with Europe: visual art in Glasgow 1890–1990', in *RSA Journal* 139:5417 (1991), 330–42.

Billig, Michael, *Banal Nationalism* (London: Sage, 2013 [1995]).

Blair, George, *Biographic and Descriptive Sketches of Glasgow Necropolis* (Glasgow: Maurice Ogle & Son, 1857).

Blaikie, Andrew, *The Scots Imagination and Modern Memory* (Edinburgh: Edinburgh University Press, 2010).

Bonnell, Thomas F., *The Most Disreputable Trade: Publishing the Classics of English Poetry 1765–1810* (Oxford: Oxford University Press, 2008).

Boschloo, Anton W. A. et al., *Academies of Art Between Renaissance and Romanticism* (The Hague: SDU, 1989).

Bowie, Karin, 'Public Opinion, Popular Politics and the Union of 1707', *The Scottish Historical Review*, 82:214, Part 2 (2003), 226–60.

Broadie, Alexander, *A History of Scottish Philosophy* (Edinburgh: Edinburgh University Press, 2009).

Broadie, Alexander and Downie, Robin, *Glasgow Moral Philosophy in the Enlightenment: Ideas and their International Influence* (Glasgow: College of Arts, 2012).

Brock, C. H., 'Dr William Hunter's Museum, Glasgow University', *Journal of the Society for the Bibliography of Natural History*, 9:4 (1980), 403–12.

Brock, Helen, 'Hunter, William (1718–1783)', *Oxford Dictionary of National Biography*, <http://www.oxforddnb.com/view/article/14234> (last accessed 20 November 2019).

Bryce, T. H., 'The Hunterian Museum', *Glasgow University Students' Handbook* (Glasgow: Glasgow University, 1935).

Bueltmann, T., Hinson, A. and Morton, G., *The Scottish Diaspora* (Edinburgh: Edinburgh University Press, 2013).

Bumsted, J. M., 'Scottish and Britishness in Canada, 1790–1914', in Marjory Harper and Michael E. Vance, eds, *Myth, Migration and the Making of Memory: Scotia and Nova Scotia c.1700–1990* (Halifax: Fernwood, 1999), 89–105.

Burgess, Moira, *The Glasgow Novel, 1870–1970: A Bibliography* (Glasgow: Scottish Library Association, 1972).

Burgess, Moira, *Imagine a City: Glasgow in Fiction* (Glendaruel: Argyll Publishing, 1998).

Cairns, John W., 'John Millar and Slavery', in Neil Walker, ed., *MacCormick's Scotland* (Edinburgh: Edinburgh University Press, 2012).

Campbell, R. H., 'Scotland's Neglected Enlightenment', *History Today*, 40:5 (1990).

Campbell, R. H., 'The Making of the Industrial City', in T. M. Devine and Gordon Jackson, eds, *Glasgow, Volume I: Beginnings to 1830* (Manchester: Manchester University Press, 1995), 184–213.

Carey, Hilary M., *God's Empire: Religion and Colonialism in the British World, c.1801–1908* (Cambridge: Cambridge University Press, 2011).

Carruthers, Mary, *The Book of Memory: A Study of Memory in Medieval Culture* (Cambridge: Cambridge University Press, 2008 [1990]).

Carruthers, Gerard and Martin, Don, eds, *Thomas Muir of Huntershill: Essays for the Twenty-First Century* (Edinburgh: Humming Earth, 2016).

Carruthers, Gerard and Kidd, Colin, eds, *Literature and Union: Scottish Texts, British Contexts* (Oxford: Oxford University Press, 2018).

Cass, Jeffrey, 'John Galt, Happy Colonialist: *The Case of the Apostate; or, Atlantis Destroyed*', *Wordsworth Circle*, 41:3 (2010), 167–70.

Chitnis, Anand C., 'The Scottish Enlightenment in the Age of Galt', in Christopher A. Whatley, ed., *John Galt (1779–1979)* (Edinburgh: The Ramsay Head Press, 1979), 31–50.

Clark, Julie and Wright, Valerie, 'Urban Regeneration in Glasgow: Looking to the Past to Build the Future? The Case of the "New Gorbals"', in Julie Clark and Nicholas Wise, eds, *Urban Renewal, Community and Participation*, (Cham, Switzerland: Springer International, 2018), 45–70.

Clarke, David, *Reflections on the Astronomy of Glasgow: A Story of Some 500 Years* (Edinburgh: Edinburgh University Press, 2013).

Cleland, James, *Enumeration of the Inhabitants of Scotland taken from the Government Abstracts of 1801, 1811, 1821; containing a particular account of every parish in Scotland and many useful details respect-*

ing England, Wales and Ireland (Glasgow: James Lumsden & Son, 1823).
Cleland, James, *Enumeration of the Inhabitants of the City of Glasgow and County of Lanark. Second Edition*. (Glasgow: John Smith and Son, 1832).
Cleland, James, *Statistical Facts Descriptive of The Former and Present State of Glasgow* (Glasgow: Bell and Bain, 1837).
Cooke, Anthony, 'An Elite Revisited: Glasgow West India Merchants, 1783–1877', *Journal of Historical Studies*, 32:2 (2012), 127–65.
Cookson, J. E., 'The Edinburgh and Glasgow Duke of Wellington Statues: Early Nineteenth-Century Unionist Nationalism as a Tory Project', *The Scottish Historical Review*, 83:205, Part 1 (2004), 23–40.
Coleman, James J., *Remembering the Past in Nineteenth-Century Scotland: Commemoration, Nationality and Memory* (Edinburgh: Edinburgh University Press, 2014).
Cornish, Henry C., 'First Glasgow International Exhibition, 1888', *Old Glasgow Club Transactions, Volume V, Session 1923–1928* (Glasgow: Aird and Coghill Ltd, 1928), 42–9.
Cowan, Edward J., 'Tartan Day in America', in Celeste Ray, ed., *Transatlantic Scots* (Tuscaloosa, AL: University of Alabama Press, 2005), 318–38.
Craig, Carol, *The Tears that Made the Clyde: Well-being in Glasgow* (Glendaruel: Argyll Publishing, 2010).
Craig, David, *Scottish Literature and the Scottish People, 1680–1830* (London: Chatto & Windus, 1961).
Crampsey, Bob, *The Empire Exhibition of 1938: The Last Durbar* (Edinburgh: Mainstream, 1988).
Crawford, Robert, *On Glasgow and Edinburgh* (Cambridge, MA: Belknap Press of Harvard University Press, 2013).
Crinson, Mark, *Modern Architecture and the End of Empire* (Aldershot: Ashgate, 2003).
Daiches, D., Jones, J. and Jones, P., *A Hotbed of Genius: The Scottish Enlightenment, 1730–1790* (Edinburgh: Edinburgh University Press, 1987).
Davies, Norman, *Vanished Kingdoms: The History of Half-Forgotten Europe* (London: Allen Lane/Penguin, 2011).
Davis, Barbara, ed., *Remaking Cities: Proceedings of the 1988 International Conference in Pittsburgh* (Pittsburgh, PA: University of Pittsburgh Press, 1988).
Dawson, Graham, *Soldier Heroes: British Adventure, Empire and the Imagining of Masculinities* (London and New York: Routledge, 1994).
Devine, T. M., *The Tobacco Lords: A Study of the Tobacco Merchants of Glasgow and Their Trading Activities, 1740–1790* (Edinburgh: John Donald, 1975).
Devine, T. M., 'The Golden Age of Tobacco', in T. M. Devine and Gordon Jackson, eds, *Glasgow, Volume I: Beginnings to 1830* (Manchester: Manchester University Press, 1995), 139–83.

Devine, T. M., 'The Urban Crisis', in T. M. Devine and Gordon Jackson, eds, *Glasgow, Volume I: Beginnings to 1830* (Manchester: Manchester University Press, 1995).
Devine, T. M., *Scotland's Empire: 1600–1815* (London: Allen Lane, 2003).
Devine, T. M., ed., *Recovering Scotland's Slavery Past: The Caribbean Connection* (Edinburgh: Edinburgh University Press, 2015).
Devine, T. M. and Rossner, Philip R., 'Scots in the Atlantic Economy, 1600–1800', in John M. MacKenzie and T. M. Devine, eds, *Scotland and the British Empire* (Oxford: Oxford University Press, 2011), 30–55.
Dickson, W. C., ed., *John Knox's History of the Reformation in Scotland*, vol. 2 (London: Nelson, 1949).
Dobson, David, *Scottish Emigration to Colonial America, 1607–1785* (Athens, GA: University of Georgia Press, 1994).
Donovan, Arthur, *Philosophical Chemistry in the Scottish Enlightenment: The Doctrines and Discoveries of William Cullen and Joseph Black* (Edinburgh: Edinburgh University Press, 1975).
Dresser, Madge, 'Remembering Slavery and Abolition in Bristol', *Slavery & Abolition*, 30:2 (2009), 223–46.
Duncan, Alexander, *Memorials of the Faculty of Physicians and Surgeons of Glasgow* (Glasgow: James MacLehose & Sons, 1896).
Duncan, Ian, *Scott's Shadow: The Novel in Romantic Edinburgh* (Princeton, NJ: Princeton University Press, 2007).
Duffill, Mark, 'The Africa trade from the ports of Scotland, 1706–66', *Slavery & Abolition*, 25:3 (2004), 102–22.
Dziennik, Matthew P., 'Whig Tartan: Material Culture and its Use in the Scottish Highlands, 1746–1815', *Past & Present*, 217 (2012), 117–47.
Edward, Mary, *Who Belongs to Glasgow?* (Glasgow: Glasgow City Libraries, c.1993).
Eisenstein, Elizabeth L., *The Printing Press as an Agent of Change* (Cambridge: Cambridge University Press, 1979).
Efland, Arthur D., *A History of Art Education: Intellectual and Social Currents in Teaching the Visual Arts* (New York and London: Teachers College Press, 1990).
Emerson, Roger L., 'Aberdeen Professors 1690–1800: Two Structures, Two Professoriates, Two Careers', in Jennifer J. Carter and Joan J. Pittock, eds, *Aberdeen and the Enlightenment* (Aberdeen: Aberdeen University Press, 1987), 155–67.
Emerson, Roger L., *Academic Patronage in the Scottish Enlightenment: Glasgow, Edinburgh and St Andrews Universities* (Edinburgh: Edinburgh University Press, 2008).
Emerson, Roger L. and Wood, Paul, 'Science and Enlightenment in Glasgow 1690–1802', in Charles W. J. Withers and Paul Wood, eds, *Science and Medicine in the Scottish Enlightenment* (Phantassie, East Lothian: Tuckwell Press, 2002), 79–142.

Erll, Astrid, *Memory in Culture*, trans. Sara B. Young (Basingstoke: Palgrave, 2011).

Eyre-Todd, George, *History of Glasgow, Volume III: From the Revolution to the Passing of the Reform Acts 1832–33* (Glasgow: Jackson, Wylie & Co., 1934).

Fairfull-Smith, George, *The Foulis Press and The Foulis Academy: Glasgow's Eighteenth Century School of Art and Design* (Glasgow: The Glasgow Art Index in association with the Friends of Glasgow University Library, 2001).

Fawcett, Arthur, *The Cambuslang Revival: the Scottish Evangelical Revival of the Eighteenth Century* (London: The Banner of Truth Trust, 1971).

Fenton, Alexander, 'The People Below: Dougal Graham's Chapbooks as a Mirror of the Lower Classes in Eighteenth Century Scotland', in Alisoun Gardner-Medwin and Janet Hadley Williams, eds, *A Day Estivall: Essays on the Music, Poetry and History of Scotland and England & Poems Previously Unpublished* (Aberdeen: Aberdeen University Press, 1990), 69–80.

Ferguson, Hugh, *Glasgow School of Art: The History* (Glasgow: The Foulis Press of Glasgow School of Art, 1995).

Findling, John E., ed., *Historical Dictionary of World's Fairs and Expositions, 1851–1988* (New York: Greenwood Press, 1990).

Forbes, Archibald, *Colin Campbell Lord Clyde* (London: Macmillan and Co., 1895).

Foreman, Carol, *Lost Glasgow: Glasgow's Lost Architectural Heritage* (Edinburgh: Birlinn, 2002).

Fraser, W. Hamish, 'Introduction: "Let Glasgow Flourish"', in W. Hamish Fraser and Irene Maver, eds, *Glasgow, Volume II: 1830–1912* (Manchester: Manchester University Press, 1996), 1–7.

Freeman, F. W., 'Robert Fergusson: Pastoral and Politics at Mid Century', in Andrew Hook, ed., *The History of Scottish Literature Volume 2, 1660–1800* (Aberdeen: Aberdeen University Press, 1987), 141–55.

Fry, Michael, *The Scottish Empire* (Phantassie, East Lothian: Tuckwell Press, 2001).

Fry, Michael, *Glasgow: A History of the City* (London: Head of Zeus, 2017).

Fryer, Linda D., 'Documents Relating to the Formation of the Carolina Company in Scotland, 1682', *The South Carolina Historical Magazine*, 99:2 (1998), 110–34.

Fuhrer, Therese, Mundt, Felix, and Stenger, Jan, eds, *Cityscaping* (Berlin: De Gruyter, 2015).

Fulton, Henry L., 'Smollett's Apprenticeship in Glasgow, 1736–1739', *Studies in Scottish Literature*, 15:1 (1980), 175–86.

Fulton, Henry L., 'John Moore, the Medical Profession and the Glasgow Enlightenment', in Andrew Hook and Richard B. Sher, eds, *The Glasgow Enlightenment* (Phantassie, East Lothian: Tuckwell Press, 1995), 176–189.

Gaskell, Philip, *A Bibliography of the Foulis Press* (Dorset: St Paul's Bibliographies, 1986).

Geyer-Kordesch, Johanna and MacDonald, Fiona, *Physicians and Surgeons in Glasgow: The History of the Royal College of Physicians and Surgeons of Glasgow* (London: Hambledon, 1999).
Gilbert, Adrian, *The Encyclopedia of Warfare: From Earliest Time to the Present Day* (London: Fitzroy Dearborn, 2000).
Gifford, D., Dunnigan, S., and McGillivray, A., eds, *Scottish Literature in English and Scots* (Edinburgh: Edinburgh University Press, 2002).
Glendinning, M., MacInnes, R., and MacKechnie, A., *A History of Scottish Architecture: From the Renaissance to the Present Day* (Edinburgh: Edinburgh University Press, 1996 [2002]).
Gomme, Andor and Walker, David, *Architecture of Glasgow* (London: Lund Humphries, 1968).
Gordon, Ian, 'John Galt', in Christopher A. Whatley, ed., *John Galt 1779–1979* (Edinburgh: The Ramsay Head Press, 1979), 19–30.
Gouriévidis, Laurence, 'Representing the Disrupted Past of Northern Scotland: The Highland Clearances in Museums', in *History & Memory*, 12:2 (2000), 122–41,
Gouriévidis, Laurence, *The Dynamics of Heritage: History, Memory and the Highland Clearances* (Farnham: Ashgate, 2010).
Grigor, Murray, 'Not in architectural order', *RSA Journal*, 144:5473 (1996), 39.
Gristwood, Anthony, 'Commemorating empire in twentieth-century Seville', in Felix Driver and David Gilbert, eds, *Imperial Cities: Landscape, Display and Identity* (Manchester: Manchester University Press, 1999), 155–73.
Guinness, Desmond, *Georgian Dublin* (London: Batsford, 1979)
Guyatt, Mary, 'The Wedgwood Slave Medallion: Values in Eighteenth-Century Design' *Journal of Design History*, 13:2 (2000), 93–105.
Halbwachs, Maurice, *The Collective Memory* (New York: Harper and Row, 1980).
Halbwachs, Maurice, *On Collective Memory*, ed. Lewis A. Coser (Chicago: University of Chicago Press, 1992 [1941]).
Hamilton, David, *The Healers: A History of Medicine in Scotland* (Edinburgh: Mercat, 2003).
Hammerton, J. A., *Sketches from Glasgow* (Glasgow and Edinburgh: John Menzies & Co., 1893).
Hanlon, P., Walsh, D., and Whyte, B., *Let Glasgow Flourish: A comprehensive report on health and its determinants in Glasgow and West Central Scotland* (Glasgow: Glasgow Centre for Population Health, 2006). <https://www.gcph.co.uk/assets/0000/0377/LetGlasgowFlourish_full.pdf> (last accessed 20 November 2019)
Hardie, John L., 'Thomas Campbell and Glasgow', *Old Glasgow Club Transactions, Volume VII, Session 1933–1934* (Glasgow: Aird and Coghill Ltd, 1934), 18–28.
Harper, Marjory and Vance, Michael E., 'Introduction', in Marjory Harper and

Michael E. Vance, eds, *Myth, Migration and the Making of Memory: Scotia and Nova Scotia c.1700–1990* (Halifax: Fernwood, 1999).

Harper, Paul, 'Tobias Smollett and the Practice of Medicine', *Yale Journal of Biology and Medicine*, 2:6 (1930), 408–16.

Harvey, Christopher, 'Scott and the Image of Scotland,' in Raphael Samuel, ed., *Patriotism: The Making and Unmaking of British National Identity, Volume II: Minorities and Outsiders* (London and New York: Routledge, 1989), 173–92.

Harvey, Wallace, *Chronicles of Saint Mungo; Or, Antiquities and Traditions of Glasgow* (Glasgow: John Smith & Sons, 1843).

Hendrix, Harald, 'The Early Modern Invention of Literary Tourism: Petrarch's Houses in France and Italy', in Harald Hendrix, ed., *Writers' Houses and the Making of Memory* (New York: Routledge, 2008), 15–30.

Hichberger, J. W. M., *Images of the Army: The Military in British Art, 1815–1914* (Manchester: Manchester University Press, 1988).

Hillyard, Brian, 'The Glasgow Homer', *The Edinburgh History of the Book in Scotland, Volume 2: Enlightenment and Expansion, 1707–1800* (Edinburgh: Edinburgh University Press, 2012), 70–80.

Hobsbawm, Eric, 'Mass-Producing Traditions: Europe, 1870–1914', in Eric Hobsbawm and Terence Ranger, eds, *The Invention of Tradition* (Cambridge: Cambridge University Press – Canto, 1996 [1983]), 263–307.

House, Jack, *The Heart of Glasgow* (London: Hutchinson, 1965).

Houston, R. A., *Scottish Literacy and the Scottish Identity: Illiteracy and Society in Scotland and Northern England, 1600–1800* (Cambridge: Cambridge University Press, 1985).

Huhtamo, Erkki, 'Global Glimpses for Local Realities: The Moving Panorama, a Forgotten Mass Medium of the 19th Century' (2002), <http://gebseng.com/-media_archeology/reading_materials/Erkki_Huhtamo-Moving_Panorama.pdf> (last accessed 20 November 2019),

Hunter, Michael, 'Aikenhead, Thomas (bap. 1676, d. 1697)', *Oxford Dictionary of National Biography*, <http://www.oxforddnb.com/view/article/225> (last accessed 20 November 2019).

Hutton, Patrick, 'Recent Scholarship on Memory and History', *The Memory Teacher*, 33:4 (2000), 533–48.

Huyssen, Andreas, *Twilight Memories: Marking Time in a Culture of Amnesia* (New York: Routledge, 1995).

Inglis, Lucy, *Georgian London: Into the Streets* (London: Penguin/Viking, 2013).

Insh, George Pratt, *Scottish Colonial Schemes 1620–1686* (Glasgow: Maclehose, Jackson & Co., 1922).

Ingamells, John, 'Tobias Smollett', *A Dictionary of British and Irish Travellers in Italy 1701–1800* (New Haven: Yale University Press, 1997).

Irwin, David and Irwin, Francina, *Scottish Painters: At Home and Abroad, 1700–1900* (London, Faber and Faber, 1975).

Jackson, Gordon, 'Glasgow in transition, c.1660 to c.1740', in T. M. Devine and Gordon Jackson, eds, *Glasgow, Volume I: Beginnings to 1830* (Manchester: Manchester University Press, 1995), 63–105.

Jackson, Gordon, 'New Horizons in Trade,' in T. M. Devine and Gordon Jackson, eds, *Glasgow, Volume I: Beginnings to 1830* (Manchester: Manchester University Press, 1995), 214–38.

Jauss, Hans Robert, 'Literary History as a Challenge to Literary Theory', *New Literary History*, 2:1 (1970 [1967]).

Jones, Jean, 'James Hutton and the Forth and Clyde Canal,' *Annals of Science*, 39:3 (1982), 255–63.

Jones, Richard, *Tobias Smollett in the Enlightenment: Travels Through France, Italy and Scotland* (Lewisburg, PA: Buckness University Press, 2011).

Kansteiner, Wulf, 'Finding Meaning in Memory: A Methodological Critique of Collective Memory Studies', *History and Theory*, 41:2 (2002), 179–97.

Kavanagh, Gaynor, 'History in the Museum – and out of it', in Timothy Ambrose, ed., *Presenting Scotland's Story* (Edinburgh: Scottish Museums Council, 1989), 27–37.

Kay, Jackie, 'Missing faces', *The Guardian*, 24 March 2007.

Keppie, Lawrence, *William Hunter and the Hunterian Museum in Glasgow, 1807–2007* (Edinburgh: Edinburgh University Press, 2007).

Kilpatrick, James A., *Literary Landmarks of Glasgow* (Glasgow: At the St Mungo Press, 1898).

Kinchin, Perilla and Kinchin, Juliet, *Glasgow's Great Exhibitions: 1888, 1901, 1911, 1938, 1988* (Oxon: White Cockade, 1988).

King, Mervyn, 'Trusting in Money: From Kirkcaldy to the MPC', delivered 29 October 2006, <https://www.bankofengland.co.uk/speech/2006/trusting-in-money-from-kirkcaldy-to-the-mpc> (last accessed 20 November 2019).

King, Reyahn et al., *Ignatius Sancho: An African Man of Letters* (London: National Portrait Gallery Publications, 1997).

Knapp, Lewis M., *Tobias Smollett: Doctor of Men and Manners* (Princeton, NJ: Princeton University Press, 1949).

Knight, Charles, ed., *Penny magazine of the Society for the Diffusion of Useful Knowledge*, March 1832–December 1845; London, vol. 1, iss. 25, (25 August 1832).

Lamont, Craig, 'Finding Galt in Glasgow', in Gerard Carruthers and Colin Kidd, eds, *International Companion to John Galt* (Glasgow: Association for Scottish Literary Studies, 2017), 34–43.

Lamont, Craig, 'Allan Ramsay and Edinburgh: Commemoration in the City of Forgetting', *Scottish Literary Review*, 10:1 (2018), 117–37.

Lamont, Craig, 'Cultivating the Classics "in a cold climate": The Foulis Press & Academy in Glasgow', *Journal of the Edinburgh Bibliographical Society* (Edinburgh: Edinburgh Bibliographical Society, 2019), 45–66.

Landsman, Ned C., 'Evangelists and Their Hearers: Popular Interpretation of

Revivalist Preaching in Eighteenth-Century Scotland', in *Journal of British Studies*, 28:2 (1989), 120–49.

Landsman, Ned C., 'Presbyterians and Provincial Society: The Evangelical Enlightenment in the West of Scotland, 1740–1775', in John Dwyer and Richard B. Sher, eds, *Sociability and Society in Eighteenth-Century Scotland* (Edinburgh: The Mercat Press, 1993), 194–209.

Lane, Paul J. and MacDonald, Kevin C., 'Introduction: Slavery, Social Revolutions and Enduring Memories', in Lane and MacDonald, eds, *Slavery in Africa: Archaeology and Memory* (Oxford: Published for the British Academy by Oxford University Press, 2011), 1–22.

Lawrence, Christopher, 'Ornate physicians and learned artisans: Edinburgh medical men, 1726–1776', in W. F. Bynum and Roy Porter, eds, *William Hunter and the Eighteenth-Century Medical World* (Cambridge: Cambridge University Press, 1985), 153–76.

Lawrence, Christopher, 'Lister, Joseph, Baron Lister (1827–1912)', *Oxford Dictionary of National Biography*, <http://www.oxforddnb.com/view/article/34553> (last accessed 20 November 2019).

Lenman, Bruce P., 'The Teaching of Scottish History in the Scottish Universities', *The Scottish Historical Review*, 52:154 (1973), 165–90.

Lenman, Bruce P., *Integration and Enlightenment: Scotland 1746–1832* (Edinburgh: Edinburgh University Press, 1981).

Lindsay, Maurice, *Illustrated Guide to Glasgow, 1837* (London: Robert Hale, 1989).

Luckhurst, Kenneth W., *The Story of Exhibitions* (London: The Studio Publications, 1951).

Lugo-Ortiz, Agnes and Rosenthal, Angela, eds, *Slave Portraiture in the Atlantic World*, (Cambridge: Cambridge University Press, 2013).

McArthur, Colin, 'The dialectic of national identity: The Glasgow Empire Exhibition of 1938', in Tony Bennett, Colin Mercer and Janet Woollacott, eds, *Popular Culture and Social Relations* (Milton Keynes and Philadelphia: Open University Press, 1986), 117–34.

McCosh, James, *The Scottish Philosophy: Bibliographical, Expository, Critical from Hutcheson to Hamilton* (Carlisle, MA: Applewood, 2009 [1875]).

McCracken-Flesher, Caroline, 'Future Scotts: The Aliens have Landed', The Bottle Imp, 16, <https://www.thebottleimp.org.uk/2014/11/future-scotts-the-aliens-have-landed/> (last accessed 20 November 2019).

McEwan, Peter J. M., *The Dictionary of Scottish Art and Architecture* (Ballater: Glengarden Press, 2004).

Macfarlane Lizars, Robina and Kathleen, *In the Days of the Canada Company: The Story of the Settlement of the Huron Tract and a View of the Social Life of the Period, 1825–1850* (Toronto: William Briggs, 1896).

MacGregor, George, *The History of Glasgow, from the Earliest Period to the Present Time* (Glasgow: Thomas D. Morison, 1881).

McIlvanney, Liam, 'The Glasgow Novel', in Gerard Carruthers and Liam McIlvanney eds, *The Cambridge Companion to Scottish Literature* (Cambridge: Cambridge University Press, 2012), 217–32.

McKenzie, Alan T., '*Robert Burns*' (review) and '*A Hotbed of Genius: The Scottish Enlightenment, 1730–1790*' (review), *Eighteenth-Century Studies* 22:2 (1988–9), 253–6.

Mackenzie, Charles, *Interesting and Remarkable Places; with Historical & Topographical Descriptions* (London: John Reynolds, 1849).

MacKenzie, John M., *Propaganda and Empire: The Manipulation of British Public Opinion, 1880–1960* (Manchester: Manchester University Press, 1984).

MacKenzie, John M., 'Essay and Reflection: On Scotland and the Empire', *The International History Review*, 15:4 (1993), 714–39.

MacKenzie, John M., 'Empire and National Identities: the Case of Scotland', *Transactions of the Royal Historical Society*, 8 (1998), 215–31.

MacKenzie, John M., '"The Second City of the Empire": Glasgow – imperial municipality', in Felix Driver and David Gilbert, eds, *Imperial Cities: Landscape, Display and Identity* (Manchester: Manchester University Press, 1999), 215–37.

McKenzie, Ray et al., *Public Sculpture of Glasgow: Public Sculpture of Britain, Vol. 5* (Liverpool: Liverpool University Press, 2002).

McLay, Farquhar, ed., *The Reckoning: Beyond the Culture City Rip Off* (Glasgow: Independent/Workers City Movement, 1990).

Maclean, Magnus, ed., *Archaeology, Education, Medical, & Charitable Institutions of Glasgow* (Glasgow: Published by the Local Committee for the Meeting for the British Association, 1901).

McLean, R., Young, R. and Simpson, K., eds, *The Scottish Enlightenment and Literary Culture* (Lewisburg, PA: Bucknell University Press, 2016).

MacLeod, Christine, *Heroes of Invention: Technology, Liberalism and British Identity, 1750–1914* (Cambridge: Cambridge University Press, 2007).

McNeil, Kevin, 'Time, Emigration, and the Circum-Atlantic World: John Galt's *Bogle Corbet*', in Regina Hewitt, ed., *John Galt: Observations and Conjectures on Literature, History, and Society* (Lewisburg, PA: Bucknell University Press, 2012), 299–322.

Maier, Charles S., 'A Surfeit of Memory? Reflections on History, Melancholy and Denial', *History & Memory*, 5:2 (1993), 136–52.

Mann, A. J., 'Gibson, Walter (b. c.1645, d. in or after 1717)', *Oxford Dictionary of National Biography*, <http://www.oxforddnb.com/view/article/67516> (last accessed 20 November 2019).

Markus, Thomas A., 'Domes of Enlightenment: Two Scottish University Museums', *The International Journal of Museum Management and Curatorship* 4:3 (1985), 215–42.

Maver, Irene, 'The Guardianship of the Community: Civic Authority prior to 1833,' T. M. Devine and Gordon Jackson, eds, *Glasgow, Volume I:*

Beginnings to 1830 (Manchester: Manchester University Press, 1995) 239–77.

Maver, Irene, *Glasgow* (Edinburgh: Edinburgh University Press, 2000).

Meighan, Michael, *Glasgow in 50 Buildings* (Stroud: Amberley, 2016).

Meusburger, Peter, 'Knowledge, Cultural Memory, and Politics', in Peter Meusburger, Michael Heffernan and Edgar Wunder, eds, *Cultural Memories: The Geographical Point of View* (London: Springer, 2011), 51–69.

Miller, David Philip, '"Puffing Jamie": The commercial and ideological importance of being a "Philosopher" in the case of the reputation of James Watt (1736–1819)', *History of Science*, 38:119 (2000), 1–24.

Miller, David Philip, *James Watt, Chemist: Understanding the Origins of the Steam Age* (London: Pickering & Chatto, 2009).

Milne, Hugh M., *Boswell's Edinburgh Journals, 1767–1786* (Edinburgh: John Donald, 2013 [2001]).

Misztal, Barbara A., *Theories of Social Remembering* (Maidenhead: Open University Press, 2003).

Mingay, G. E., *Georgian London* (London: Batsford, 1975).

Mitchell, James Oswald, *Old Glasgow Essays* (Glasgow: James Maclehose and Sons, 1905).

Moore, James Carrick, *The Life of Lieutenant-General Sir John Moore, K. B.*, vol. I. (London: John Murray, 1833).

Moore, James, and Silverthorne, Michael, eds, *The Meditations of the Emperor Marcus Aurelius Antoninus,* trans. Francis Hutcheson and James Moore (Indianapolis: Liberty Fund, 2008).

Morris, Michael, 'Joseph Knight: Scotland and the Black Atlantic', *International Journal of Scottish Literature*, 4 (Glasgow: Association for Scottish Literary Studies, 2008).

Morris, Michael, 'Multi-directional Memory, Many-Headed Hydras and Glasgow', in Katie Donington, Ryan Hanley, Jessica Moody, eds, *Britain's History and Memory of Transatlantic Slavery: Local Nuances of a 'National Sin',* (Liverpool: Liverpool University Press, 2016), 195–215.

Morrison-Low, A. D., '"Feasting my eyes with the view of fine instruments": Scientific Instruments in Enlightenment Scotland, 1680–1820', in Charles W. J. Withers and Paul Wood, eds, *Science and Medicine in the Scottish Enlightenment* (Phantassie, East Lothian: Tuckwell Press, 2002), 17–53.

Morton, H. V., *In Search of Scotland* (London: Methuen, 2000 [1929]).

Mullen, Stephen, *It Wisnae Us: The Truth About Glasgow and Slavery* (Edinburgh: The Royal Incorporation of Architects in Scotland, 2009).

Mullen, Stephen, 'A Glasgow-West India Merchant House and the Imperial Dividend, 1779–1867', *Journal of Scottish Historical Studies* 33.2 (2013), 196–233.

Mullen, Stephen and Newman, Simon, *Slavery, Abolition and the University of Glasgow* (University of Glasgow report: 2018), <https://www.gla.ac.uk/media/media_607547_en.pdf> (last accessed 20 November 2019).

Muir, James Hamilton, *Glasgow in 1901* (Glasgow and Edinburgh: William Hodge & Company, 1901).

Murphy, Paula, *Nineteenth-Century Irish Sculpture: Native Genius Reaffirmed* (New Haven and London: Yale University Press, 2010).

Murray, David, 'Some Letters of Robert Foulis', *The Scottish Historical Review*, 14:54 (1917), 97–115.

Murray, David, 'Some Letters of Robert Foulis (continued)', *The Scottish Historical Review*, 14:55 (1917), 249–71.

Nora, Pierre, *Realms of Memory: Rethinking the French Past*, ed. Lawrence D. Kritzman (New York: Columbia University Press, 1989 [1984–1992]).

O'Brien, G. and O'Kane, Finola, eds, *Georgian Dublin* (Dublin and Portland, OR: Four Courts, 2008).

O'Connor, Anne, *Florence: City and Memory in the Nineteenth Century* (Florence: Città di Vita, 2008).

O'Neill, Mark, 'Museums, Meaning and Money in Glasgow', *Journal of Irish Studies*, 2:2 (2009), 139–52.

Oakley, C. A., *The Second City* (London and Glasgow: Blackie and Son, Limited, 1946).

Olick, Jeffrey K., 'Social Memory Studies: From "Collective Memory" to the Historical Sociology of Mnemonic Practices', *Annual Review of Sociology*, 24 (1998), 105–40.

Olson, James S. and Shadle, Robert, eds, *Historical Dictionary of the British Empire A–J* (Westport, CT: Greenwood Press, 1996).

Orr, Julie, *Scotland, Darien and the Atlantic World, 1698–1700* (Edinburgh: Edinburgh University Press, 2018).

Osborough, W. N., *Law and the Emergence of Modern Dublin: A Litigation Topography for a Capital City* (Dublin: Irish Academic Press in association with the Irish Legal History Society, 1996).

Paces, Cynthia, 'The Fall and Rise of Prague's Marian Column', *Radical History Review*, 79 (2001), 141–55.

Paxman, Jeremy, *Empire: What Ruling the World Did to the British* (London: Penguin, 2011).

Pittock, Murray, 'Historiography', in Alexander Broadie, ed., *The Cambridge Companion to The Scottish Enlightenment* (Cambridge: Cambridge University Press, 2003), 258–79.

Pittock, Murray, 'Ramsay, Allan (1684–1758)', *Oxford Dictionary of National Biography*, <http://www.oxforddnb.com/view/article/23072> (last accessed 20 November 2019).

Pittock, Murray, *Scottish and Irish Romanticism* (Oxford: Oxford University Press, 2008).

Pittock, Murray, *The Road to Independence? Scotland Since the Sixties* (London: Reaktion Books, 2008).

Pittock, Murray, *Material Culture and Sedition, 1688–1760: Treacherous Objects, Secret Places* (Basingstoke: Palgrave Macmillan, 2013).

Pittock, Murray, *Enlightenment in a Smart City: Edinburgh's Civic Development, 1660–1750* (Edinburgh: Edinburgh University Press, 2018).
Pittock, Murray and Whatley, Christopher A., 'Poems and Festivals, Art and Artefact and the Commemoration of Robert Burns, c.1844–c.1896', *The Scottish Historical Review*, Volume XCIII, 1: No. 236 (2014), 56–79.
Quinault, Roland, 'The Cult of the Centenary, c.1784–1914' in *Historical Research*, 71:176 (1998), 303–23.
Pick, Daniel, *War Machine: The Rationalisation of Slaughter in the Modern Age* (New Haven and London: Yale University Press, 1993).
Porter, Roy, 'Medical Lecturing in Georgian London', *The British Journal for the History of Science*, 28:1 (1995), 91–9.
Prebble, John, *The Darien Disaster* (London: Secker & Warburg, 1968).
Readman, Paul, 'The Place of the Past in English Culture *c.*1890–1914', *Past & Present*, 186 (2005), 147–99.
Reid, J. M., *Glasgow* [British Cities and Towns Series] (London: B. T. Batsford, 1956).
Rembold, Elfie, 'Negotiating Scottish Identity: The Glasgow History Exhibition 1911', *National Identities*, 1:3 (1999), 265–85.
Richards, Thomas, *The Commodity Culture of Victorian England: Advertising and Spectacle, 1851–1914* (Stanford, CA: Stanford University Press, 1990).
Rice, C. Duncan, *The Scots Abolitionists, 1833–1861* (Baton Rouge: Louisiana State University Press, 1981).
Rigney, Ann, 'Plenitude, scarcity and the circulation of cultural memory', *Journal of European Studies*, 35:1 (2006), 11–28.
Robinson, Eric and McKie, Douglas, eds, *Partners in Science: Letters of James Watt and Joseph Black* (London: Constable, 1970).
Robson, Brian, 'Roberts, Frederick Sleigh, first Earl Roberts (1832–1914)', *Oxford Dictionary of National Biography*, <https://doi.org/10.1093/ref:odnb/35768> (last accessed 20 November 2019).
Rolfe, W. D. Ian, 'William and John Hunter: breaking the Great Chain of Being', in W. F. Bynum and Roy Porter, eds, *William Hunter and the Eighteenth-Century Medical World* (Cambridge: Cambridge University Press, 1985), 297–319.
Rowland, Lawrence S. et al., 'English, Scots, and Yemassee at Port Royal', *The History of Beaufort County, South Carolina: Volume 1, 1514–1861* (Columbia: University of South Carolina Press, 1996), 58–79.
Samuel, Raphael, *Theatres of Memory, Volume 1: Past and Present in Contemporary Culture* (London and New York: Verso, 1994).
Scott, Paul Henderson, 'Galt, John (1779–1839)', *Oxford Dictionary of National Biography* <http://www.oxforddnb.com/view/article/10316> (last accessed 20 November 2019).
Scott, William Robert, *Francis Hutcheson: His Life, Teaching and Position in the History of Philosophy* (Cambridge: Cambridge University Press, 1900).
Sexton, Alexander Humboldt, *The First Technical College: A Sketch of the*

History of 'The Andersonian', and the Institutions Descended from It, 1796–1894 (London: Chapman & Hall, 1894),

Shain, Charles E., 'John Galt's America', *American Quarterly*, 8:3 (1956), 254–63.

Sher, Richard B., *Church and University in the Scottish Enlightenment: The Moderate Literati of Edinburgh* (Princeton, NJ: Princeton University Press, 1985).

Sher, Richard B., 'Commerce, Religion and the Enlightenment in Eighteenth-Century Glasgow', in T. M. Devine and Gordon Jackson, eds, *Glasgow: Volume 1: Beginnings to 1830* (Manchester: Manchester University Press, 1995), 312–59.

Sher, Richard B., 'Images of Glasgow in Late Eighteenth-Century Popular Poetry', Andrew Hook and Richard B. Sher, eds, *The Glasgow Enlightenment* (Phantassie, East Lothian: Tuckwell Press, 1995), 190–213.

Simpson, Kenneth, *The Protean Scot: The Crisis of Identity in Eighteenth Century Scottish Literature* (Aberdeen: Aberdeen University Press, 1988).

Small, David, *By-gone Glasgow* (Glasgow: Morison Brothers, 1896).

Smith, Craig, 'Adam Smith: Left or Right?', *Political Studies*, vol. 61 (2012) 784–9.

Smitten, Jeffrey, '*Church and University in the Scottish Enlightenment: The Moderate Literati of Edinburgh* (review)', *Eighteenth-Century Studies*, 19:4 (1986), 580–3.

Smout, T. C., 'The Anglo-Scottish Union of 1707. I. The Economic Background', *The Economic History Review*, New Series, 16:3 (1964), 455–67.

Smout, T. C., 'The Glasgow Merchant Community in the Seventeenth Century', *The Scottish Historical Review*, 47:143, Part 1 (1968), 53–71.

Smout, T. C., 'Born Again at Cambuslang; New Evidence on Popular Religion and Literacy in Eighteenth-Century Scotland', in *Past & Present*, 97:1 (1982), 114–27.

Soltow, J. H., 'Scottish Traders in Virginia, 1750–1775', *The Economic History Review*, 12:1 (1959), 83–98.

Somerville, Thomas, *George Square, Glasgow; and the lives of those whom its statues commemorate* (Glasgow: John N. MacKinlay, 1891).

Sowerby, Scott, *Making Toleration: The Repealers and the Glorious Revolution* (Cambridge, MA: Harvard University Press, 2013).

Spicci, Mauro, 'Museums, Memory and the Shaping of Identity: a conversation with Professor Eviatar Zerubavel', *Altre Modernità*; 5 (2011), 115–18.

Stallworthy, Jon, ed., *The New Oxford Book of War Poetry* (Oxford: Oxford University Press, 2014).

Stark, David, *Charles Rennie Mackintosh and Co: 1854 to 2004* (Catrine, Ayrshire: Stenlake, 2004).

Stelter, Gilbert A., 'John Galt: The writer as Town Booster and Builder', in Elizabeth Waterston, ed., *John Galt: Reappraisals* (Guelph: University of Guelph, 1985), 17–43.

Strang, John, *Glasgow and its Clubs: or, glimpses of the condition, manners, characters, and oddities of the city, during the past and present centuries* (London and Glasgow: Richard Griffin & Co., 1855).
Stronach, George, 'Wilson, Alexander (1714–1786)', rev. Roger Hutchins, *Oxford Dictionary of National Biography*, <http://www.oxforddnb.com/­view/article/29633> (last accessed 20 November 2019).
Summerfield, Penny, 'Culture and Composure: Creating Narratives of the Gendered Self in Oral History Interviews', *Cultural and Social History*, 1:1 (2004), 65–93.
Summerson, George, *Georgian London* (London: Pleiades Books, 1945).
Swaminathan, Srividhya, 'Adam Smith's Moral Economy and the Debate to Abolish the Slave Trade', *Rhetoric Society Quarterly*, 37:4 (2007), 481–507.
Swaminathan, Srividhya and Beach, Adam R., eds, *Invoking Slavery in the Eighteenth-Century British Imagination* (Aldershot: Ashgate, 2013).
Sweetman, John, 'Moore, Sir John (1761–1809)', *Oxford Dictionary of National Biography*, <https://doi.org/10.1093/ref:odnb/19132> (last accessed 20 November 2019).
Taylor, Alan, ed., *Glasgow: An Autobiography* (Edinburgh: Birlinn, 2016).
Todd, George-Eyre, *The Glasgow Poets: Their Lives and Poems* (Paisley: Alexander Gardner, 1906 [1903]).
Thomas, Alfred, *Prague Palimpsest: Writing, Memory, and the City* (Chicago: University of Chicago Press, 2010).
Trumpener, Katie, *Bardic Nationalism: The Romantic Novel and the British Empire* (Princeton, NJ: Princeton University Press, 1997).
Trumpener, Katie, 'Annals of Ice: Formations of Empire, Place and History in John Galt and Alice Munro', in Michael Gardiner and Graeme Macdonald, eds, *Scottish Literature and Postcolonial Literature: Comparative Texts and Critical Perspectives* (Edinburgh: Edinburgh University Press, 2011), 43–56.
Uglow, Jenny, *The Lunar Men: The Friends Who Made the Future, 1730–1810* (London: Faber and Faber, 2002).
Walvin, James, *Britain's Slave Empire* (Stroud: Tempus, 2000).
Ward, Stephen V., *Selling Places: The marketing and promotion of towns and cities, 1850–2000* (London: Routledge – E. & F. N. Spon, 1998).
Waterston, Elizabeth, '*Bogle Corbet* and the Annals of New World Parishes', in Elizabeth Waterston, ed., *John Galt: Reappraisals* (Guelph: University of Guelph, 1985), 57–62.
Watson, Nicola J., *The Literary Tourist: Readers and Place in Romantic & Victorian Britain* (Basingstoke and New York: Palgrave Macmillan, 2006).
Weart, Spencer R., *Nuclear Fear: A History of Images* (Cambridge, MA: Harvard University Press, 1988).
West, Christina, 'Memory—Recollection—Culture—Identity—Space: Social Context, Identity Formation, and Self-construction of the Calé (Gitanos) in Spain', in Peter Meusburger, Michael Heffernan and Edgar Wunder, eds,

Cultural Memories: The Geographical Point of View (London: Springer, 2011), 101–19.
Westover, Paul, *Necromanticism: Travelling to Meet the Dead, 1750–1860* (Basingstoke: Palgrave Macmillan, 2012).
Whatley, Christopher A., *The Industrial Revolution in Scotland* (Cambridge: Cambridge University Press, 1997).
Whatley, Christopher A. *Scottish Society, 1707–1830: Beyond Jacobitism, Towards Industrialisation* (Manchester: Manchester University Press, 2000).
Whatley, Christopher A., 'Contesting Memory and Public Places: Albert Square and Dundee's Pantheon of Heroes', Christopher A. Whatley, Bob Harris, and Louise Miskell, eds, *Victorian Dundee: Image and Realities*, second edition, (Dundee: Dundee University Press, 2011 [2000]), 173–96.
Whatley, Christopher A., 'Contested Commemorations: Robert Burns, Urban Scotland and Scottish Nationality in the Nineteenth Century', in Gerard Carruthers and Colin Kidd, eds, *Literature and Union: Scottish Texts, British Contexts* (Oxford: Oxford University Press, 2018), 221–43.
Whewell, William, 'On the General Bearing of the Great Exhibition', *Lectures on the Results of the Great Exhibition of 1851* (London: David Bogue, 1852), 3–25.
Whyte, Iain, *Scotland and the Abolition of Black Slavery* (Edinburgh: Edinburgh University Press, 2006).
Wilson, Patricia J., '*Ringan Gilhaize:* A neglected masterpiece?', in Christopher A. Whatley, ed., *John Galt (1779–1979)* (Edinburgh: The Ramsay Head Press, 1979), 120–50.
Wilson, Patricia J., '*Ringan Gilhaize:* the product of an informing vision', *Scottish Literary Journal*, 8:1 (1981), 52–68.
Wilson, Ross J., 'Still fighting in the trenches: "War Discourse" and the memory of the First World War in Britain,' *Memory Studies*, 8:4 (2015), 454–69.
Winch, Donald, 'Smith, Adam (bap. 1723, d. 1790)', *Oxford Dictionary of National Biography*, <http://www.oxforddnb.com/view/article/25767> (last accessed 20 November 2019).
Winter, Jay, 'Sites of Memory', in Susannah Radstone and Bill Schwarz, eds, *Memory: Histories, Theories, Debates* (New York: Fordham University Press, 2010), 312–24.
Withers, Charles W. J., and Wood, Paul, eds, *Science and Medicine in the Scottish Enlightenment* (Phantassie, East Lothian: Tuckwell Press, 2002).
Wood, Marcus, 'Significant Silence: Where was Slave Agency in the Popular Imagery of 2007?', Cora Kaplan and John Oldfield, eds, *Imagining Transatlantic Slavery* (New York: Palgrave Macmillan, 2010), 162–90.
Wood, Paul, 'Anderson, John (1726–1796)', *Oxford Dictionary of National Biography*, <http://www.oxforddnb.com/view/article/481> (last accessed 20 November 2019).
Wood, Paul and Withers, Charles W. J., 'Introduction: Science, Medicine and the Scottish Enlightenment: An Historiographical Overview', in Charles

W. J. Withers and Paul Wood, eds, *Science and Medicine in the Scottish Enlightenment* (Phantassie, East Lothian: Tuckwell Press, 2002), 1–16.

Worsdall, Frank, *The City that Disappeared: Glasgow's Demolished Architecture* (Glasgow: The Molendinar Press, 1981.)

Wright, Beth S., '"Seeing with the Painter's Eye": Sir Walter Scott's Challenge to Nineteenth-Century Art', in Murray Pittock, ed., *The Reception of Sir Walter Scott in Europe* (London and New York: Bloomsbury, 2007), 293–312.

Yoshikawa, Saeko, *William Wordsworth and the Invention of Tourism, 1820–1900* (Farnham: Ashgate, 2014).

Index

Note: *italic* indicates figure

Aberdeen, 115
  Common Sense philosophy, 48
  Enlightenment and, 33, 35, 53
Aberdein, Jennie
  on *Bogle Corbet*, 128
Abrams, Lynn
  on 'composure', 41
Adam, Robert, xi, 22, 71
Adam, Stephen
  stained glass panels, 148, 177–8
Adam, William (*bap.* 1689, *d.* 1748), 43
Adam Smith Theatre, 95
African Holocaust, 102
Age of Reason, 71
Aikenhead, Thomas, 50
Aird, Provost, 15, 16
Albert, Prince (1819–61), 66
Alexander, Boyd, 92
Alexander, Claud (1724–72), 92
Alexander, Wilhelmina, 92
Alexander, Sir William, Earl of Stirling, 114
Allan, David, 44–8, *44*
  Fine Art Exhibition in the Court of Old College (1761), *44*, 198–9
  The Foulis Academy of the Fine Arts (1760), 46, 47, 48
American War of Independence (1775–83), 21, 92
An Address . . . Concerning the African Slave Trade, xi
Anderson, Benedict, 153
Anderson, Prof. John (1726–96), xi, 33, 50, 97, 141

Anderson Institution, 97–8, 141
Annan, Thomas, 45–6, 47, 58n, 192
anti-Catholic riots, 67
anti-Catholic societies, 26
anti-Union riots, x
Arbuckle, James
  Glotta (1721), 146–7
Arbuckle Coffee Company, *35*, 36
Assmann, Aleida, 33, 101, 119, 202
  Cultural Memory and Western Civilization (2011), 46
Assmann, Jan, 33, 89–90
  Religion and Cultural Memory (2006), 41
Atget, Eugène
  photographs, 192
Atlantic world, 15
Auschwitz, 90
Aveline, François Antoine (1718–62), 43

Bagnall, Robert, 21
Bainbridge, Simon
  British Poetry and the Revolutionary and Napoleonic Wars (2003), 154
Baird, John, 25
Ballochmyle estate, 92
Barber, Jude and Welsh, Louise
  'Empire and Glasgow', 205
Barbados, 91–2
Barclay, John
  on Glasgow, 145–6
Barclay, Robert, of Ury, 114–15
  Apology for the True Christian Divinity (1678), 115

Index

Barfoot, Mike, 59n
  on Glasgow University networks, 51
Barnaby, Paul
  'Timeline of the European Reception of Sir Walter Scott, 1802–2013', 118
Barthes, Roland, 46
Battle of Corunna (1809), 155
Battle of Culloden (1746), 118
Battle of Sheriffmuir (1715), x, 16
Battle of Trafalgar (1805), 156
Belfast, 191
Bell, Henry, 75
  PS *Comet*, xii, 24
Bellamy, Martin
  on shipbuilding, 186
Benjamin, Walter, 46
Berry, Christopher, 95
  The Idea of Commercial Society in the Scottish Enlightenment (2013), 93
Bible, 40, 42, 99, 171
Bickham, Troy, 100
Billig, Michael, 204
  Banal Nationalism (1995), 160
Black, Joseph (1728–99), 18, 33, 43, 48, 51–2, 65–6, 73, 76, 77
  Essays and Observations (1756), 51
Black Lives Matter movement, 88, 194
Blaikie, Andrew
  The Scots Imagination and Modern Memory (2010), 7
Blair, George
  Biographic and Descriptive Sketches of Glasgow Necropolis (1857), 149–50
Blake, George
  The Shipbuilders, 176
Blake, William, 106
Boswell, James, 3, 21–2, 56n, 99
  No Abolition of Slavery; or, the Universal Empire of Love (1791), 99–100
  Tour of Corsica (1768), 99
Boyd, Zachary, 27n
Brexit vote, 7
Bristol, 16, 88, 91, 104
British Empire, 26, 104, 122, 154, 184, 195, 202
  Dublin and, 153–4, 158
  Glasgow and, 24, 77–8, 90, 91, 119, 105, 127, 142, 154, 161–2, 174, 184, 205
  Scotland and, 87, 173, 178, 179, 184–5
  writers and, 119, 123, 125–8
  see also Glasgow; Glasgow Exhibitions
British Museum, 102, 106

Broadie, Alexander
  on Thomas Reid, 93
Browne, James
  Works of Tobias Smollett (1872), 62
Buchanan, Archibald, 24
Buchanan, Robert and Mackenzie, A. C.
  'The new Covenant', 173–4
Bruce, Robert
  Bruce Report, 4
Bruce, Robert the, 191
Bryce, Thomas Hastie (1862–1946), 74
Bueltmann, Hinson and Morton
  The Scottish Diaspora (2013), 85
Burgess, Moira, 3
  Imagine a City (1998), 3
  The Glasgow Novel (1972), 3
Burns, Robert (1759–96), 24, 28n, 143–4, 148, 179, 182, 191–2
  statues, 66, 67, 159, 160
  Poems, Chiefly in the Scottish Dialect (1806), 22
  'The Bonnie Lass o' Ballochmyle', 92
  'The Slave's Lament', 106
  'To a Mouse', 22

Cairns, John, 93, 94–5
Caldicott, Edric and Fuchs, Anne
  Cultural Memory (2003), 6
Caledonia; or, the Pedlar turn'd Merchant (1700), 117–18, 121
Caledonian Mercury, 170
Calton Weavers' Strike (1787), 97
Cambuslang Revival, 40–2, 68
Cameronians Memorial (1924), 162
Campbell, Archibald, Duke of Argyll (1682–1761), 52
Campbell, Colin, Baron Clyde (1792–1863), 66, 159, 160, 161, 162
Campbell, Daniel, x, 17
Campbell, Roy, 52
  on Glasgow and industry, 172
  'Scotland's Neglected Enlightenment' (1990), 34
Campbell, Thomas (1777–1844), 64, 66, 143, 144, 146, 150, 159, 164n, 179
  'Elegy Written in Mull' (1795), 144–5
Campbell, William, 23, 70, 80n
Canada, 114, 122, 125–7, 128–129, 130, 131
Canada Company, 129
Canton, China, 26
Cardiff, 191
Carlyle, Thomas, 182

Carolina, 114–16
Carolina Company, 115
Caroline, Queen, 25
Carswell, Catherine, 206
Cass, Jeffrey
  on Galt, 129
Catholic Relief Act, xi
Certain Propositions Relating to the Scots Plantation of Caledonia (1700), 117
Chalmers, Thomas, 25
Chantrey, Francis Leggatt, 74
Charles Edward Stuart, Prince, x
Charles Town, 114, 116
Cicero, 75
City of Glasgow Union Railway Company, 77
Clark, Rev. James, 15
Clark and Wright
  'Urban Regeneration in Glasgow' (2018), 193, 194
Clarke, David, 77
Clarkson, Thomas, 99
Cleland, James, 155
Cochrane, Andrew (1693–1777), 95
Cochrane, William (1738–85), 74, 80n
Coleman, James
  Remembering the Past in Nineteenth-Century Scotland (2014), 7, 67
Colston, Edward (1636–1721), 104, 112n
commemoration, 5, 18, 66, 67, 104, 106, 108n, 144, 148, 149, 151, 153, 154, 158, 160–1, 171, 175, 203; *see also* cultural memory
Commonwealth Games name changes, 195
Company of Scotland Trading to Africa and the Indies, 14, 116
Connell, Lord Provost Arthur (1772–4), 199
Cooke, Anthony, 103
Cookson, J. E.
  on Wellington statues, 162–3
Cooper, Richard (1701–64), 43
Cora Linn, 146
coronation (1953), 159
Covenanters, 39, 40, 49, 115, 116, 124, 171
Craig, Carol
  The Tears that Made the Clyde (2010), 193
Craig, David
  on Smollett, 55
Crampsey, Bob
  on Highland Association Bazaar (1907), 180

Cowan, Edward J.
  'Myth of Scotch Canada' (1999), 114
Crawford, Robert
  On Glasgow and Edinburgh (2013), 2
Cullen, William (1710–90), 18, 48, 50, 59n, 64, 73, 74, 76, 77, 80n, 198
cultural memory, 41, 45, 46, 52, 53, 63–79, 85–6, 87–9, 92, 103, 108, 115, 119–21, 131, 149, 152, 154, 160–1, 170, 183, 185, 194, 199–200, 203–6
  commemoration and, 18, 33, 45, 66, 149, 158–9, 171–2, 185; *see also* commemoration
  exhibition and, 4, 45, 199, 174, 175, 183–4, 201–2
  Glasgow and, 4, 5, 52, 64, 65, 67, 69, 73, 74, 86, 120, 128, 148, 150, 163, 171, 193, 201–6
  Georgian Glasgow and *see* Georgian Glasgow
  Glasgow Enlightenment and, 33, 38, 63, 64–5, 66–7, 74–5, 77
  memory studies and, 6–7, 33, 90, 201
  monuments and, 63, 70, 105, 153–4, 158–60, 162, 163
  memorials and, 67–8, 143, 162
  paintings and, 6, 45, 66–7, 120, 132, 202
  sites of memory, 45, 85, 89, 143
  statues and, 6–7, 66, 69, 153–4, 156, 159, 161–2, 163, 194–5, 202, 205
  topography of, 64, 68, 120
  writers and, 115, 119–20, 123, 131–2, 144–55, 161
  see also slavery
Cunninghame, William, 20, 21, 87–8

Daiches, David, Jones, J. and Jones, P.
  A Hotbed of Genius: The Scottish Enlightenment (1986), 33–4, 44
Dale, David, 22
Darien Company, 116, 132
Darien Scheme (1698–1700), 14, 87, 116–17, 120–22, 124
Davis, David Brion
  on Millar, 95
Davis, Margaret Thomson, 206
Dawson, Graham, 161
  Soldier Heroes (1994), 7, 153
Declaration of Arbroath (1320), 125
Defoe, Daniel, 3, 124, 135n
  Tour Through the Whole Island of Great Britain (1724), x, 18

Index

Derrida, Jacques, 202
Devine, T. M., 87, 105, 116, 169
  Recovering Scotland's Slavery Past, 89
Devine, T. M. and G. Jackson
  Glasgow, Vol. I: Beginnings to 1830 (1995), 2, 34
Dewar, Donald, 64
Donovan, Arthur, 50–1, 53
  Philosophical Chemistry in the Scottish Enlightenment (1975), 48–9
Dreghorn, Allan, xi, 20
Dresser, Madge
  on Bristol commemoration, 104
Duffill, Mark
  on Darien scheme, 87
Dundas, Henry, 8n
Dunlop, William, 115–16
Dunlop, William (1792–1848)
  Statistical Sketches of Upper Canada (1832), 128

East Kilbride, 53, 63
Easter Rising of 1916, 158
Edinburgh, 20, 67, 70, 85, 117, 154, 169, 174–5, 191, 192, 201
  Academy of St Luke, 20, 43
  anti-Catholic riots, 21–2
  Commonwealth Games (1970), 195
  Georgian era scholarship and, 2
  literati, 20, 50
  Scottish Enlightenment and, 2, 33–5, 38–9, 43–4, 49–51, 53, 96, 99, 118
  UNESCO City of Literature (2004), 143
  University, 43, 55, 178
Edinburgh Committee for the Abolition of the Slave Trade, 100
Edinburgh Society for the Encouragement of Arts, Sciences, Manufactures and Agriculture, 42
Edward, Mary
  Who Belongs to Glasgow? (1993), 108
Eisenstein, Elizabeth
  The Printing Press as an Agent of Change (1979), 42
Emerson, Roger L.
  on King's College, 48–9
emigration, 114, 120, 126, 128, 131
Erll, Astrid
  on collective texts, 125
Erskine, David Steuart, 11th Earl of Buchan (1742–1829), 33, 43–4
Erskine, Henry, Lord Cardross, 115–16
  Seal of the House of Cardross 133n

Fagen, Graham, 106
Fairfield Shipbuilding & Engineering Company, 64, 177
Fawcett, Arthur
  The Cambuslang Revival (1971), 40–1, 42
Fearless Girl (2017), 163, 168n
Ferguson, Adam, 50
Findling, John E.
  Historical Dictionary of World's Fairs (1990), 181–2
Finlay, Kirkman, 26
Flaxman, John, 155, 166n
Fleming, Robert, 65, 68
Florence, 5, 43, 146, 149
Floyd, George (1973–2020), 88
Forbes, Archibald
  on Baron Clyde, 161
Foreman, Carol
  Lost Glasgow, 201
Forth and Clyde Canal, 23
Foucault, Michel, 170
Foulis, Andrew (1712–75), 20, 39
Foulis, Robert (1707–76), 20, 39, 42–4, 48, 64, 65
Foulis brothers, xi, 20, 38–9, 42, 43, 46, 48, 49, 54, 65, 70, 73, 196
Foulis Press, 38–40, 42, 48, 65
  A Catalogue of Books Imported (1740), 39
Fraser, Hamish W.
  Glasgow, Volume II:1830–1912 (1996), 178
French Revolution, 119, 128
Fry, Michael, 8n, 87, 116
  Glasgow: A History of the City (2017), 2
  Scottish Empire (2001), 1

Gaitens, Edward, 3
  Dance of the Apprentices (1948), 3, 97
Galileo, 75
Galt, John (1779–1839), 5, 115, 118–20, 122–32
  Annals of the Parish (1821), 119, 120, 123, 127
  Bogle Corbet (1831), 125–128, 129–30
  Lawrie Todd (1830), 125
  Ringan Gilhaize (1823), 115, 124–5
  The Autobiography of John Galt (1833), 129
  The Ayrshire Legatees (1821), 123
  The Entail (1823), 120, 124, 125, 127
  The Literary Life (1843), 122
  The Steam-Boat, 127

Gaza, 160
General Assembly (1638), 13, 40, 68
George I, King, x, 1, 15, 91
George II, King, 153
George IV, King, 26
   visit to Edinburgh, 120–1, 129, 131, 180
George VI, King and Queen Elizabeth
   visit to 1938 Exhibition, 183
George, Prince of Wales, 15
Georgian era, x, xii, 1, 7, 13, 26, 52, 66, 85, 124, 141
   books and, 2
   cultural identity and, 131
   cultural memory and, 89, 204
   Enlightenment and, 35, 73
   exhibitions and, 198–9, 202–3, 204
   Merchant City and, 196, 204
   religious troubles and, 172
   scholarship and, 97
   texts and, 119, 124, 201
Georgian Glasgow, 2, 4, 14, 20, 27, 34, 39, 87, 95, 97, 194, 202, 203, 205, 206
   architecture, 2, 4, 5, 14, 33, 148, 205
   cultural memory and, 5, 33, 52, 66, 85, 89, 97, 123, 132, 141–2, 170, 196, 199–201, 204
   exhibitions and, 195–203, 205
   in literature, 3, 118–32, 114, 146–51, 153, 155, 206
   location, 196
Geyer-Kordesch, J., and MacDonald, F., 48–50, 51, 71
Ghana, 102
Gibb, Robert
   Thin Red Line (1881), 131, 132
Gibson, John
   History of Glasgow (1777), xi
Gibson, Walter, 115–16
Gifford, D., Dunnigan, S., and McGillivray, A.
   on Scott,118
Gladstone, William Ewart (1809–98), 66, 158, 159
Glasgow
   architecture, 33, 46, 72, 105, 169, 176, 177, 186, 193, 197
   and Birmingham, 186, 191
   character, 2, 15, 43, 51, 69, 73, 97 170–1, 172 177–8, 185–6, 196, 199, 201, 204
   City of Culture (1990), 104, 193
   cityscape, 4, 23, 77, 127, 145–6
   class tensions, xi, xii, 22–3, 25, 97, 141

commerce, 1, 14, 17, 20, 27, 34, 43, 76–7, 85, 92–3, 98, 114, 148, 169–72, 181, 197
Commonwealth Games (2014), 90, 163, 194–5, 205
cultural memory and *see* cultural memory
early history, 13–14
foundation story, 13, 148–9
identity, 5, 18, 19, 148, 149, 150, 163, 169, 177, 192, 194
image, 2, 3, 4, 5, 33, 35, 38, 65, 68, 76–7, 85, 97, 124, 141, 146, 149, 170, 182, 191–5, 204
imperialism and, 5, 104, 114–15, 123, 153, 160
industry, 5, 35, 77, 105, 141, 169, 170, 172, 174, 176, 179, 181, 191, 192, 197, 199, 201
manufacturing,17, 20, 38, 118, 163
merchants, 13–16, 18, 20–2, 26, 48, 52, 85, 87–8, 91–2, 95, 103–5, 122, 147, 155, 171, 177, 196–7, 198, 206
New Lanark project, 22
novel, 3, 123
Orange march (1822), 26, 171
population, x, xi, xii, 13, 14, 18, 20, 21, 22, 23, 25, 26, 35, 117, 118, 169–71
Presbyterianism and, 4, 17, 49, 50, 69, 122
Protestant character, 13–14, 21, 25
Red Clydeside, 97
regeneration, 105, 181, 193–4
religious identity, 42, 150, 170–1
riots, x, 17, 19, 21, 22, 67
Roman Catholics and, xi, 21, 22, 26 25, 67, 171
royal burgh (1636), 130
Scottish Enlightenment and *see* Scottish Enlightenment
'Second City of the Empire', 5, 24, 132, 141, 143, 154, 169–72, 181, 186, 191, 202
sectarianism, 21
self-perception, 85
shipbuilding, 5, 35, 64, 98, 141, 142, 147, 163, 169, 176, 186, 197, 199
slave trade and *see* slave trade
slavery and *see* slavery
slum clearances, 192
social problems, 24, 193, 197
spinning, 17, 22, 123
stereotypes, 193
sugar trade, 18, 92, 103, 114, 196, 205

Index

technology, 121, 162, 174–5, 179, 197
tobacco, 3, 21, 22, 87, 88, 91, 92, 106, 196
'Tobacco Lords', 3, 21, 25, 87, 98, 196, 198
topography, 3, 64, 68, 70, 147
town council, xi, 17, 18, 19, 88
Victorian, 3, 22, 86n, 171, 196, 198, 199, 203–4
weaving, xi, 22, 23, 24, 25, 97, 128
Workers City movement, 104
'Workshop of the World', 22, 141, 171
writers and, 3, 26, 35, 142, 143, 147–8
see also British Empire; Georgian era; Georgian Glasgow; Glasgow Enlightenment
Glasgow Advertiser, xi
Glasgow Anti-Slavery Society, 103
Glasgow Boys, 2–3, 177, 197
Glasgow Built Preservation Trust, 105
Glasgow Centre for Population Health, 193
Glasgow Chamber of Commerce, 22
Glasgow City Council, 13, 64, 105, 193
Glasgow City Heritage Trust, 205
Glasgow City Improvements Act (1866), 123–4
Glasgow Colonial Society, 122
Glasgow Committee for the Abolition of the Slave Trade, 100
 An Address to the Inhabitants of Glasgow . . . Concerning the African Slave Trade (1791), xi, 100
Glasgow City Council, 13, 64, 105, 106, 193
Glasgow Courant, x, 16, 70
Glasgow Emancipation Society, 103
Glasgow Enlightenment, xi, 2, 21, 33, 38, 48, 63, 64–7, 74–7, 85, 92, 97, 124, 141, 151, 196, 204
 scholarship and, 33–5
 see also cultural memory; Georgian Glasgow; Scottish Enlightenment
Glasgow exhibitions, 5, 65, 163, 172, 181, 184, 192, 196, 197, 203
 and Bishop's Castle, 172–3, 174, 180
 Burns Exhibition (1896), 45
 and Clachan, 179–80, 182–3
 Downpresser (2007), 106
 Empire Exhibition (1938), 181–85
 Empire Exhibition Scotland – 1938, Official Guide, 182
 Foulis Academy Exhibition (2001), 77, 196
 Glasgow and the World, 203

 'Glasgow Stories', 4, 199–201
 How Glasgow Flourished 1714–1837 (2014), 4, 195, 197–202, 200, 204–5
 International Exhibition (1901), 174–7, 181, 185, 203
 International Exhibition of Science, Art and Industry (1888), 172–4, 181
 and lion rampant, 184, 185
 Mackintosh Exhibition (1996), 177
 Mind-Forg'd Manacles: William Blake and Slavery (2007), 106
 Pen and Ink Notes at the Glasgow Exhibition (1888), 172–3
 and Mary Morrison of Barra, 183
 Scottish Exhibition (1911), 178–181, 196
 and souvenirs, 180, 184
 and tartanry, 180
 The Glassford Family Portrait: A Hidden Legacy (2007–8), 106
 and Tower of Empire 182–183, 185
Glasgow Herald, ix, 170, 183
'Glasgow Homer', 42
Glasgow Ladies' Auxiliary Society, 103
Glasgow Ladies' Emancipation Society, 106
Glasgow Life, 195, 199, 201, 205
Glasgow Literary Society, 28n, 51, 94
Glasgow Museums and City Council
 Towards Understanding Slavery – Past and Present (2007), 106
Glasgow Museums Resource Centre, 202
Glasgow named places
 Anderson's Institution, xi, 97–8, 141
 Anderson's Museum, 72
 Argyle Arcade, xii
 Argyle Street, xii, 37
 Assembly Rooms, 70
 Asylum for Lunatics, xii, 24–5
 Bank of Scotland, 17
 Bath Street, 74
 Bellahouston Park, 181
 Bishop's Castle, 20, 23
 Bishop's Palace Memorial Pillar, 69
 Bridgeton, 75
 Briggait, 205
 Burrell Collection, 106
 Calton, xi, 22–3
 Cathedral Square, 69, 98
 Celtic Park, 194
 Cenotaph, 66, 159, 160, 162
 Central Station, 4, 20, 37
 Charlotte Street, 22
 City Chambers, 2, 4, 22, 66, 159–60, 172, 177, 184, 185, 192, 197

Glasgow named places (*cont.*)
  Clyde, River, 4, 5, 13, 17–18, 37, 67, 141, 143–8, 150, 153, 169, 170, 176, 197
  Clyde Street, x, xii, 25, 69
  Clydeport Building, 75
  Corunna Street, 24, 155
  East End, 106, 194
  Elmbank Street, 75
  Emirates Arena, 194
  Finnieston Crane, 163, 192
  Foulis Building, 65
  Gallery of Modern Art, 21, 88, 106, 163
  Gallowgate Street, 37
  George Square, xi, xii, 4, 7, 22, 24, 66–8, 74, 143, 150, 155–6, *156*, 158, 159–60, 162, 194–5, 204
  Gilmorehill, 37
  Glasgow Arms Bank, 20
  Glasgow Cathedral (St Mungo's), xi, 13, 37, 38, 39, 65, 67–8, 69, 128, 149, 150, 151 170
  Glasgow City Art Gallery, 177
  Glasgow Cross, xi, 15, 19, 20, 22, 88, 124, 127, *127*
  Glasgow Grammar School, 151
  Glasgow Green, 26, 75, 147, 156, 194
  Glasgow School of Art, 65, 176
  Glassford Street, xi, 5, 23, 196, 204
  Grahamston, 20, 37
  Havannah Street, 21
  High Street, 20, 21, 24, 37, 38, 69, 192, 196, 204
  Hutcheson's Bridge, 70
  Hutcheson's Hospital, 27
  Ingram Street, 5, 65
  Jamaica Street, 21, 89, 123, 204
  Kelvin Way, 38
  Kelvin Way Bridge, 76, *76*
  Kelvingrove Art Gallery and Museum, 4, 95, 106 , 174, 176, 195, 196, 197, 199, 202–3, 204
  Kelvingrove Park, 76, 162, 178, 180, 181
  La Belle Place, 76
  McLellan Galleries, 176, 177
  McPhun Park, 75
  Maryhill Burgh Halls, 177
  Mechanics' Institute and Technical College of Science, 74–5
  Mercat Cross, 37, 38
  Merchant City, 21, 85, 104–5, 196, 197, 201, 204, 205
  Mitchell Library, 28n, 65, 80n, 196, 204
  Molendinar Burn, 68, 128, 146
  Necropolis, 13, 67, 148, 149–51, 170, 197
  Nelson Mandela Place, 75, 76
  Parliamentary Road, 25
  People's Palace, 25, 106, 108, 196
  Physic Garden, 71
  playhouse, 20
  Pollokshaws, 24
  Port Glasgow, 13, 16–17
  Provand's Lordship, 65, 106
  Queen Street Station, 4
  Ramshorn Church, 65
  Robertson Street, 75
  Royal Bank of Scotland, 22
  Royal Exchange, 21, 163
  Royal Infirmary, xi, 69, 70–1, *71*
  St Andrew's Church, xi, 20, 205
  St Andrew's Roman Catholic Cathedral, xii, 25, 69
  St Enoch Square, 4
  St Mungo Museum of Religious Life and Art, 106
  St Nicholas Garden, 65
  Saltmarket Street, 20, 37, 196
  Sauchiehall Street, 176
  Shawfield Mansion, x, 17, 19, 21, 23, 87
  Ship Bank, 20
  Stirling Library, 21
  Strathclyde House, 75
  Tolbooth, 15, 22, 170
  Tontine Buildings, x, 22, 128
  Town Hall, 22
  Trades Hall, xi, 5, 25, 71, 196
  Trades House, 13
  Toun's Hospital, x, 17–18, 25
  Tron Kirk, 15
  Trongate, x, 18, 37, 69, 127, *127*, 128, 148, 151, 196
  University Avenue, 38, 64
  University of Strathclyde, xi, 97–8
  Virginia Street, 21, 89, 123, 204
  York Street Riding School, 70
  West End, 37, 172, 181, 203
  see also University of Glasgow buildings
Glasgow Ohio Company, 122
'Glasgow School' of fiction, 119
Glasgow West India Association, 103
Glassford, John, 18, 20, 21, 23, 87, *107*, 112–13n
'Glorious Revolution' (1688), 1, 18, 116
Goldsmith, Alastair Lindsay
  on Tower of Empire, 182

Index

Gomme and Walker
  Architecture of Glasgow (1968), 105
Gordon, Ian
  on Galt, 130
Gordon, Sir Robert, of Lochinvar, 114
Gouriévidis, Laurence
  on the Clachan, 183
  on National Museum of Scotland, 202
Graham, Dougal
  A Full, Particular and True Account of the Rebellion in the Years 1745–1746, 19
Graham, J.
  on Nelson monument, 157
Graham, Thomas (1805–69), 66, 159
Grassby, Charles Benham, 75
Gray, Alasdair
  Lanark (1981), 3–4, 205–6
Great Exhibition (Crystal Palace) of 1851, 172, 173, 175
Gregory, James, 93
Greenock, 17, 24, 91
Greenshields, John, 74–5
Grenada, 90
Grigor, Murray, 177
  Scotch Myths (1981), 131
Gristwood, Anthony, 180
Groom, Brian
  on Second City debate, 191
Guelph, 128–30, *130*, 132
Guinness, Desmond
  Georgian Dublin (1975), 2
Gulag, 90
Gulliver, Stuart
  'Merchant City: the Recolonization of Central Glasgow', 105
Guyatt, Mary
  on Wedgwood medallion, 102

Halbwachs, Maurice, 6, 33, 68–9, 89, 122
Hamilton of Gilbertfield, William (c.1665–1751), 39–40
Hamilton, David, 55, 156
Hamilton, Duke of, 24, 66
Hamilton, Gavin, 39, 67
Hamilton, Robert, 51
Hamilton, Thomas (1789–1842)
  Cyril Thornton (1827), 73, 119, 142n
Hammerton, J. A.
  Sketches from Glasgow (1893), 162
Hanlon, Walsh and Whyte
  Let Glasgow Flourish, 193
Hanoverian monarchy, 16, 23, 25, 45, 63, 129–30

Hardie, Andrew, 25
Harvie, Christopher
  on Scott, 180
Haussmann, Georges-Eugène, 124, 192
Havelock, Sir Henry, 153, 161
Hemans, Felicia
  'To my Younger Brother, on his return from Spain' (1812), 155
Henderson, Francis, 69
Hendrix, Harald
  on Petrarch, 144
Hichberger, Joan
  on Scots in British army, 131
Highland clearances, 202
Highland Light Infantry Memorial for the Boer War (1906), 162, 168n
Hill, Burton J., 40
Hind, Archie
  The Dear Green Place (1966), 3
Hobsbawn, Eric, 182
Hodge, Albert Hemstock, 75
Hogg, James, 119
  Private Memoirs and Confessions of a Justified Sinner (1824), 119
Hollywood and Scottish history, 126
Holocaust, 6, 90
Home, John, 70
Homer, 75
Hook, Andrew, and Sher, R.
  The Glasgow Enlightenment (1995), 34
House, Jack
  The Heart of Glasgow (1965), 2
Houston, R. A.
  Scottish Literacy and the Scottish Identity (1985), 42
Howitt, William
  Homes and Haunts of the Most Eminent British Poets (1877), 144
Huhtamo, Erkki, 147
Hull, 104
Hume, David, 34, 44, 50, 95, 96
Hunter, John (1728–93), 50, 53
Hunter, William (1718–83), 24, 38, 48, 50, 51, 53–4, 55, 63, 64, 72–74, 141
  Anatomy of the Gravid Uterus (1774), 54
Huron Tract, 129
Hutcheson, Francis (1694–1746), 17, 34, 39, 50, 53, 74
  The Meditations of the Emperor Marcus Aurelius Antoninus, 39
Hutcheson brothers, Thomas and George, 27n, 156
Hutton, James, 23

Iberoamerican Fair (1929), 180–1, 183
'Improvement' age of, 141, 2
Independence Referendum (2014), 7, 194
Indian Rebellion (1857), 161
Ingamells, John
   on Smollett, 55
Inglis, Lucy, 2
Ingram, Archibald, 18, 20
Insh, George Pratt
   on Carolina Covenanters, 115
International Slavery Museum, 103

Jacobite Rising (1715), x, 16
Jacobite Rising (1745), x, 18–19
Jacobite Risings, 1
Jacobite story, 120–1
Jacobites, 19, 63, 191, 206
Jacobitism, 44
James I & VI, King, 114
James II & VII, King, 14
James III & VIII, King, 16, 178
Jauss, Hans Robert
   on literary works in their time, 124–5
Jewish Ghetto, Prague, 192
Johnson, Samuel, 62, 99
Johnston, Arthur
   dedication to Glasgow (1642), 145
Johnston, John
   on the Clyde, 145, 164n
Jones, George
   The Burial of Sir John Moore after Corunna (c.1834), 152
Jones, Richard, 55

Kames, Lord
   Sketches of the History of Man (1774), 100
Kansteiner, Wulf
   on memory studies, 126
Kavanagh, Gaynor
   on museum images, 205
Kay, Jackie
   'Missing Faces' (2007), 105
Kelman, James, 104
Kelvin, Lord, 173
Kennedy, John F., 68
Kilpatrick, James
   Literary Landmarks of Glasgow (1898), 143
Kinchin, Perilla and Kinchin, Juliet, 179, 181, 186
King, Elspeth
   on Glassford family portrait, 108

Kingdom of Strathclyde, 13
Kirkcaldy Penny, 95
Knight, Joseph, 99
Knox, John, 13, 67, 150, 165n
   monument, 13, 67, 148, 150, 170
Knox, John (artist) (1778–1845), 157
   Old Glasgow Cross or The Trongate (1826), 127, *127*, 136n
   The Nelson Monument Struck by Lightning (1810), 157, *157*
Kyle, Elizabeth
   The Tontine Belle (1951), 88

Lake District, 144
Landsman, Ned C.
   on converts and the Bible, 42
Lane, Paul J. and MacDonald, Kevin C.
   on slavery, 90
Lavery, John
   Modern Glasgow, 3
   Potter at Work, (1888), 179
Lee, Arthur
   Essay in Vindication of the Continental Colonies of America (1764), 93
Leeds, 170
Leith, 50, 91
Lenman, Bruce
   on Galt, 119–20, 132
   on the Scottish Exhibition (1911), 178
Limond, Brian, 142n
Lincoln, Abraham, 99
Lindsay, Maurice, 77
   Illustrated Guide to Glasgow, 1837 (1989), 26
Lister, Joseph, 71
Liverpool, 16, 88, 91–2, 100, 103–4, 154, 157
Livingstone, David, 69, 98, 98 f10, 99, 101, 106, 149, 171, 182
Locke, John, 95
London, x, 16, 18, 51, 53, 85, 104, 146, 175
   Georgian, 2
   Scottish Enlightenment and, 34, 43, 53, 73
   Scottish colony, 52
Longstaff, Will
   Immortal Shrine/Eternal Silence (1928), 162
   Menin Gate at Midnight (1927), 162
Luckhurst, Kenneth, 184
   on the Empire Exhibition (1938), 184

McArthur, Colin
   on Empire Exhibition (1938), 182–3

Index

McArthur, John
  Plan of the City of Glasgow, xi
Macarthur, Mary, 155
  elegies on Robert Burns, 150
  Necropolis: An Elegy (1842), 150–1
  'The Clyde' (1842), 143
  'The Hero and his Sword', 151–3
McArthur, Alexander and Long, H. Kingsley
  No Mean City (1935), 35, 193
McCracken-Flesher, Caroline
  on Scott, 154
McCulloch, William, 40–1
MacDonald, John Blake
  James Watt Portrait, 78
McEwan, Peter
  Dictionary of Scottish Art and Architecture (2004), 42
Macfarlane, Alexander, 52
McGavin, William 'The Protestant', 25
MacGregor, George, 70
  History of Glasgow (1881), 69
McIlvanney, Liam
  on Galt, 123
Mackenzie, Charles
  Interesting and Remarkable Places (1849), 148
MacKenzie, John M., 170, 179, 183, 184
  Imperial Cities (1999), 169
McKenzie, Ray
  on Frederick Sleigh, 161–2
Mackintosh, Charles Rennie, 176–7
Mackintosh, Colin, 180
McLauchlan, Archibald
  The Glassford Family Portrait (c.1767), 106–8, *107*, 112–13n
McLay, Farquhar
  The Reckoning: Beyond the Culture City Rip Off (1990), 104
MacLehose, James
  on Foulis Academy, 44
MacLeod, Christine, 81n
  Heroes of Invention (2007), 74
McLellan, Archibald, 176
McNeil, Kenneth
  on *Bogle Corbet*, 126, 128
Macpherson, James
  The Works of Ossian (1765), 131
Macrae, James, 18
M'Ure, John
  A View of the City of Glasgow (1736), x, 18
Maier, Charles, 90, 104
Malt Tax, x, 17, 19

Mandler, Peter
  '"Faust comes to town"' (2012), 124
Marian Column, Prague, 158
Markus, Thomas, 71–2, 73
Mary, Queen of Scots, 173, 191
Maver, Irene
  on symbols, 184
Mayne, John
  'Glasgow: A Poem (1783; 1803), 37, 64, 127, 146, 147–8, 165n
Melville, Andrew, 13
memory studies, 6–7, 33, 90, 126, 201
  collective memory, 6, 7, 33, 40, 45, 89, 119, 120, 121, 122, 125, 174, 179, 202, 203
  see also cultural memory
Mennons, John, xi
Meusberger, Peter
  on slavery and trauma, 90
migration, 85
Millar, John (1735–1801), 33, 48, 64
  Observations Concerning the Distinction of Ranks in Society (1771), 94–5
Miller, David Philip
  on Watt, 75
Miller, James, 188n
Milan Cathedral, 148
Milton, John, 95
Mingay, G. E., 2
  Georgian London (1975)
Mitchell, James, 54
Mitchell Library, 65
Misztal, Barbara A., 121
  Theories of Social Remembering (2003), 6–7
Moir, D. M., 125
Monkland Canal, 23
Monteith, John, 24
Montford, Paul, 76
Moor, Prof. James (*bap.* 1712, *d.* 1779), 39, 46
Moore, Dugald, 132, 151, 179
  'Stanzas to the Clyde' (1833), 146
  sonnet on Glasgow's Cathedral (1831), 150
  The Bard of the North (1833), 87
Moore, Dr John (1729–1802), 18, 24, 28n, 50–1, 53, 66, 73, 151, 179
Moore, Sir John (1761–1809), 24, 66, 151–2, 153, 155–6, 158–9, 160–1
  statues, xii, 66, 155, 156, *156*, 159, 162
  The Diary of Sir John Moore (1904), 160
  The Life of Lieutenant-General Sir John Moore (1833), 160

Moore, John and Silverthorne, Michael
  *The Meditations of the Emperor Marcus
    Aurelius Antoninus* (2008), 39
Morning Chronicle, 169
Morton, Graeme, 130
Morton, H. V., 85, 86n
Mossman, John, 75–6, 76, 98
Muir, James Hamilton
  Glasgow in 1901, 175–6
Muir, Thomas, of Huntershill (1765–99), 23
Mullen, Stephen, 92, 106, 108n, 110n
  It Wisnae Us, 105
Murphy, Paula
  Nineteenth-Century Irish Sculpture
    (2010), 153, 158

Napoleonic wars, 171, 175
National Army Museum, 159
National Defence League, 194
National Galleries of Scotland, 46
National Trust for Scotland, 106
'necro-tourism', 144
Nelson, Admiral Horatio, 70, 151 153, 156–8, 157
New Canadian Library, 126
New South Wales, 122
Nora, Pierre, 89, 143
  Les Lieux de mémoire, 6, 45
North America, 114, 120, 125, 131
  Presbyterian essence, 122
Northern Looking Glass (1825), 156
Nova Scotia, 114, 131
  'Scottish Day', 131
New Lanark Project, 22
Newton, Sir Isaac, 95

Oakley, C. A.
  The Second City (1946), 143
O'Brien, Gillian and O'Kane, Fionola
  Georgian Dublin (2008), 2
O'Connell, Daniel, 158
O'Connor, Anne
  on Dante, 149
O'Neill, Mark
  on Glasgow's cultural sites, 197
Ohio
  Scottish Street names, 123
Old Calton Burial Ground, Edinburgh, 99
Olick, Jeffrey K and Robbins, J
  on memory studies, 7
Orr, Julie
  on Darien Scheme,117, 134n
Oswald, James (1779–1853), 66, 159

Owen, Wilfred, 154
Oxford Dictionary of National Biography, 161

Paces, Cynthia
  on Marian Column, 158
Pains and Penalties Bill (1820), 25
Paisley, xi, 37, 100, 169
Palestine, flag of, 159–60
Papists Act (1778), 21–2
Paris, 43, 54, 146, 192
  Père Lachaise Cemetery, 67, 149
Park, Patric
  on Moore statue, 155
Parliament, xi, xii, 16, 94, 99–100
Parliamentary Commission of Visitation
    (1690), 49
Paul, Robert (1739–70), 43, 198, 199
  *A View of St. Andrew's Church from the
    Battlements of the Old Town House*, 198
  *From the South on the East Side of St.
    Mungo's Church*, 198
  Views of Glasgow from the South East
    (1760s), 198
Paxman, Jeremy
  Empire (2012), 103
Pearce, Sir William, 64
Peel, Sir Robert (1788–1850), 66, 159
Pick, Daniel
  on codes and images, 175
Phipps, Elvira Anna
  Memorials of Clutha (1842), 148
Pittock, Murray, 67, 126, 170, 184
  The Invention of Scotland (1991), 131
Point Pleasant Park, 131
Pollokshaws Printfield Company, 18
Ponte dei Sospiri, 151
Porter, Roy
  on Hunter brothers, 53
Prebble, John
  on Darien Scheme, 116
Presbyterian exiles, 115
Prescott, John, 104
Preudhomme, Jean, 67
Privy Council, 114

Quakerism, 114–15, 133n
Quinault, Roland
  'The Cult of the Centenary' (1998), 174

Radical Martyrs, 25
Radical War (1820), xii, 97

Index

Ramsay, Allan, snr. (1684–1758), 20, 43, 146–7
  'Clyde's Welcome to his Prince' (1721), 146
  The Gentle Shepherd (1725), 146
  'To the Ph— an Ode' (1721), 146
Readman, Paul
  on history in English culture, 196
Reeve, Antonia, 46
reform, 141
Reform Act for Scotland (1832), xii, 26
Reformation, 1, 13, 20, 25, 42, 68, 124
Reid, Thomas (1710–96), 48, 64–5, 93
religious intolerance, 50
religious persecution, 14, 115–16, 117
Rembold, Effie
  on Scottish Exhibition (1911), 178–9
remembrance, 45, 62–3, 66, 67, 104, 142, 149, 155, 159, 197, 202; *see also* cultural memory
Renaissance, 5, 46, 101
Reston, Jane, 41
Revolutionary Wars, 23
Reynolds, Sir Joshua (1723–92), 73–4
Rice, C. Duncan, 95, 99, 103
Richards, Thomas, 184
  The Commodity Culture of Victorian England (1990), 174
Rigney, Anne
  on cultural memory, 170
Riley-Smith, Ben
  'Call for memorial to Glasgow slave trade', 112n
Robertson, J.M., 55
Robinson, Eric and McKie, Douglas
  Partners in Science (1970), 52
Robison, John, 52
Roche, Alexander Ignatius
  Legendary Glasgow, 3
Roderic Random (slave name), 91
Rolfe, W. D. Ian
  on the Hunter brothers, 73
Romanticism, 141, 146, 155
Royal Glasgow Volunteers, 23
'Rule Britannia', 194
Ruskin, John, 175
Rutherglen, 37

St Kentigern, 13
St Lucia slave insurrection (1796), 160
St Mungo, 3, 13, 18
St Paul's Cathedral, 156
Saltire, 159–160

Samuel, Raphael, 197
  Patriotism: The Making and Unmaking of British National Identity (1989), 180
Sanborn, Jim (b. 1945), 96
Sassoon, Siegfried, 154
Scotland
  culture and, 20, 35, 42, 105, 126
  empire and, 87, 173, 184
  Highlands and Lowlands, 1, 35, 145, 179, 180, 183, 191
  Independence Referendum (2014), 7, 194
  identity, 130–2, 195
  invention of, 120–1, 131
  Reformation and 13–14, 67
  religious identity, 124
  slavery and *see* slavery
Scott, Andrew, 25–6
Scott, Michael (1789–1835)
  Tom Cringle's Log (1829–34), 119
Scott, Sir Walter (1771–1832), 66, 67, 119, 122, 127, 143, 127, 154–5, 159, 166n, 178, 179, 180, 182
  Abbotsford, 144, 148
  Scott monument, Edinburgh, 144
  Old Mortality (1816), 115, 125
  'The Field of Waterloo' (1815), 154
  Waverley (1814), 118, 120, 151
Scottish Development Agency, 105
Scottish diaspora, 85, 108, 122
Scottish Enlightenment, 2, 3, 4, 7, 43, 45, 52, 53, 54–5, 62, 73, 132, 141, 198
  Aberdeen and 33, 35, 48, 53
  Edinburgh and *see* Edinburgh, Enlightenment
  Glasgow and, 15, 20, 22, 24, 26–7, 33–35, 36, 49–51, 53, 65–7, 93, 95
  London and, 73
  networks of, 38, 48, 50–4
  scholarship and, 49–50
  slavery and *see* slavery
  topography of, 118
  University of Glasgow and, 34, 37–9, 48–9, 52–3, 74, 94, 95, 141
Scottish history, 1, 2, 4, 63, 178–9, 192
Scottish National Portrait Gallery, 95
  Heraldic Exhibition (1891), 175
Scottish nationalism
  parties, 184–5
Sellars, James and Barr, James
  International Exhibition designers, 172
Senegal, 91
Shain, Charles
  on Galt, 125

Shelley, Percy B.
  'Ozymandias' (1818), 163
Sher, Richard, 34, 49, 50
  Church and University in the Scottish Enlightenment (1985), 49
  'Commerce, Religion and the Enlightenment in Eighteenth-Century Glasgow', 34
  The Glasgow Enlightenment (1995), 34
Silverthorne, Michael, 39
Simpson, Kenneth
  on Smollett, 55
Simson, Prof. Robert, 51
slave trade, xi, 81n, 88, 89, 103, 104, 108n, 112–13n, 118, 205, 206
Slave Trade Act (1807), xi, 103
slavery, 6, 24, 76, 88, 93, 104, 105, 108, 116, 123, 141, 171, 195, 199, 202
  abolition of, 8n, 16, 26, 90, 97, 99, 100, 103, 141
  abolitionists, 93, 94, 99, 102, *102*, 186n, 104
  anti-slavery movement, xi, 94, 97, 99, 100, 103
  Boswell, James and, 99
  cultural memory and, 79, 85, 89–90, 103, 128, 201–2, 203–4
  emancipation societies and, 99, 103, 106, 171
  Glasgow and, xi, 5, 8n, 16, 20–1, 26, 77–9, 85, 87, 88, 89, 90, 92, 98, 99, 100, 103, 104, 106–8, 108–9n, 110n, 112–13n, 118, 161, 171, 196, 198, 203–6
  memory studies and, 90
  Millar, John and, 94–5
  Moore, Sir John and, 160–1
  scholarship and, 88–9, 90, 92
  Scottish Enlightenment and, 2, 93, 94, 199, 203, 204
  slave ships, 91–2, 100–1, *101*, 105
  Smith, Adam and, 92–4, 97, 196
  'Triangular Trade', 90
  University of Glasgow and, 81n, 88, 94–5, 108–9n
  Watt, James and, 76, 81n
Slavery Abolition Act (1833), xii, 26, 103
Slavery and Abolition (1980), 90
Slavery in Africa (2011), 90
Sleigh, Frederick, Earl Roberts (1832–1914), 161–2
Smellie, William, 50, 53
  A Treatise on the Theory and Practice of Midwifery (1752–64), 53

Smith, Adam (1723–90), 33, 43, 48, 51, 53, 54–5, 64, 65–6, 73, 92–99, 148, 197
  and slavery *see* slavery
  statues, 34, 65, 95, 96, 96–7
  Lectures on Jurisprudence (1762), 94
  Theory of Moral Sentiments (1759), 93, 100
  The Wealth of Nations, 20, 93–4, 95, 101
Smith, Craig
  'Adam Smith: Left or Right?' (2013), 94
Smith, John, 64
Smollett, Tobias (1721–71) 38, 48, 50, 53, 54–5, 62–3, 73, 74, 80n, 118, 179, 196
  monument, 62–3
  An Essay on the External Use of Water (1752), 54
  Ode to Independence, 38
  The Adventures of Roderick Random (1743), 91
  The Expedition of Humphry Clinker (1771), 20, 34, 54–5, 63, 118
  'The Tears of Scotland', 63, 118
  Travels through France and Italy (1766), 55
Smout, T. C., 40, 117
Soldier Hero, 142, 151, 153, 154–5, 158, 160–2, 170
Somerville, Thomas, 155
Southern Carolina, 114–16
Southey, Robert
  History of the Peninsular War (1823), 152
Sowerby, Scott
  on Scots colony, 115
Stelter, Gilbert
  on Galt 128, 129
Stewart, Dr Charles, 52
Stewart, Provost John, 149
Stirling, 16
Stuarts Town, 114–16
Stuart, Prince Charles Edward, 15, 18–19, 155
Stuart, James Francis Edward, 15–16
Stuart Kings, 1
Summerson, John
  Georgian London (1945), 2
Sutherland, T.
  Death of Sir John Moore (1815), 152
Swaminathan, Srividhya, 93–4
  Invoking Slavery in the Eighteenth-Century British Imagination (2013), 89

Tait, Thomas Smith, 182, 183, 186
Tartan Day, 131
Tassie, James (1735–99), 43, 95
Taylor, Alan
  Glasgow: An Autobiography (2016), 2
Taylor, Jason
  Molinere Bay Underwater Sculpture Park (2006), 90
The Protestation of The Generall Assemblie of the Church of Scotland (1638), 13, 39, 179
Telford, Thomas, 75
Thom, Rev William, of Govan
  The Defects of an University Education (1762), 97
Thomas, Alfred
  on Prague, 192
Timothy, H. B.
  The Galts: A Canadian Odyssey, John Galt 1779–1839 (1977), 126
Titanic disaster (1912), 121
Trumpener, Katie
  on Galt, 125, 129
Turner, William, 146
Twain, Mark, 154

Uglow, Jenny
  Lunar Men (2002), 77
UNESCO World Heritage Sites, 22
Union, Acts of 1, 14, 15, 16
Union, Articles of, 15
Union, Regal (1603), 1
Union flag, 159–60, 170
Union of Parliaments (1707), 1, 17, 87, 118, 124, 201
unionists, 118, 160, 162, 194
University of Glasgow, xi, 13, 16, 35, 45, 69, 71, 77, 95, 97, 114, 116, 123, 141, 170, 196
  Hutcheson, Francis and, 17, 33, 39, 53, 74
  networks, 51–3
  teachers and, 18, 33
  see also Glasgow Enlightenment; Scottish Enlightenment; slavery
University of Glasgow buildings
  Adam Smith Building, 66, 95
  Adam Smith Business School, 66
  Foulis Academy of Fine Arts, xi, 20, 21, 34, 42–8, 47, 54, 65, 73, 80n, 95, 176, 198, 199, 201
  Gilbert Scott Building, 64–5
  Gilmorehill campus, 37–8, 64
  Hunterian Museum and Art Gallery, xi, 24, 46–8, 54, 55, 58n, 66, 71, 72, 73–4, 77, 141, 203, 204
  Joseph Black Building, 66
  Lion and Unicorn Staircase, 64
  Macfarlane Observatory, xi, 20, 52, 70, 141
  Memorial Gates, 64, 95
  Old College, 16, 20, 38, 39, 40, 44–5, *44*, 52, 64, 66, 69, 73, 77, 99, 128, 141, 146, 147, 148
  Pearce Lodge, 38, 64
  Randolph Hall, 95

Valdelievre, Mélina
  petition,161
Victoria, Queen (1819–1901), xii, 66, 159, 170, 172
Victoria and Albert Museum, 102–3
Vienna Business School, 95
Virginia, 88

Wade, General, 17
Walkinshaw, Clementine, 19
Wall Street Bull (1989), 163
Wallace, William, 39–40, 178, 191
Walton, Edward Arthur
  Glasgow Fair, 3
Walvin, James
  on slavery, 88, 103
Warburg, Aby (1866–1924)
  Mnemosyne Atlas, 101
Warburton, Eliot
  Darien; or, The Merchant Prince (1852), 121–2
Ward, Stephen
  Selling Places (1998), 196–7
Waterston, Elizabeth
  Galt text,126–7, 128
Watson, Nicola
  The Literary Tourist (2006), 144
Watt, James (1736–1819), xi, 4, 38, 48, 50, 52–3, 64, 73, 74–77, 78, 81n, 105, 124, 141, 182
  statues, xii, 66, 74–5, *76*, 77, 156, 159
Weart, Spencer R.
  on Chicago International Exposition (1893), 175
Wedderburn, John, 99
Wedgwood, Josiah (1730–95), 102, *102*
Wellington, Duke of
  statues, 152, 162–3
West, Benjamin
  The Death of General Wolfe (1770), 152

West Country Intelligence, 16; *see also Glasgow Courant*
Westover, Paul
　Necromanticism (2012), 144
Whatley, Christopher, 67, 162, 160
　Scottish Society: 1707–1830 (2000), 1
　The Industrial Revolution in Scotland (1997), 171
Whewell, William
　on 1851 Great Exhibition, 173
Whyte, Iain
　Scotland and the Abolition of Black Slavery, 1756–1838 (2006), 103, 108
Wilberforce, William, 100
Wilberforce House, 104
Wilkes, John
　The North Briton, 118
Wilkie, David
　The Penny Wedding (1818), 120
William IV, King, 26
William of Orange, 1, 14, 25, 49, 50, 69
　statue, x, 18, 19, 69, 150, 153, 156
Wilson, Prof. Alexander (1714–86), xi, 20, 38, 42, 52, 65, 70, 73
Wilson, James, 25
Wilson, John
　'Clyde' (1764), 146
Wilson, Patricia
　on Galt, 124
Wilson, Ross
　on war discourse, 154

Winter, Jay, 159
　on sites of memory, 45
Withers, Charles W. J. and Paul Wood
　Science and Medicine in the Scottish Enlightenment (2002), 48
Wolfe, Charles
　'Burial of Sir John Moore',153
Wood, Paul
　The Aberdeen Enlightenment (1995), 35
Wordsworth, Dorothy, 144
Wordsworth, William, 144, 146
World Trade Centre, 68
World War I, 45, 175, 181
World War II, 6, 182
World's Fairs, 169, 172, 175
Wright of Derby, Joseph
　An Experiment on a Bird in the Air Pump (1786), 63

Yoshikawa, Saeko
　William Wordsworth and the Invention of Tourism (2014), 144

Zerubavel, Eviatar
　on museums, 202
Zoffany, Johann (1733–1810)
　Portrait of Claud Alexander and his Brother Boyd with an Indian Servant (1784), 92

EU representative:
Easy Access System Europe
Mustamäe tee 50, 10621 Tallinn, Estonia
Gpsr.requests@easproject.com